BOOK ONE

Covert Operations
In the War on Drugs
A True Story

NICK JACOBELLIS, SENIOR SPECIAL AGENT
U.S. CUSTOMS SERVICE, RETIRED

Controlled Delivery, Book I

Copyright ©2018 by Nick Jacobellis

ISBN 978-0-9982956-4-0 (print)
ISBN 978-0-9982956-5-7 (ebook)

All rights reserved. This book or any portion thereof may not be reproduced or used in any manner whatsoever without the express written permission of the publisher except for the use of brief quotations in a book review.

Book design by www.StoriesToTellBooks.com

Email: badgepublishing@gmail.com

Website: www.badgepublishing.com

CONTROLLED DELIVERY

FOREWORD

A controlled delivery is the ultimate sting operation. In the 1980s and 1990s, undercover operations known as a controlled delivery became an effective tactic to use to dismantle Colombian based smuggling organizations.

The story Controlled Delivery is not your ordinary police procedural and depicts the actions of one of the most unique undercover operations ever mounted by the United States Customs Service. In addition to being the author of this book, I am also the U.S. Customs Agent who initiated, directed and participated in the undercover operation that is the main focus of this two-part true story.

While serving in an undercover capacity, my colleagues and I waged a secret war on the drug merchants who threatened our borders on a regular basis. Whenever we went operational, we became the portable front lines of The Drug War and achieved a victory for our side. The undercover personnel featured in this book were The Dirty Dozen With Wings, a group of self trained covert operators, who performed a mission that most people of sound mind would shy away from.

In order to understand how this true story came about, I need to take you back in time, to when I was a kid growing up in the Flatbush section of Brooklyn. It was during this period of time, that I had two dreams in life. One was to become a federal agent and the other was to learn how to fly. To be more specific, whenever I thought about the future, I always imagined myself wearing a military style flight suit and being involved in a law enforcement aviation pursuit of some kind.

After years of wondering how this vision of the future would materialize, I knew exactly how I was going to achieve my goals, when I read a magazine article about the missions that were performed by the U.S. Customs Service. The more I learned how this federal agency used uniformed officers, a special agent force and a fleet of vessels and aircraft to combat acts of smuggling, I knew exactly what I wanted to do for a career. After getting a college degree and working in city and state law enforcement positions, the day finally came when I was hired by the U.S. Customs Service.

After being assigned to the Resident Agent in Charge (RAC) Office at JFK Airport and the RAC Long Island, I requested a transfer to the front lines of The Drug War in South Florida. While the main focus of our efforts were in the ports of entry and along our borders, some of us also aggressively pursued smugglers beyond our shores.

My first assignment when I arrived in Miami was to serve as a member of the Freighter Intelligence Search Team aka FIST. FIST was the unit that interdicted acts of smuggling along the Miami River, as well as in the Port of Miami. On certain occasions, we also conducted vessel boarding operations in Customs Waters (within 12 miles of the shoreline).

After serving in the Miami Freighter Intelligence Team, I experienced deja vous in megaton proportions when I received my wings and I became a U.S. Customs Air Officer. As an Air Officer, I flew interdiction missions throughout the Caribbean, in search of smugglers who used private aircraft and high speed "go fast" boats, to smuggle drug contraband into the United States.

While residents and tourists enjoyed South Florida beaches and nightlife, an armada of U.S. interdiction assets engaged drug smugglers on a daily basis throughout the Caribbean. In time, the blue and green water of the Bahamas became littered with the rusting hulks of smuggling aircraft that didn't make it to their intended destination. Contraband occasionally washed up on the beach and the thunder of high-speed boats could always be heard rumbling off shore throughout the night.

After being promoted to the rank of Special Agent, I was assigned to the newly formed Miami Air Smuggling Investigations Group 7. Group 7 was located in a trailer complex behind the Miami Air Branch facility at Homestead Air Force Base. After a successful run at making several significant cases, I set my sights on more elusive targets.

During the period that I refer to as The Miami Vice Era of The Drug War, smugglers used various methods to penetrate our Southeast border at all hours of the day and night. While their goal was to "shotgun" as many drug shipments as possible into the United States, our mission was to stop them from doing so.

By the late 1980s and early 1990s, U.S. and Bahamian drug interdiction forces were very effective in forcing air and marine smugglers to operate further away from our shores. At the same time, it became more challenging for U.S. interdiction forces to operate farther away from their bases. Before our success in the Caribbean, the smugglers came to us, sometimes in droves. In fact, the smugglers seemed to subscribe to the theory, "If you throw enough shit against the wall, some of it was bound to stick."

During the period of time that it took to drive the smugglers away from South Florida and various locations in the Bahamas, smuggling organizations suffered significant losses of planes, vessels and crews. This was a serious blow to their operations, because transportation is the key element in any act of smuggling. As a result, without transportation, the smugglers were unable to bring their products to market.

While serving in this successful interdiction effort, I saw an opportunity for a group of undercover operatives to offer their services to unsuspecting violators (criminals). In order to conduct a successful infiltration operation, we had to convince our "clients" that we had ability to smuggle drug shipments into the CONUS (Continental United States), while avoiding U.S. interdiction assets. However, this plan would only work, if we utilized private aircraft that could carry large shipments of drug contraband. These planes also had to be capable of flying long distances without needing to be refueled.

In the last two decades of the 20th Century, South Florida was a labyrinth of intrigue that included a large number of informants, domestic drug traffickers, smugglers and law enforcement officers in the local population. As a result, my colleagues and I were in the right place at the right time to put our feelers out and draw attention to ourselves. Our targets were Colombian based smuggling organizations and their stateside representatives/receivers. My plan was to strike deep into the heart of the enemy through the effective use of covert operations.

In order to fund this operation, I intended to use the "front money" aka the expense money that was given to us by our Colombian "clients." This money would be used to pay the expenses that we incurred, when we provided the transportation services to "smuggle" drug shipments from Colombia to the United States. Once we were "hired" by a smuggling organization and we picked up a drug shipment in Colombia, we would maintain complete "control" over the contraband at all times. This included when we executed the "delivery" phase of every operation. It is also important to note, that whenever we went operational, my colleagues and I had to act like real smugglers without breaking the law.

Once an undercover aircraft and crew returned to the CONUS, my plan was to use the drug shipment as bait, to lure out as many drug smugglers and stateside receivers as possible. To add insult to injury, my colleagues and I would wait until we were paid a sizable amount of drug money for services rendered, before we agreed to deliver any of the contraband. Once the delivery was made, a small army of U.S. Customs Agents and other law enforcement officers would move in and arrest the subjects of our investigation. If everything went according to plan, the undercover operatives would ride off into the sunset, devise a new cover story, get introduced to another group of unsuspecting smugglers and repeat the same process as many times as possible.

Because we could not confide in the Colombian government, it was imperative for us to utilize the services of contract aircrews and sources of information to operate covertly on foreign soil. To be more specific, due to the risks involved, sworn law enforcement officers were not allowed to operate in an undercover capacity in places like Colombia. This policy necessitated the use of non-sworn civilian personnel, who were formally documented as confidential sources of information and contract employees.

In order to make my idea a reality, I turned to my most trusted network of airport contacts and documented sources of information. Up until this time in my career, my sources of information had helped me make a number of cases and seizures. The day I approached my private aviation contacts, they all agreed to serve and provide me with planes, crews, hangars, mechanics and office space. All I needed now was authorization from my superiors and we would be in business.

In October of 1988, I requested permission to form an undercover air unit that would be responsible to infiltrate smuggling organizations, for the purpose of executing as many controlled deliveries as possible. After presenting my plan to the Special Agent in Charge (SAC) in Miami and the Regional Commissioner, my "Trojan Horse" operation was approved. Clearly, at that time, the U.S. Customs Service was an agency that encouraged individual initiative.

With no prior military experience and an expired student pilot's license in hand, I became the ad hoc commanding officer of my very own undercover air unit. Looking back, I was probably the last person who should have been put in charge of a covert air operation, considering the fact that I only had about a dozen hours of flight training and three solo flights under my belt in single engine aircraft. The simple truth is, I got this job because it was my idea and no one else apparently wanted to assume the responsibility.

Having authorization to do anything in federal service was more important than anything else. Fortunately, a recent change in federal law allowed federal law enforcement agencies to establish proprietary corporations and create phony bank accounts, in the same way that intelligence agencies are known to operate. In addition, this new law authorized agencies to use trafficker directed funds, or money that was provided by violators (criminals) during undercover sting operations, as expense money to conduct undercover operations. This meant, that we could react to situations without delay, because we did not have to apply for traditional government funding through normal channels. While conducting these high risk undercover operations, every penny that we recovered from our drug smuggling "clients" would be deposited in a certified undercover bank account and would be strictly controlled.

In order to go operational, I recruited a cadre of contract personnel who were willing to play by the rules, despite the fact that on the surface we had to act like the smugglers we were targeting. Our contract crews included, war heroes, convicted felons, three defendant informants, a former Colombian drug cartel pilot, experienced private pilots, commercial airline pilots and a smuggler who never got caught.

While mounting these highly specialized covert operations, we assembled an impressive fleet of undercover aircraft that were "leased" to the U.S. Customs Service on a case-by-case basis. Because some of my contacts were aircraft brokers, we were able to rent any aircraft that we needed that we did not have in "inventory."

Officially, we were assigned to the U.S. Customs Service Miami Air Smuggling Investigations Group 7. After we completed our first mission, we became known as The Blade Runner Squadron, a nickname that we adopted because we flew on the edge. The original logo for this operation depicted an undercover aircraft taking off on the edge of a knife blade; the same knife that would be used to execute our crews, if their real identities became known to our adversaries.

When I wasn't working alone, I had at least one special agent, sometimes two or three, assigned to help me run this rather unorthodox covert air operation. When we went operational, we teamed up with other special agents from Group 7, from other Customs units in Miami, as well as with special agents from other agencies and from other Customs offices throughout the country.

In the process of executing a succession of transportation cases aka controlled deliveries, we made history on a number of occasions. The stakes were always very high and despite what one of our critics had to say, we took calculated risks because we were in a risky business, but we never took chances and believe me there's a difference between the two. Everyone who worked for us also proved to be incredibly trustworthy. This is evident by the fact, that we transported tons of cocaine and handled millions in untraceable cash without experiencing any integrity problems.

As you can imagine, participating in undercover operations involving multi-hundred and multi-thousand kilogram shipments of cocaine would prove to be a very dangerous and demanding experience. What was even more bizarre was that none of us were specially trained to do what we did. You see, despite the fact that controlled deliveries were the "meat and potatoes" of the U.S. Customs Service, there was no formal training available, that prepared us to mount safe and successful covert operations using undercover aircraft.

To be more specific, there was no specialized training program entitled Controlled Delivery 101. The undercover school that did exist provided very basic training at best. Worse yet, a number of special agents who were stationed in South Florida, weren't sent to undercover school in a timely fashion. As an example, I wasn't sent to undercover school until September of 1991. This meant that my colleagues and I were largely self-taught and learned our trade in the field. We learned how smugglers conducted business and how they behaved, by investigating acts of smuggling and interdicting smugglers in the act of violating the law. Working with reliable informants and documented sources of information also helped us to hone our skills as undercover operatives. The next hurdle was to learn how to negotiate smuggling ventures and drive hard bargains with Colombian based smugglers and their stateside representatives.

In order to learn the business of directing undercover air operations, I relied on my experience as a U.S. Customs Air Officer and what little training and experience that I had as a student pilot. Just like I was a self-taught undercover agent, I was a self-taught director of flight operations as well. Since no school existed that could train me to serve in this capacity, I spent my spare time devouring flight manuals and talking to U.S. Customs Pilots and private pilots, to learn about the flying characteristics of different types of aircraft. In doing so, I learned how far different aircraft could fly, while carrying the required crew compliment and various amounts of fuel and cargo.

I also became well versed on the capabilities of different types of aircraft, to safely land and take off on different kinds of runways. This included while taking off with a "full bag" of fuel and a cargo bay bulging with drug contraband. I also had to become familiar with seaplane operations. In addition, I learned how to navigate and plot courses on a map/air chart so I could plan operations down the last gallon of aviation fuel. Last but not least, I also learned about the weather and other factors that related to the safe operation of aircraft. This included learning how to successfully penetrate Colombian airspace undetected.

Luckily, I was a people person. This made it easy for me to recruit, direct and control an eclectic group of the informants, sources of information and contract personnel. Even though there were times when I felt like the headmaster of a school for wayward boys, I accepted the antics of our "hired hands" as a way to let their hair down before going in harm's way.

While directing and participating in this undercover operation, I came to believe that pilots are a special breed, because each and every time they got airborne they defied gravity. I also believe that because I tried my hand at flying, I elevated my standing a notch or two with the experienced pilots that I recruited to serve in our UC OP.

Looking back, this dream of mine was only a success because I had the best people imaginable working by my side. In time, I saw us gel into an effective undercover force that never compromised its integrity and was able to fly under the most adverse conditions imaginable without experiencing the loss of life. We had close calls, but fortunately for us, being close only counts while playing horseshoes and throwing hand-grenades.

Everyone who agreed to work with us was treated with respect, regardless of their past mistakes and crimes against society. The special agents who were involved in this operation received a few quality step increases and monetary awards amounting to a few thousand dollars. A few of the Group 7 Special Agents who were actively involved in this certified undercover operation were eventually promoted and became Senior Special Agents. None of us asked for, or received any medals and none were handed out, even though many of the things that we did warranted being formally decorated.

In order to receive substantial monetary payments, a person had to be directly responsible for helping U.S. Customs Agents arrest major violators and seize significant amounts of contraband, drug money and valuable assets. If necessary, sources of information and contract personnel also had to be prepared to testify, if that's what it took to prosecute a case in federal court.

From the time that I started investigating acts of smuggling in South Florida until our undercover operation was disbanded, I was authorized to pay my sources of information and contract aircrews approximately $2.5 million dollars for services rendered. That figure alone should give you some idea of how successful we were. I say this, because the federal government does not authorize this amount of money to be paid to informants, sources of information and contract personnel unless they provide a very valuable service.

During this undercover operation, my colleagues and I provided the specialized assistance necessary that enabled U.S. Customs Agents, FBI Agents and DEA Agents, to arrest dozens of major violators and seize a number of multi-hundred and multi-thousand kilogram shipments of cocaine, thousands of pounds of marijuana and large quantities of drug money. In addition to helping me seize a number of drug smuggling aircraft, my cadre of informants and sources of information also made it possible for me and other agents to seize over thirty vehicles, two go fast vessels, dozens of firearms and other drug assets valued in the millions of dollars. Clearly, whatever amount of money we paid our "hired hands" was only a fraction of what they enabled the government to seize. In fact, in some respects, it is difficult to put a price on certain aspects of our success.

When these operations were being conducted, we never released any information that explained how these major drug seizures and arrests were actually made. When the media wanted to know more, our response was, "No comment." To their credit, the reporters who covered our press conferences didn't push for more clarification.

After reading this true story, some of you might ask why I never walked away from this incredibly stressful and dangerous assignment, in order to become a so-called "regular agent." One reason is because this operation was my idea. I should also mention that this operation didn't happen overnight. As you will read, it took several years of participating in interdiction missions and conducting different types of smuggling investigations, before I requested permission to form an undercover unit that specialized in executing controlled deliveries using private aircraft. By the time we completed our first high risk controlled delivery, I was hooked and wanted to stay in the game as long as possible. Quite frankly, I always believed that I would know when it was time to move on. Until that day came, I had every intention of honing my own skills and developing the capabilities of The Blade Runner Squadron.

One of the reasons I was drawn to covert operations, was because every controlled delivery required a great deal of "Yankee" ingenuity. I was also seduced by the taste of the hunt and the challenge of participating in the ultimate sting operation. I also enjoyed the adrenaline rush that was always present while working in high risk drug enforcement operations.

To give you an idea of where I am coming from, consider that one of my favorite movies is The Dirty Dozen. The theme of this unusual war movie should give you a better idea of what made me tick as a human being. The idea of taking a dozen misfits, eccentrics and social outcasts and grooming them to become a force to be reckoned with, was something that got my creative juices flowing and made it worthwhile for me to get out of bed in the morning.

As a result of my Catholic upbringing, I also believed in forgiveness. Having this mindset enabled me to treat the informants, sources of information and contract personnel who had a "tainted" past with respect, providing they followed the rules and served with distinction. In fact, one of my sources of information who was a convicted felon, performed so admirably, I would have gladly given this guy a full pardon, if I had the authority to do so. I also worked with certain defendant informants, who I thought deserved to be formally pardoned.

From a professional standpoint, running the undercover operation that is the main subject matter of this book was the high point of my entire law enforcement career. In fact, nothing that I did before was as exciting and nothing I would ever do in the future, would peg my intrigue meter more, than being involved in covert air and marine operations.

There was also a bit of the rebel in me, who hated wearing suits and ties and working 9 to 5 as a "regular" agent. Call me crazy, but I preferred to make my own hours and work 12 to 18 hours days, instead of working 8 hours a day in an office pushing paper. If maintaining this level of activity meant that I had to work with little or no quality time off, then so be it. I was also a bit of an eccentric, who preferred working with other eccentrics.

I also liked the idea of cultivating my own cases, instead of being handed a stack of cases to investigate. In this regard I loved being proactive. I also like being creative and what was more creative than concocting cover stories and invading Colombia. I was also very loyal to the U.S. Customs Service and saw my involvement in cutting edge undercover operations, as a way to help keep my agency on the front page of the national news. In this regard, I was no different than any other professional, who did his best to make his team look good.

In order for us to get to the point where we were ready to go operational, my colleagues and I spent many days and nights learning the ropes of running successful undercover operations. We also learned early on, that failure to cover some small detail could result in the loss of life and a variety of other problems.

Any federal agent, who needed an undercover crew to infiltrate a smuggling organization and successfully transport a shipment of drug contraband, had to believe in our capabilities. In order to develop and maintain a favorable reputation, we had to execute every mission without making any mistakes, or causing an international incident. This was critically important, because making mistakes and creating international incidents were not tolerated. In this regard, only time would tell if my colleagues and I would always have the so called "right stuff."

In the late 1980s and the early 1990s, the U.S. Customs Service was evolving into an agency that was heavily involved in certified undercover operations. High ranking Customs managers liked having investigative groups under their command involved in successful covert operations for two main reasons. As I briefly mentioned before, one reason for this, was because successful UC ops generated the money aka trafficker funds that enabled agents to pay for a variety of legitimate expenses. In our case, this included rental fees for undercover vehicles, aircraft and vessels, as well as paying fuel bills, cell phone bills and travel expenses. In order to document every legitimate expense that we made, my colleagues and I obtained receipts whenever possible. In fact, we became so judicious about documenting our legitimate expenses, our unofficial motto became, "GET A RECEIPT!"

Having access to this outside source of revenue made local SAC and RAC Offices less dependent on headquarters for funding. Because the U.S. Customs Service had a knack for running successful undercover operations or special ops, annual cash awards and Quality Step Increases (QSI Awards), that were mini promotions, were handed out to the most active agents, as well as to their superiors. Naturally, the bosses received the larger cash awards, while the smaller amounts went to the worker bees.

It is also important to note, that in my opinion, the statistics generated during The Drug War should be viewed as being even more impressive, when you consider that a smaller number of agents were actually responsible for initiating the most significant cases. The bulk of the remaining agents provided valuable support, with some agents doing as little as possible. In other words, the heaviest load was actually carried by a smaller number of agents than you are aware of. I say this because, when a major case breaks on the local or national news and you hear that fifty federal agents were involved in an enforcement action, this case was probably made by one or two hard charging special agents, but forty eight others were needed to conduct surveillance's and execute search and arrest warrants. Like it or not, that's the way it was.

INTRODUCTION

I started writing this book in February of 1989. From the inception of this rather unusual undercover operation, I documented our adventures, trials and tribulations as they occurred, with the hope of one day sharing these events with the general public. With the exception of periodic editing, I wrote this true story while I was actively involved in directing and participating in drug interdiction missions, smuggling investigations and undercover operations. One reason why it took so long for me to publish Controlled Delivery Book I and II, is because this is not an easy story for me to tell.

Whether boarding tall ships in New York Harbor during the early days of our country, or preventing the smuggling of different types of contraband in more modern times, the agency known as the U.S. Customs Service had an outstanding reputation for protecting the revenue and the national security of the United States. After the terrorist attacks on 9/11/01, the U.S. Customs Service that I worked for was merged with the Immigration and Naturalization Service (INS) and transferred from the Treasury Department to the newly formed Department of Homeland Security. Today, an agency called U.S. Customs and Border Protection (CBP) represents the uniformed side of the original or "Legacy" U.S. Customs Service and the "Legacy" INS. An agency called Homeland Security Investigations (HSI) and U.S. Immigration and Customs Enforcement (ICE) are the entities that perform a combined Customs/Immigration and DHS enforcement and investigative mission. This is strictly my opinion, but I hope the day comes when ICE/HSI are merged into CBP. Doing so, would enable us to have ONE federal agency that performs every Customs and Immigration mission.

For the purposes of contributing to the amazing history of the "Legacy" U.S. Customs Service, I will keep things as they once were and use the agency name that dates back to 1789 when I tell this true story. Putting the present situation aside, the U.S. Customs Service is often the last agency to capture the mind of the average person, when one considers the contribution made by the federal government in undercover drug enforcement operations. Far too many people believe that Customs "Agents" are the folks who go through your luggage at the airport when you return from a trip overseas. Although uniformed Customs Inspectors (now called CBP Officers) perform a necessary and at times a dangerous job, they are not part of the investigative side of the house. Only Special Agents and certain Customs Officers conducted criminal investigations and worked undercover. Hopefully, this book will shed some light, on one of the missions of the "Legacy" U.S. Customs Service that very few people are aware of.

The story Controlled Delivery takes you through several years of adventure and intrigue as seen through my eyes, while performing the duties of a U.S. Customs Patrol Officer, Air Officer, Special Agent and Senior Special Agent.

In the beginning of this true story, I'll take you on the same journey that I took, when I graduated from the ranks of being a more traditional law enforcement officer and I became an undercover agent.

For security reasons, this story could not be told when these undercover operations were being conducted. After waiting over two decades to tell this story, the time has come to let the world know, how a relatively small group of undercover operatives executed a number of highly successful controlled delivery operations, that resulted in the seizure of over 22,000 pounds of cocaine, 11,000 pounds of marijuana, the arrest of dozens of major violators and the recovery of approximately $3 million dollars in trafficker directed funds (drug money). Of all the individuals who were arrested and sentenced as a result of our sting operations, two major violators received life sentences in federal prison for their "Drug War" crimes. I decided to go with a figure of 22,000 plus pounds of cocaine, because this is the amount that was transported on our undercover aircraft. An additional quantity of cocaine was air dropped to an undercover vessel, by the Colombian based targets of a Miami Group 7 investigation. This airdrop occurred after one of our undercover aircraft picked up an initial shipment of 500 kilos. This case is included in *Controlled Delivery Book I*.

While working in an undercover capacity, my colleagues and I made record-breaking drug seizures in different locations and broke our own record four times in the New England area alone. As you will read, our efforts were not without sacrifice. The question is, why have so many law enforcement officers given so much, for what at times seems to be such a hopeless cause? First, I think that we all respectively love our jobs. Our strong work ethic and upbringing molded us into people who are not afraid of a little hard work, even when the odds are against us. Second, I believe that we live in a world of extremes and are attracted to a combative existence when the cause is noble and just.

Law enforcement officers also enjoy protecting society from harm. In fact, one of the most gratifying aspects of our job was to seize a large drug shipment, or a significant amount of drug money. To put things in a more modern perspective, law enforcement officers from my generation considered drug smugglers to be no different than the terrorists that we are fighting today. Simply put, drug smugglers were the enemy and we engaged them to the best of our ability on a daily basis. As a result, we enjoyed being in a profession where we could bring major violators to justice and make them trade their Rolex watches, for an inexpensive pair of Smith & Wesson handcuffs.

All good things come to an end and as such, our operation did not last forever. The sanctioned undercover operation that was unofficially known as The Blade Runner Squadron was disbanded on May 12, 1993. Looking back, there was never a dull moment. I also have to state for the record, that I was actually grateful when I was transferred to other duties. I felt this way, because I had no more to give and I needed a change in scenery.

During my law enforcement career I was a chain-smoking workaholic, who would have preferred to work twenty-four hours a day if such a thing was possible. I guess you can say that I was an adrenaline junkie, who eagerly ran into harm's way each and every time an opportunity presented itself. By the time I joined the U.S. Customs Service and transferred to Miami, I lived by the motto that was made famous by Operation Greenback Agents (a money laundering operation in Miami); "So many Colombians, so little time."

As a result of my involvement in covert operations, I learned that being an undercover agent is a lot like being a stand-up comic, in a place where the audience gets to kill you if your jokes aren't funny. I also learned that working undercover can make the Grand Canyon look more like a shallow grave than a National Treasure.

Even after my line of duty spinal injuries got worse, I pushed myself as hard as humanly possible. I knew plenty of other law enforcement officers who would have gladly traded places with me and retired early, until the first time they were unable to walk right, or were in excruciating pain. After I turned down the first offer to medically retire, I used prescription medication and a cane to help me stay on the job and get around when my injuries flared up. In the process, a bad situation made worse, when I was re-injured for a third time in the line of duty.

After a long and very successful law enforcement career, I was forced to medically retire after I failed a medical fitness for duty examination. Since I had no say in the matter, I graciously accepted the set of retired special agent's credentials that came in the mail to my home. It was time for me to move on to the next phase of my life.

Once I retired, I went from doing 100 miles an hour in a 25 mile an hour speed limit, to a crawl. While it took some time to get used to a much slower pace, I eventually saw my situation as a blessing in disguise instead of a curse. As a retired agent, I used my free time to immerse myself in the lives of my family members. You might say that I made up for lost time, even though time is something that you can never really make up.

The first step that I took to accomplish this was to apologize to my two sons for being away so much. Even when I was technically off duty and at home, all of our lives were constantly interrupted by phone calls and emergencies that caused me to return to work. The day I made this apology, my youngest son Michael, who was 10 years old at the time, responded with all of the innocence of a child when he looked up at me and said, "Don't worry, Dad. You were fighting for our country." I still get choked up to this day whenever I think of my youngest son's kind words.

The story Controlled Delivery takes you back to a time when a relatively small number of U.S. Customs Agents and private contractors took the fight to the enemy through covert means. Whether my colleagues and I were very lucky, or good at what we did, is up to you to decide. Personally, I believe that God was our Co Pilot and that my colleagues and I were protected by a higher authority whenever we went operational. If you doubt this is true, I suggest you read on.

I also sincerely hope that you will find the information in this book to be even more interesting, because it was written by a special agent and not by a journalist who tagged along and documented these events through inexperienced eyes. It is also my hope, that after reading Controlled Delivery, you will have a greater insight into the efforts that were made by a few good men to successfully engage a very elusive enemy. Enjoy!

A NOTE FROM THE AUTHOR

Due to the volume of information that I received written authorization to publish, I decided to divide the true story Controlled Delivery into two parts. Doing so enabled me to include some additional information, that provides a more detailed description of what it was like to serve during The Miami Vice Era of The Drug War.

In order to conceal the identities of the government personnel that I worked with, I used their first name, followed by the first letter of their last name to identify them. I also used nicknames to identify the contract pilots, crew chiefs, informants and sources of information who helped us accomplish our mission. The bad guy's identities have also been changed, as are some of the details of certain events to protect trade craft.

When I decided to write this book, I sought immediate direction from the Office of Regional Counsel in 1988, regarding the publication of written material by a U.S. Customs Officer/Agent. In order to comply with agency policy and obtain written permission to publish the story Controlled Delivery, manuscripts that contained additional information were provided to the U.S. Customs Service for official review. The first letter of authorization that I received from an agency administrator is dated March 19, 1991, the second is dated July 15, 1994 and the third letter is dated June 10, 1996.

The photographs that are included in CD Book I and II were taken by various agents and undercover operatives in the field and were provided to me over the course of several years. *Copies of documents that authenticate the information in this book will be posted on my website: badgepublishing.com.

The story Controlled Delivery was written from my perspective and is based on what I did, what I observed, what I was told and what I documented when these events occurred. This includes, when I performed certain duties on my own and with other law enforcement officers, as well as when I recruited, debriefed, directed and worked with various informants, sources of information and contract personnel. I also made sure to give credit where credit was due, by acknowledging the contribution that was made by the law enforcement officers, contract personnel and sources of information, who served with great distinction during various enforcement actions, investigations and sanctioned undercover operations. When it was appropriate to do so, I also included my opinion and some personal information. I also left a few things out of this story, in order to comply with certain instructions that were relayed to me by the U.S. Customs Service. Regardless, I promise you won't be disappointed.

I should also mention, that documenting what we did was easy, compared to the process of editing the mountain of raw material that I was given authorization to publish. While I continued to prepare this story for publication, I also sanitized the contents well beyond what was required. This process included deleting and sanitizing certain information that I was previously authorized to publish.

In the years that I waited to publish CD Book I and CD Book II, I further developed my skills as a freelance writer, by publishing over 170 magazine articles and two historical fiction books; *The Frontline Fugitives Book I, The Khaki Cops* and *The Frontline Fugitives Book II, Cops In A Combat Zone*. Currently, *The Frontline Fugitives Book III and The Frontline Fugitives Book IV* are in their final stages and will be published in 2018.

Contents

Foreword		i
Introduction		xviii
A Note from the Author		xxv
Acknowledgments		xxx
1	In the Beginning	1
2	A Dream Come True	19
3	Air Ops	33
4	The Air War over the Bahamas	36
5	Pursuing Air Smugglers on the Ground	53
6	Making the Transition to Undercover Agent	78
7	Breaking Away from the Pack	88
8	Operation White Christmas	96
9	Our First Mission	105
10	Open for Business in Miami	123
11	The Very Thin Blue Line	131

12	Necessity is the Mother of Invention	135
13	The Greed Factor	139
14	General Puma	142
15	Informants	193
16	The Greatest Show on Earth	199
17	Standing By to Stand By	208
18	Ready, Set, Go!	216
19	Shaken Not Stirred	227
20	Anchors Away	245
21	Victory at Sea	254
22	Welcome to Colombia	270
23	Born to Be Wild	281
24	Go West Young Man Go West	291
25	Mayday Mayday We're Going Down	302
A Preview of Controlled Delivery Book II		326

ACKNOWLEDGMENTS

Controlled Delivery Book I and Book II are dedicated to my wife, my sons, the members of The Blade Runner Squadron, as well as to the U.S. Customs Agents, U.S. Customs Pilots, U.S. Customs Officers, FBI Agents, DEA Agents, police officers, sheriff's department detectives, federal prosecutors and U.S. military personnel who participated in the investigations, enforcement actions and undercover operations described in this true story.

THE BLADE RUNNER SQUADRON MOTTO

We fly at night if the price is right, no load too great, no distance too far, I'm the man for your contraband, one plane in, one plane out, last call!

CHAPTER 1
IN THE BEGINNING

Some of the reasons why I decided to become a law enforcement officer are simple, while others are more complex. For starters, I think a lot of it had to do with my fascination with secrets and my religious upbringing.

As an Italian American I was raised in the Flatbush section of Brooklyn, New York where I went to Catholic School and majored in guilt. Whether I wanted to go or not, my parents dragged me and my four younger brothers to Holy Cross Church every Sunday to attend Mass. Like clockwork, the priest would use a loud and authoritative voice, to order everyone who stood in the aisles and the back of the church to find seats; everyone except the New York City Police Officers, who were attending part of the Mass before they went back on patrol. Seeing this happen week after week, made me realize at an early age, that police officers were special people in the eyes of God.

I also realized something interesting about the police, when I was a young boy growing up in Brooklyn and I observed two detectives arrest a man on the street where I lived. A crowd formed and everyone whispered back and forth trying to speculate why the police were taking our neighbor into custody. The moment I observed the two detectives in action, I realized that only they knew why they were on East 29th Street. From that moment on, I knew that the police lived in their own world and that anyone who wasn't a cop was an outsider. If you wanted to know the secrets you had to be a victim, a perpetrator, or a policeman. For obvious reasons, I decided never to be a victim and didn't want to know the secrets bad enough to get myself arrested. Instead, I wanted to become one of them, a member of the secret society that carried a badge and gun.

My first career break came when I was in high school and I managed to get hired in a part time Neighborhood Youth Corps position at the 17th Precinct in Manhattan. When a wave of police corruption resulted in the creation of the Knapp Commission, I decided to re-consider my career options and see if there were any other agencies where I might like to serve, besides the N.Y.P.D.

As I said earlier, my quest for a career ended when I learned about the missions that were performed by the U.S. Customs Service. Since I was still in high school at the time, I decided to ask my father, if I could take flying lessons with a buddy of mine, who later became an Air Force Pilot. When my request was denied, I waited to graduate, so I could enlist in the Marines and train to become a helicopter pilot. Since my father was a World War II veteran, I thought for sure that he would approve. I was wrong. As far as my father was concerned, there was no reason for me to enlist, when the War in Vietnam was winding down and almost over. Unless my lottery number was selected, I was going to college.

Fortunately, a brand new city university called John Jay College of Criminal Justice was taking applications from students who wanted to pursue a career in law enforcement. After receiving a Bachelor of Science Degree in Police Science, I spent several years working in different city and state law enforcement positions, while I waited to be hired by the U.S. Customs Service.

A Twist Of Fate

As I look back over my career as a police officer and federal agent, I can remember a number of times when I risked my life, never giving it a second thought until later on. Taking action when you're on duty is dangerous business. Getting involved in a hair-raising situation when you are off duty is a horse of a completely different color.

After working a 3x11 tour of duty in the Bronx as a New York State Park Police Officer, I decided to drive through Manhattan and stop for a cold one on the way home. Actually, I was doing what a lot of cops did back then when they got off duty, especially after getting off duty late at night. Rather than go home to a dark house, cops were famous for doing a little bar hopping to unwind. Right or wrong, this was the way it was.

As a native New Yorker, I always thought Manhattan was especially spectacular at night, when the city was virtually empty of pedestrians and vehicles. Once the masses of people went home, you could cruise through the mountains of well-lit skyscrapers with the greatest of ease and enjoy the sights as if you were a tourist with special privileges. Toss in a light dusting of snow in Manhattan at night and you have the perfect Christmas.

The last thing that I expected to run into, while I was cruising around Manhattan was a robbery in progress. The moment I turned my brand new fire engine red diesel powered VW Rabbit eastbound on East 47th Street, I spotted two young Hispanic men leave a brownstone building and enter a yellow cab. I cannot explain how or why, but I knew these guys were "dirty" and a crime had just been committed.

While the cab sped away, I pulled up to the building, just as a well dressed man frantically ran out to the street and started yelling that he had been robbed. As I rolled the window down and identified myself, I could see the look of relief on the man's face, when he realized that an off duty cop had come to his rescue. While I kept one eye on the yellow cab as it stopped at the traffic light on the corner, I listened to the victim report that two Hispanic males just robbed him and that they had a gun. The moment I spotted the taxi cab start to pass through the intersection, I put my car in gear and told the victim to call the police.

As I worked my way through the gears, I went in hot pursuit as fast as my little diesel engine was able to propel me down the street. At first, my hopes were high that I would spot a police car and get some help. After driving a few blocks cross-town, I was beginning to wonder where the entire midnight tour had gone off too.

I knew that cops were known to doze off on a late tour, but what were the odds that every cop in Manhattan was sound asleep before 1AM. Simply put, I couldn't help but shake my head when I realized that there is never a cop around when you needed one. Since I had not taken any action yet, there was still time to get some help. Rather than give up, I continued to look in all directions for a passing police car, while I followed the bad guys cross-town.

As the cab approached Rockefeller Center, the two Hispanic bad guys turned and looked right at me. The cat was out of the bag as they say. So much for the element of surprise. The good news was, that even though the two perps (perpetrators) knew that they were being followed, they did not leap out of the cab and haul ass. The bad news was that I was still alone. As I prepared to take these guys down, I spotted one of the holdup men lean over and instruct the cab driver to pull over. This was it, show time, I thought to myself, as I prepared to go into action.

When the cab pulled over to the curb, both perps remained in the back seat and kept an eye on me rather than get out. Rather than appear overly concerned or hesitant to take action, I decided to come on like gangbusters. I immediately jammed on the brakes and exited my car the same way I would if I was at work. As I came across the hood with my revolver in hand, I identified myself as a police officer and ordered both men to freeze.

The words, "Police! Don't Move!" were never said with more authority. Much to my amazement both perps complied. Without giving it a second thought I charged their position. With my five shot .38 Special S&W .Model 36 revolver in hand, I quickly approached the rear of the taxi and ordered the two perps to exit the vehicle and assume the position up against the side of the yellow cab.

When the shorter perp hesitated and tried to get back into the cab, I became very concerned about him taking the cab driver hostage. As I screamed as loud as I could, I aimed my off duty revolver at the second perp and yelled, "Get out! Let's go, move it!"

I was still in control. My commands must have hit home. The shorter one listened and joined his partner outside by the side of the Checker cab. While sounding as calm as possible, I told the cab driver to call his dispatcher and get me some help. While the old cabby picked up his radio, I turned my full attention back to the Hispanic version of Butch Cassidy and the Sundance Kid.

When the shorter of the two perps started whining, "My wife's in the hospital. She's bleeding bad, man," and his plea fell on deaf ears, he became aggressive and yelled, "What's your problem?" While I continued to hold them at gunpoint, I responded in a raised voice and said, "There's been a robbery and someone said you two did it!"

While I listened for the sound of police sirens, the seconds passed like hours. I never felt more alone in my life. The next one to comment was the taller perp. "We're leaving." A second later the shorter one with the big mouth remarked, "I'll sue your ass."

I didn't flinch, even though I must admit that I felt as if the situation was about to go from bad to worse. In fact, all I could think about was being on the front page of the newspaper, after I shot one or both of these assholes when they jumped me.

While I continued to cover them with my revolver, I decided it was time to raise my voice in a last ditch effort to exert control. The second I yelled, "Don't move!" the two perps said something to each other in a low voice before they turned on me. As they advanced toward my position, I took a defensive step back with my right foot and tucked my revolver close to my side.

I was just about to open fire, when I pointed to the ground with my left hand, while I screamed at the top of my lungs and said, "You see that fucking line? Step over it and I'll fucking shoot! Come on you mother fuckers! Come on! One more step!" As the two perps froze, they actually looked down at the imaginary line that I warned them not to cross.

During this encounter I felt like a cave man facing a pair of saber tooth tigers with a club in his hand. On top of being very concerned about my personal safety, I was literally a breath away from pulling the trigger. It was almost as if I could see the temptation in their eyes deciding whether or not they should continue to lunge at me and attack. As soon as they looked at each other, I felt the threat diminish a bit, when they reeled back around and went back up against the side of the cab. Just about the time that I thought they were complying with my commands, I heard the one with the big mouth say, "He won't shoot us in the back." With that they were off and running.

As I took off after them, I remember commenting under my breath that I hate to run. When the two bad guys reached 6th Avenue, one went south and the one with the big mouth went north. Great! Now what?

It is truly amazing how your mind can compute information in a matter of seconds, to give you the answers that you need when you are in a dangerous situation. I decided to forget about pursuing the taller one, because he ran into a subway station. Instead, I opted to go after Mr. Big Mouth, because he was heading uptown where the streets were well lit. Then, out of nowhere, an unmarked car pulled up next to me and I heard the crackle of a police radio.

As I turned to my right, I saw two guys in plainclothes who looked like cops. A split second later on of them called out and said, "Hey, are you the off-duty cop who needs help?

My response was quick and to the point, "Yea!"

After hearing what I had to say, one of them called out, "Get in, we're Rockefeller Center Security."

Without hesitation I jumped into the unmarked security car and was quickly introduced to two Retired New York City cops who were now working for the Rockefeller Center security force. "Make a right," I said as their car reached the corner. As we drove toward the next traffic light, I scanned the streets and locked in on my target. There he was, Mr. Big Mouth standing on the corner nervously looking around for me.

The security car was still rolling to a stop when I leaped out and ran toward Mr. Big Mouth. Thank God he did not see me until I was right on top of him. Everything I learned in the police academy and on the street came pouring out of me, as I threw myself on top of this guy like a cheap suit. The second I flipped the robbery suspect to the ground we were engaged in a fierce street fight.

As crazy as this may sound, the effects of tunnel vision prevented me from feeling any of this bad guy's punches, while I focused my mind on one thing, my survival. Things started to really get ugly when I began to get tired of fighting and I realized that this particular perpetrator was trying to grab my revolver. With my life clearly on the line, I rallied every ounce of strength that I had left and poured it on until I heard someone yelling from behind, "It's OK, he's giving up!" When I turned around, I saw a sea of New York City Police Officers and the two security officers standing over and all around me.

While I sat on top of the perp and pushed his face against the concrete, I locked his hands behind his back and extended my free hand like a doctor in an operating room when I asked someone for a pair of handcuffs. As soon as someone slapped a pair in my hands, I had the "bracelets" on Mr. Big Mouth. As I started to slowly come out of the effects of tunnel vision, I could hear and see more that was going on all around me. Even though the cavalry was a little late coming to the rescue, the presence of such a large number of cops and police cars on scene was a very impressive sight to behold.

Since I was too tired to pick my prisoner off the ground, I literally dragged the perp over to the curb and deposited him in the back of the closest RMP (New York City Police Radio Motor Patrol car). The moment I heard a police radio broadcast the call to disregard the report of a Signal 10-13 Assist Police Officer, I wondered if my brand new VW was still parked where I left it. "Holy shit, my car," I said to the cop who was driving. As soon as I told the two cops that I left my car in the middle of the street with the engine running, the driver said, "Let's go." A split second later I was being taken back to Rockefeller Plaza so I could recover my car.

After racing over to Rockefeller Plaza, I was amazed to see that my brand spanking new fire engine red Volkswagen Rabbit was still running with the driver's door wide open and the headlights on. I guess no self respecting car thief would want to admit, that he stole a VW with a diesel engine that was left running in the middle of the street with the door open. This could only happen in New York City.

No matter how hard I tried I could not give this arrest away. When an NYPD Lieutenant told me that this collar (arrest) was too good to give away, I was forced to process the arrest. Personally, I didn't care about getting credit for this arrest, because I had three days off and wanted to get away from New York for some R&R.

To make a long story short, Mr. Big Mouth wanted to cooperate, but I had no intentions of listening. Finally, two New York City Police Detectives convinced me to speak to my prisoner. The next day I went to the Manhattan District Attorney's Office and after testifying in the Grand Jury I was given an arrest warrant for the bad guy who got away.

After visiting the local police precinct and getting some plainclothes cops to give me a hand, we raided a fleabag apartment building on the west side and arrested the second robber. I will never forget the look on this guy's face, when he saw me standing in the open doorway to his shithole of an apartment, while armed with something a little more substantial than a five shot thirty-eight.

As a result of this particular off duty arrest, I met Mario Cozzi, the Assistant Chief Investigator for the New York (Manhattan) District Attorney's Office. At the time, I was on my way to visit a friend from college who worked in the DA's Office, when I heard a cranky voice blurt out, "Hey, Trooper, where's your horse?" Since New York State Park Police Officers wore the same snappy gray uniforms as State Troopers, it was common to be referred to us as a cowboy of some kind, especially since we also wore those light coffee colored Stetson hats.

The second I turned around to see who was talking to me, I spotted an older gentleman sitting behind a pile of reports. Since the sign on his door identified Mario as the Assistant Chief Investigator, I walked over and introduced myself. The moment we met, Mario asked me what I was up to. After I gave him a brief rundown of the off-duty incident that I was involved in, Mr. Cozzi leaned across his cluttered desk and asked if I liked being a uniformed cop, which I did. When Mario asked me if I had any other aspirations, I responded without hesitation and said that my dream in life was to become a U.S. Customs Agent. As soon as I told Mr. Cozzi what my long term career goal was, he smiled wide as he reached into his shirt pocket and removed a black leather commission book, like the type that federal agents carried. After accepting the worn leather ID case I flipped it open and almost died.

While I examined the retired credentials, Mario told me about his twenty plus years of service as a U.S. Customs Agent, which included time as an Attaché at our Embassy in Italy. I couldn't believe it. Here I was sitting across the desk from a man who retired from the job that I wanted in the worst way.

"Hey, you want to be a detective in the meantime?" he blurted out.

"Sure," I said as I sat back still in shock.

"OK, fill this out, send it to me and we'll be in touch," he said as he fumbled for a wrinkled application form and passed it to me.

That day I left the Manhattan DAs office totally amazed and more convinced than ever, that there was a God and that he liked policemen. Some three months later, while working another 3X11 tour in the Bronx, I received a phone call right after roll call. As soon as I took the call, I heard the scratchy and overpowering voice of Mario Cozzi almost yelling as he said, "Hey, hey, you start Monday. See ya!" As I hung up the phone, I smiled and thought to myself, what a colorful guy.

That Monday I sat across from his cluttered desk and watched Mr. Cozzi rummage through a desk drawer, while he asked me what badge number I liked. Not knowing what to say, I sat patiently as Mr. Cozzi held up a gold investigators shield displaying the number 109 before he tossed it over to me and said, "Hey, you like that one?" As I admired the gold badge, I responded and said, "Yes, Sir." In that instant I became an Investigator for the famous New York District Attorney's Office. As I left Mario's office to get my ID card photograph taken, it felt like I just received a battlefield commission.

MY FIRST LOOK AT THE BIG PICTURE

While working with an informant who was purchasing illegal firearms in Manhattan, my partner Ralph M. and I were told that an Arab social club owner wanted some assistance in kidnapping a wealthy New York businessman. The main reason why this businessman was targeted was because he was Jewish. (I should mention that our informant was a real character. When we documented this guy and told him that he was officially known as CI 6, he immediately asked what happened to CI 5.)

Once CI 6 briefed us about his conversation with the Arab social club owner, my partner Ralph M. and I eagerly volunteered to go undercover as the Mafia hit men that the subject of our investigation was looking to hire. However, before my partner and I went undercover, we needed to get the recorded conversations between our informant and the subject of our investigation "officially" translated from Arabic into English. In order to accomplish this, arrangements were made through our superiors at the DA's Office for me to meet an official from the Israeli government at the Lexington Hotel.

While I sat across from this Israeli official, I instinctively knew that I was in the presence of a very interesting and intelligent man. Even though this Israeli operative was much older than I was, he gave me the distinct impression that he was no stranger to a good fight.

Being a true professional, this Israeli official paid very close attention to everything that I said, when I briefed him about our investigation. He seemed to be especially interested in the part of the story that involved the Arab social club owner's vendetta against a wealthy New York businessman, because he was Jewish. Just like in the movies, I turned the tapes over to the Israeli official, shook his hand and left the room.

Shortly after my meeting with a representative of the Israeli government, I was contacted by an Israeli Police General stationed at the United Nations. Even though General Y.M. and his men were very busy, he personally made sure that I had every recorded conversation transcribed in time for my partner and I to make our next move.

MY FIRST UNDERCOVER RODEO

Going undercover as a young Mafia hit man was easy for me, because I had a vivid imagination and years of growing up in New York City under my belt. It also helped that I was a full blooded Italian American, who had plenty of opportunities as a kid to observe the local mobsters in action. I say this because back in the day, you would have to be deaf, dumb and blind, not to notice the traditional organized crime mobsters, who operated in New York City when I was a kid. In those days the mob guys were everywhere. Almost every aspect of life back then was in some way, shape, or form influenced by the Mafia, or so it seemed. What made them amazing characters, was how blatant they could be when they wanted to telegraph their presence, which of course was most of the time.

(All four of my grandparents immigrated from Italy to the United States in the early 1900s. My real family name is Iacobellis and is pronounced Yacobellis. Personally I regret that it was ever "Americanized" and changed to Jacobellis.)

In order to give you an idea of how I received my education about traditional organized crime aka The Mafia, permit me to take you back in time to the 1960s. I began learning about the Mafia and the impact that their activities had on life in New York City, when I walked into my aunt's house and I spotted a brand new color TV in the corner of the living room. While I admired this magnificent piece of "modern" technology, the nearby dining room table was filled with family members. Before I continue, you have to understand that back in the early to mid 1960s, it was quite common for middle class families to own a black and white television set. In other words, to own a color television set at that time was a big deal.

As I slowly extended my index finger, to touch the largest color television set that I ever laid eyes on, my father called out to me and said something about how the TV was a little warm and that I should be careful not to touch it, or I would burn my fingers. Of course everyone had a laugh at my naive expense.

As I looked at my father with young innocent eyes, I wondered what he meant, because my aunt's brand new color TV wasn't emitting any heat at all. I was twice as confused when my father called out, "It fell off a truck, son. Don't worry about it."

I was even more perplexed when I examined the brand new color TV and I was unable to find a scratch on it, let alone the type of damage that one would expect to see, if a television set fell off the back of a truck when it was being delivered. I was also surprised to hear, that my aunt and uncle would buy a TV that fell off the back of a delivery truck, even if there wasn't a scratch on it.

The day eventually came when my father explained, that the local mobsters were routinely selling hijacked truckloads of sought after items, to otherwise law abiding people at discounted prices. Buying stolen items of value was part of life back then. As my father would one day explain, plenty of good decent people supported the Mafia, by patronizing their underground black-market activities. Naturally, this included purchasing all sorts of luxury items, from fur coats to television sets in order to save money.

As a kid, I grew up in the black and white world of the 1950s and 60s, where you were either a good guy or a bad guy. There was simply no in-between. As I said before, you could be a victim, a suspect, an innocent bystander, or the detective handling the case. I should also mention, that despite the Mafia's negative impact on society, the streets in certain neighborhoods were safe, because criminals were more afraid of answering to the Italian mob than the police. In fact, back then, only a complete fool would mug an old lady, stick up an Italian deli, or burglarize a home in a neighborhood where the Mafia dons lived and operated. Like it or not, there wasn't a police precinct in New York City, that sent that kind of message out to the criminal element and everyone knew it.

Besides, back then, far too many cops accepted free meals and received all kinds of gratuities to look the other way and not enforce certain laws. Things really got out of control when some cops allowed themselves to be corrupted by drug traffickers and a few went on to commit other serious crimes. Still, no matter how sharp the mob guys looked with their flashy cars, clothes and jewelry, I never once wanted to be a part of their lifestyle. Years later, when it came time for me to act like a young Mafia hit man, all I had to do was remember the days when television sets "fell off the back of trucks" and never received a scratch.

During my first undercover assignment I had a chance to "break bread" with a real bad guy and pretend to be someone else, while I wore a Nagra recording device known as a "wire." What made this undercover operation even more interesting, was that we were assisted in our investigation by Israeli Intelligence Officers. Being assisted by the Israelis was my first opportunity to participate in a "big picture" undercover operation.

The first time I worked undercover, my partner and I met CI 6 and the subject of our investigation for lunch in Teresa's (Italian) Restaurant, in the Little Italy Section of lower Manhattan. During this meeting, I was relaxed and incredibly comfortable in my roll as a young Mafia hit man. Unlike my favorite movie stars, I had no script or cue cards to follow when I spoke to the subject of our investigation. Whatever we did worked, because Ralph M. and I made enough of an impression on the Arab social club owner to become part of his kidnapping and extortion plan.

When it came time to carry out this crime, Ralph and I met with CI 6 and the Arab Social Club owner to execute the kidnapping of the Jewish businessman. On the way to the victim's home in the Marine Park section of Brooklyn, we stopped the undercover car and placed the Arab social club owner under arrest.

An interesting turn of events occurred, when our prisoner didn't believe that we were police officers. Instead, the Arab social club owner thought that we were testing him, to see if he would give us up if he was taken into custody. When our prisoner continued to refuse to believe that we were police officers, we called our back up team over to convince the subject of our investigation that we were real Mc Coy. The moment the Arab social club owner was taken away in handcuffs, I knew that I found my niche in life. Simply put, I loved working undercover and couldn't wait to do it again.

Several years later I visited my friends in the DA's office and made a point to stop by and see Mr. Cozzi. When the Chief Investigator joined us and asked if I would like my old job back, Mr. Cozzi remarked with pride, "He's not going anywhere. He's got the best job in law enforcement. He's a Special Agent with the U.S. Customs Service."

CHAPTER 2

A DREAM COME TRUE

After waiting eight long years, I was finally offered a position as a U.S. Customs Patrol Officer in 1983. The day I reported to 2 World Trade Center, a young secretary in an empty office handed me U.S. Customs Patrol Officers Badge # 198 and my temporary U.S. Treasury ID card. Even though this wasn't much fanfare for a job that I waited so long to get, it was definitely a moment worth waiting for.

The day I reported for duty I met Jack L., the Assistant Special Agent in Charge at JFK Airport. When Jack asked me what I wanted to do in Customs, I wasted no time in telling him that I wanted to fly. As soon as Jack L. explained in a fatherly way, that my superiors would not want to hear that someone they just hired was eager to transfer to Customs Air Operations, I agreed to keep my aspirations to myself. After working in plainclothes at JFK Airport and out on Long Island, I was sent to the Federal Law Enforcement Training Center (FLETC) in Brunswick, Georgia.

EARNING MY WINGS

While I never knew exactly how it would happen, I was convinced the day would come when I would learn how to fly. The opportunity of a lifetime took place, when I was going through training at FLETC and I became friends with the four U.S. Customs Pilots who were in my class. When a Customs Pilot by the name of Bob W. heard me express an interest in learning how to fly, I was airborne in less than 24 hours.

At 31 years of age I was too young to be afraid and too gung ho to think that I could get killed while trying to learn how to fly. Regardless, I eagerly climbed into the cockpit of a Cessna 150 and started the engine with the help of my flight instructor. As we taxied out to the 10,000 foot runway, I learned the hard way that a plane is steered with your feet and not with your hands when it was on the ground. After I sloppily managed to make it to the runway, Bob W. showed me how to run up the engine and prepare for takeoff. In a matter of minutes I was airborne.

After about ten hours of flight instruction, Bob W. was ready to cut me loose for my first solo flight. On the morning of March 26, 1984, the weather broke and Bob W. decided that I had waited long enough. Just to be sure that I was ready to solo Bob and I took off for some additional practice runs. After completing a number of "touch and goes" Bob told me to stop the plane halfway down the runway. While speaking with a Texas drawl, Bob grinned and said, "I'll wait here for you," as he calmly exited the plane, closed the door, walked over to the side of the runway and sat down.

After I looked around the small cockpit, I checked the controls, scanned the instruments and applied full power, without giving my decision to solo a second thought. As I rolled by my flight instructor, I got the thumbs up sign for good luck. Before I knew it the single engine Cessna was picking up more and more speed. At the time, I was so excited I never noticed that I was alone inside the cockpit. When I reached the point of no return, I knew what had to happen next. At just the right time, I gently pulled the controls back into my chest and rotated the plane into the air. I was as euphoric as a human being could be without using drugs. I was flying on my own with no one else in the cockpit. Clearly, this was one of the greatest moments of my life.

After I successfully completed three solo "touch and goes" I parked my plane by a small crowd of Customs Patrol Officers and Pilots; all friends who supported me through my flight training. My T-shirt was ripped off Army style and inscribed with the date of my first solo.

In addition to being one of my greatest personal achievements, learning how to fly put me one step closer to getting a transfer to Air Operations. Learning how to fly would also come in handy, when I began to plan and direct the undercover air operations that are the primary focus of this true story.

After completing 13 weeks of training, I returned to New York. Initially, I worked in plainclothes at the International Arrivals Building at JFK Airport. I was eventually transferred with two of my friends to the RAC Long Island at Republic Field. My first assignment at the RAC Long Island was to work with Jimmy Z., a U.S. Customs Patrol Supervisor from the Marine Unit. Shortly after we met, I gave Jimmy Z. the nickname "Otto" because he looked like a German U-Boat commander whenever he wore his white Irish wool sweater.

OTTO

The ride over to the U.S. Coast Guard Base on Governors Island, on the thirty six foot U.S. Customs patrol boat, was a relatively smooth trip. Our mission that night was to establish a floating surveillance platform, to observe the stern of a Colombian freighter that some Special Agents believed was transporting 100 kilos of cocaine.

Once we arrived on Governors Island, we tied up next to the U.S. Coast Guard Cutter Dauntless and set up our beach chairs to wait out the night. To fight off the boredom one of our fellow crewmen, an older Customs Patrol Officer (CPO) broke out his fishing pole, while Kenny C. and I went to the base Burger King to fill up on fast food. After we ate, we took turns watching the stern of the Colombian freighter from across the river.

By 3 AM or so we were getting ready to call this surveillance off, when I took one last look at the murky water around the stern of the large black freighter. As I looked through the binoculars, I could not believe my eyes when I saw a diver wearing a black wet suit in the water. Just to make sure that I wasn't seeing things, I asked Kenny C. to take a look. Sure enough, Kenny confirmed my observations. Since we had no radios, we had to run half way around the base, to return to the pier where "Otto" was sitting on a lounge chair.

As soon as we ran up to Jimmy Z., he could tell that we were excited. In between huffing and puffing, I spoke as fast as I could, as I pointed toward the Colombian freighter and said, "Jim, there's a diver in the water. I'm sure I saw one."

Otto was calm, cool and very collected as he asked, "What did you see?" With Kenny C. backing me up, I described how I observed the head of a scuba diver bobbing up and down behind the rudder of the ship that we had under surveillance.

Jimmy Z. was a former U.S. Customs Air Security Officer aka Sky Marshal who worked his way up in rank and had a real passion for working on the water. Personally, I always thought we got along great. In fact, before I go any further, let me say that going to work with Otto was always a pleasure and something to look forward to. As a result, I was anxious to do a good job for him. I had also been in law enforcement long enough to know when I saw something, especially something as unique as a scuba diver in New York Harbor. When I filed my report I made sure to do so with confidence.

Although he seemed a bit reluctant at first, Otto began to nod his head and consider the possibility, that what we actually saw a scuba diver in the water behind a Colombian freighter, on the Brooklyn side of the harbor. After looking out into the New York Harbor, Jimmy Z. relayed our observations to the U.S. Customs Agents, who were maintaining the surveillance on the subject vessel over in Brooklyn. Soon the radio crackled with reports of noises being heard in the water around the pier area. I wasn't crazy after all. There was a diver in the water. Moments later, several special agents reported hearing splashing in the water around the freighter.

As soon as the surveillance teams tightened their perimeter around the Colombian freighter, we heard calls for assistance from the special agents who were in hot pursuit of a car that picked up a scuba diver from a nearby pier. In no time, Otto had the thirty-six foot U.S. Customs patrol boat (a former U.S. Navy Vietnam War era SWIFT boat) cranked up and heading across the harbor.

After years of plying my trade as a local law enforcement officer, I finally made it to the front lines of our nation's Drug War as a U.S. Customs Patrol Officer. While our patrol boat raced across New York Harbor at flank speed, I was screaming inside, as I thought about the days when swashbuckling U.S. Customs Officers boarded tall ships in New York Harbor, to enforce the laws of a new nation.

While the special agents on land made their arrests and recovered a duffel bag filled with cocaine, my colleagues and I on the patrol boat searched the Brooklyn side of the river, to see if there were any other divers or contraband under any of the piers. After Otto entered the filthy water to conduct a more thorough search under one of the piers, we cleared the area and returned to base.

My first surveillance and interdiction effort as a U.S. Customs Officer ended in success. Unfortunately, my morale would suffer a bit, when the U.S. Customs Service handed out commendations and cash awards, to the personnel who participated in the seizure of 75 kilos of cocaine valued at $7.5 million dollars, from a freighter called the Republica de Colombia.

I'll never forget the look on Jimmy Z.'s face when he told me that there had been a slight oversight and my name, as well as Kenny C.'s name, were not turned in for a commendation and cash award. As you can imagine, I was a bit disappointed to learn that I was overlooked, especially since I made more of a contribution to this seizure than the old patrol officer with the fishing pole, who fell asleep during the surveillance, but got recognized anyway.

Jimmy Z. was kind enough to take me and Kenny C. out for dinner where we laughed about the inadequacies of the system over Mexican food and a few beers. Later on, another veteran U.S. Customs Agent I knew told me not to worry about being overlooked, because the day would come when I would get an award when I did not deserve one. Needless to say, that never happened during my career in the U.S. Customs Service.

This type of case did not happen every day in New York City, but there was one place where it did. That night I started to think about transferring to Miami; a duty station that was filled with nonstop action.

LET THE GAMES BEGIN

The fact that I had some investigative experience came in handy, when it came time for me to conduct my first federal criminal investigation. While I was stationed at the Long Island RAC Office, I was assigned to work a collateral investigation that involved locating a fugitive. This particular investigation intrigued me, because it involved a manhunt for a fugitive, who was wanted for his involvement in a marijuana smuggling case. The RAC Long Island was contacted because this fugitive was believed to be hiding out in New York State. With not much to go on, I started digging.

Needless to say, as a newly hired CPO (Customs Patrol Officer) I wanted to make a good impression. For several days, I used every contact I had and ones that I had to make, in order to locate the fugitive who was wanted by our agents in Florida. Eventually, I was able to pinpoint the missing link's whereabouts to a business in Rockland County, New York. The day I was ready to make an arrest, I asked CPO Bob S. and CPO Kenny C. to give me a hand. Special Agent Tommy N. was sent along to keep an eye on us, a fact that reinforced my faith in the information that I developed, because Special Agents only seemed to go out in the field when things looked promising.

Being a native New Yorker meant that I was accustomed to winter weather conditions. As a result, snow storms and cold weather never bothered me. If anything, a fresh coating of snow always made me feel like it was Christmas time. Regardless of the inclement weather, we made our way up to Rockland County from our office at Republic Field on Long Island. By the time we got into position, the snow was ankle deep.

As a result of some old fashioned police work, the fugitive was located at an auto supply store. Because of the layout of the combination warehouse and showroom, we positioned ourselves in the parking lot, so we could arrest the fugitive when he left work and headed for his car. Once it started to snow again, it didn't take long before the parking lot and our cars were covered with a fresh blanket of white stuff.

At the end of his work day, the fugitive emerged from the building and headed towards his car. After days of tracking him and hours of sitting in our cars, it was time to move in. Since it was my case, I got to call the shots. As the fugitive walked to his car, oblivious of our presence in the parking lot, I picked up my Customs radio and imitated Gene Hackman when he played Detective Popeye Doyle in the French Connection and yelled, "Move in! Take him down!" Just like in the movies, all four of us converged on the fugitive's car with guns drawn.

Like many other enforcement actions, this arrest went down fast and thankfully without incident. Once I called the case agent in Florida, to let him know that we found his fugitive, I finished some paperwork and made the long drive back home on an ice cold sleet driven night. The next day this arrest made the local newspaper. The Customs Service got some ink and my colleagues and I had a little bit of fun in the process.

This arrest did not go down in the history of The Drug War as a major campaign, or for that matter anything even close to a skirmish. Successfully conducting this "collateral" investigation did enable me to further develop my investigative capabilities and provide assistance to a U.S. Customs Agent in our Jacksonville office. In the end, that was enough for me.

UNDERCOVER AGAIN AND LOVING IT

While I was assigned to the RAC Office at Republic Field, I volunteered to work undercover in a fishing village on the tip of Long Island. During this assignment, I worked undercover with Jimmy Z. aka Otto, Agent Tommy N. CPO Jim O'R and CPO Bob S. The fact that I attended the Marine Law Enforcement Training Course aka Boat School at FLETC, enabled me to gain some valuable field experience, when I had the opportunity to serve on the undercover vessels that we used during this operation.

Everyone involved in this operation was a pleasure to work with. In particular, Bob S. and Jim O'R. were fearless individuals, who looked more like pro football players than federal law enforcement officers. While Jim O'R. really did play for a college team, Bob S. was famous for telling strangers that he was in the Samoan Football League.

When one of the locals wondered if Bob was telling the truth, he responded in a very convincing tone of voice and said, "The reason you don't recognize me is because I wear a helmet when I play." Deep down inside I was hysterical laughing, when this particular local resident began to nod her head and accept his explanation. It was this type of quick witted response that made Bob S. well suited for undercover work. Simply put, you can't train people to think on their feet like this and come up with a response that sounded legitimate, even though it is was complete bullshit. Jim O'R also had moments when he was equally convincing in his undercover role.

During this operation we got to practice what it was like to adopt a fictitious identity and gather information without revealing who were really were. We also got the chance to work in a potentially dangerous environment, without carrying badges or guns and without back up.

While working in this undercover operation, Bob S. and I talked seriously about transferring to Miami. Towards the end of our assignment, we convinced our wives to let us travel to Florida to check out the office and speak to the boss.

As soon as we met the Chief of Patrol in Miami, we accepted his offer to transfer to South Florida with all moving expenses paid for by Uncle Sam. Unfortunately, everyone seemed anxious to go except my wife. In addition to having a career that she really enjoyed, my wife made a lot more money than I was making at the time. Worse yet, I was asking her to leave a job where she was recently promoted and became the first woman officer of her corporation.

My wife also knew that I was not one to work the required eight hours a day and race home for dinner. In the end, my wife reluctantly agreed to go. Years later our marriage would strain to the point of almost disintegrating, because my wife regretted not staying behind to maintain her career. In a way, I couldn't blame her.

Once the moving truck picked up the contents of our small apartment, we were off to the airport to catch our flight to South Florida. As far as I was concerned, there was something motivating me to transfer to the Sunshine State. As a result, I was 110% confident that I was doing the right thing.

A VIEW FROM THE FRONTLINES

By the mid 1980s the Drug War was escalating. Instead of the emphasis being on the Mexican Border, as depicted in the Life Magazine article that I read back in 1969, the spotlight was now on South Florida. Fortunately, the fix was in and I knew before I arrived that the Chief of Patrol assigned me and my partner Bob S. to the Miami Freighter Intelligence Search Team, otherwise known as FIST. After a trip to the range to qualify with our weapons, including the 9mm H&K MP5 submachine gun, my buddy Bob S. and I were ready to get to work.

The FIST Group covered the Miami River and the Port of Miami on a 24 hour, seven day a week basis. U.S. Customs Patrol Officers worked in plainclothes and in unmarked cars developing informants, conducting surveillance operations and raiding freighters to interdict shipments of cocaine, marijuana, U.S. currency and weapons. Naturally, it did not take long before I realized that Miami was like Morocco, a web of intrigue that was not to be compared with any other part of the country.

Every day we went to work, my partner and I spent our time stopping cars and trying to develop informants, who could let us know when drug shipments were going to be smuggled into Miami. The ships we watched ranged in size from large vessels to small coastal freighters. In addition, we covered the cruise ships and the less attractive Haitian freighters. Clearly, working along the Miami River and in the port area was a lot like being a street cop in a high crime area.

Shortly after we arrived in South Florida, my partner Bob S. and I participated in our first arrest and drug seizure. Since this case involved a freighter that was in dry dock in Port Everglades (Ft. Lauderdale), we met at Lester's Diner on State Road 84 to grab something to eat, before it was time to take up our positions.

The case we were working on that night was assigned to CPO Paul G., the most active and successful FIST member in Miami. Paul G. was a super hard working CPO, who had more informants working the Miami River and the Port of Miami, than the Catholic Church had priests in the Vatican. When Paul said that we would make a seizure, we made a seizure. This night was no different. (Just like the rest of us who served as CPOs, Paul G. would get promoted and become a Special Agent when the Customs Service expanded its investigative force.)

After we ate, we were given our assignments and made our way into Port Everglades to assume our positions. During this tactical interdiction operation, Bob S. and I were assigned to maintain the eyeball on the freighter. This meant that our job was to report any suspicious activity. After spending several hours sitting in a sweltering hot car, we spotted a smuggler walk down the gangway of the suspect vessel.

As soon as we notified the other members of our team who surrounded Port Everglades, we received requests from several CPOs to give the direction of travel of the suspect. Since Bob and I were knew to the area, we were about as lost as you could be. We barely knew the difference between north and south, especially since it was our first time inside Port Everglades. In no time, Bob and I were hysterical laughing, while we sat in our car and tried to direct our first surveillance in South Florida.

Finally, the suspected smuggler got into an old car and began to drive out of the port. Now we were on our way. To say that we were anxious and excited would be an understatement. We also instinctively knew that the car we were following had to be loaded with drugs as we headed toward the exit to the Port.

Everything was going well, until the crewman we were following turned into the on-coming traffic lane and sped toward the exit at a high rate of speed. While CPO Bob S. and I were in hot pursuit, CPOs Louie M., Scott L. and Paul G. had the exit blocked and intercepted the smuggler before he could escape. Once the driver was handcuffed and searched, we found 13 kilos of cocaine in the trunk of the old Ford Torino. This seizure was a great way to welcome us to South Florida. Even though I didn't know how or when it would happen, I would see a lot more cocaine than 13 kilos in the future.

CHAPTER 3

AIR OPS

One of the happiest moments in my career took place in April of 1986, when I was contacted by Roger G. from air operations and asked if I was still interested in becoming a U.S. Customs Air Officer. Without hesitating I accepted the position and was welcomed aboard. In addition to receiving a promotion and a pay hike, I would finally be getting my wings and a chance to live my life long dream and become an aviator for Uncle Sam.

The late 1980s and early 1990s was the period of time when the United States Government went on the offensive and decided to take the fight to the enemy. This was the height of The Drug War in South Florida and the Caribbean; an era when the U.S. Customs Service was dramatically expanded in size to meet the drug smuggling threat head on.

REPORTING FOR DUTY

The day I arrived at Homestead Air Force Base to assume my new duties, I got the distinct impression that we were a nation at war. This seemed obvious the moment I observed a number of heavily armed U.S. Customs aviators wearing military flight suits, military flight boots and military issued sunglasses. Even some of the aircraft that the Customs Service operated was either previously or currently used by the U.S. Armed Forces. The fact that we conducted ourselves in a paramilitary fashion also made The Drug War seem like a real conflict. I say this because almost every aspect of our job was influenced in some way by military tactics and military protocols. Even the way we told time and spoke on the radio, was very GI, especially when we used Zulu Time. (The military refers to Greenwich Mean Time as Zulu Time.)

Whether we were chasing smugglers through the mangrove swamps, on the open ocean, in the air, in remote border areas, or in populated urban areas, being a U.S. Customs Officer or Agent was a dangerous profession, that at times was considerably more exciting than traditional police work. Working in places like South Florida, throughout the Caribbean and along the Mexican Border also reinforced the fact that we were operating on the front lines. This was the case, because the action was non stop and always very intense in these locations. The fact that people on both sides of this conflict carried guns and used codes to communicate, further added to the intrigue and made surviving contact with the opposing forces something to celebrate.

Anyone who questions, whether it makes sense to relate to The Drug War in military terms, is either a non combatant, someone who has never been involved in drug enforcement operations, or isn't paying attention. Certainly, anyone who lost a loved one or a friend to a drug overdose, or watched a loved one or friend ruin their life by using drugs, will agree that the drug problem is far too serious of a conflict, to only be classified as a social crime dilemma.

CHAPTER 4

THE AIR WAR OVER THE BAHAMAS

Many of the men I flew with in the U.S. Customs Service were combat veterans of the War in Vietnam and had years of experience chasing smugglers. Some of our pilots and air officers also had law enforcement experience from other agencies.

For the record, U.S. Customs Air Operations was a very professionally run organization. This was the likely the case, because Air Ops was generally managed and supervised by former military pilots. Air Ops was also staffed by a rather impressive number of very capable people. This included U.S. Customs Pilots like John R., Bill P., Red D., Roger G., Gene P., Ron M., Rick B., Ralph G., Jack H., Brooks B., Robbie V., Mike S., Bob B. etc… Larry K. and Harry B. were two Special Agents, who went on to serve as Aviation Group Supervisors and provided critical support to the undercover operation that is the central focus of this true story.

My first air chase took place over the teal green waters of the Caribbean near Eleuthera Island at sunset. As soon as we intercepted the "bogie" or target aircraft, the drug smuggling pilot began to make his run. After we broke off our pursuit and circled above the air drop site, we watched the kicker crouch in the open door of the smuggling aircraft and drop several bales in a nice neat line near an awaiting vessel.

This was the moment I had waited a long time for. I was patrolling the frontlines of the Drug War in the Caribbean, in a U.S. Customs aircraft, that was ready to prevent the smuggling of contraband into the United States. Then reality set in. With no U.S. Customs, or U.S. Coast Guard patrol boats in the area, this drug shipment would likely get through. Worse yet, the act of smuggling that I just witnessed was not a crime in the United States, at least not yet.

The next airdrop that I observed was further down the Bahamian Island chain. A Beechcraft Queen Air approached from the south and executed three perfectly good passes twenty-five feet above the ocean. All I could do was watch in complete amazement, as I counted eight splashes in the water on each run. After the third airdrop, the drug plane made a sharp right turn and headed south again. It was fruitless to chase this aircraft, because the United States was in the other direction. All we could do was pass each other in the sunset sky and go about our business as if nothing happened.

A number of drug smuggling pilots and their crews weren't so lucky. In one short period of time, five drug smuggling aircraft crashed into the sea, while being pursued by U.S. Customs aircraft in the Bahamas. Each one of these smuggling aircraft crashed while trying to airdrop drug shipments to awaiting smuggling vessels. On one occasion, a Piper Navajo cart wheeled into the ocean, after the drug pilot dropped his landing gear and flaps too close to the waves, when the kicker started tossing out bales. This particular twin engine Piper Navajo exploded on impact and sank.

Even though under normal circumstances most people would be upset to observe a plane ditch or crash at sea, I never felt any remorse for the smugglers who were killed while trying to make a delivery. As far as I was concerned, drug smugglers were the enemy and if they died during the commission of a crime, so be it.

In another incident, two smugglers ditched their light twin engine aircraft during an airdrop and were lucky to evacuate the plane before it sank. Fortunately, for them and for us, a U.S. Coast Guard helicopter was on station and was able to pull the two smugglers out of the water.

This time I had a reason to get excited, because the coasties (U.S. Coast Guard) agreed to deliver the two drug smuggling aviators to Homestead Air Force Base, instead of taking their soaking wet passengers to Jacksonville Memorial Hospital in Miami. Bear in mind, that when the Coast Guard fished smugglers out of the ocean during this period of The Drug War, they usually took the "survivors" to the closest hospital. This was done so the "survivors" could get examined for exposure and injuries. By the time a team of U.S. Customs

Agents arrived to "clear" these rescued individuals through Customs, they were usually no where to be found. This time things would be different.

Even though at the time, these smugglers broke no laws in the United States, they were still obligated to "clear" Customs upon their arrival in our country. Doing so, gave us a chance to check these individuals out to see if they were wanted.

On the flight back to Homestead Air Force Base, I wondered how long my colleagues and I would have to play this deadly game of tag. At that time, the only thing we could do once a drug shipment was dropped into the ocean, was to try and have U.S. Customs or Coast Guard patrol boats pursue the marine smugglers who picked up a load. For every crash and burn, there was another daredevil with a pilot's license out there, trying to make a successful run, so he could get paid a large amount of money.

When the two smugglers were dropped off near the control tower on Homestead Air Force Base, they had no idea that I would be waiting for them. Once again, I felt like the Gene Hackman character Detective Popeye Doyle, when the "rescued individuals" jumped out of the Coast Guard helicopter and they found me standing there grinning and waving my right hand. With a contingent of U.S. Air Force Security Policemen standing by my side, I identified myself and asked the two men if they wouldn't mind clearing Customs. Naturally, they complied because they had no choice.

Instinct and experience, combined with a little training, can be a formidable tool for a law enforcement officer to possess. After conducting a brief interview, I knew these guys weren't going anywhere, until I checked them out from top to bottom and inside and out. I was also convinced, that the subject with the Swedish passport was "dirty" aka a criminal. Proving it was the hard part. The fact that what they just did in the Bahamas was not a crime in the U.S., meant that I could only hold them for so long while I checked them out.

When the Group 7 Duty Agent Special Agent Mark F. responded, he gave me a hand going over what little we had. Luckily, we were able to determine that our Swedish friend was in fact a fugitive, wanted in Florida for his involvement in a major smuggling venture. Under the circumstances, I felt great that my hunch about this guy proved to be correct. After releasing one of the rescued individuals, we arrested the fugitive and transported him to the Metropolitan Correctional Center (MCC).

WHEELS IN THE WELL

Once we were notified of a scramble, U.S Customs air crews had eight minutes to get airborne or "wheels in the well," so we could intercept an acquired target. As soon as the Command Duty Officer (CDO) announced the presence of a target that was worthy of further scrutiny, everyone on flight status grabbed their rifles and survival gear, before heading out to the flight line.

Somewhere over the Bahamas, a target was identified and was being tracked by our radar detection specialists. The U.S. Customs Citation Jet, which was already on patrol, was being diverted towards the radar blip, that was performing a series of turns over the ocean. Since we had a full compliment of personnel working the 4X12 shift, the Miami Air Branch would put up a maximum effort, to investigate the suspicious aircraft. At the very least, we wound get a chance to practice our skills, even if we found nothing. If we were lucky, we would fly smack into an airdrop of drug contraband and begin a chase that would take us in any number of directions.

So far, I had flown in every fixed wing aircraft and helicopter that the U.S. Customs Miami Air Branch had in inventory, except the old twin engine blue and white Aero Commander that we affectionately called Emily. With our Citation Jet already airborne and no seats available in the Black Hawk helicopter, I jumped in with Customs Pilot Bill P. and Customs Pilot Dennis Del G. and strapped in.

While the Pilot in Command (Bill P.) taxied the old Rockwell 560 Model Aero Commander towards the active runway, I watched as our Black Hawk helicopter got airborne. In a way, I envied my fellow Air Officers, who were lucky enough to be assigned to bust crew duty in the "Hawk" that night. Everyone knew that the chances of seeing any ground action increased when you flew in one of our helicopters. This was the case, because it was the Black Hawk's job to insert the "bust crew" into any location where a drug plane landed, especially in places where fixed wing Customs aircraft could not safely land. Naturally, when feasible, Air Officers and Customs Pilots would made arrests while operating fixed wing aircraft.

After getting over the disappointment of being excluded from helicopter bust crew duty, I paid more attention to what was going on around me. Once Customs Pilot Bill P. got the green light from the Air Force control tower to take off, he applied full power to Emily's engines and off we went into the wild blue yonder.

As excited as you can be at a time like this, you have to keep your eyes and ears open. When you are not looking for other "traffic" (other planes in the sky), you pay close attention to the radio chatter so you can follow what's taking place. You need to do this, so you will know what to do, if you are called into action.

Once everyone lifted off, we each had an assigned task. Since Emily was an air interdiction asset, we got to fly out over the ocean to rendezvous with the Citation and get into the chase. While we went feet wet and headed out over the ocean, the Black Hawk skirted the coast and waited to pounce on the smugglers if they landed stateside.

Again we were functioning like a team. While the Customs Radar Detection Specialists at our air interdiction command and control center known as C3I, continued to track the target, he directed our Citation Jet to the area where the "Judy" (target aircraft) was located. After being vectored into the area by C3I, the Customs Citation Jet jumped the target aircraft in the middle of an airdrop.

As the smuggling vessel moved in to pick up the packages that were dropped into the ocean, the crew realized that their associates in the smuggling aircraft were in trouble. This was easy to figure out, because the Citation Jet had no stealth capabilities. As a result, it was impossible to hide its presence from the smugglers on the boat below. In an effort to warn a fellow smuggler that he was in trouble, the boat captain radioed the pilot of the Aztec with the bad news that he had company on his tail.

Unfortunately for the bad guys, a smuggler flying a light twin engine Piper Aztec would never be able to outrun a Citation Jet. Under the circumstances, the pilot of the smuggling aircraft had limited options. These options included, ditching near the friendly smuggling vessel, or landing in a place where the Citation was unable to land. Smugglers also had to be concerned that there were no U.S. government helicopters in the area. They could also make a run for the U.S. coastline and try to mix in with the other air traffic, especially as night fell over South Florida.

As Bill P. eased up on the throttles, he put Emily into a slow turn and joined up on the Citation, as it continued to follow the red and white Aztec. From my vantage point in the back of Emily, I was close enough to the action to see that there were two people on board the smuggling aircraft. This was a typical flight crew for an air drop scenario. It was also our good fortune that we were headed straight for the South Florida coastline.

While I sat in the un-air-conditioned chase plane, I check my survival gear, just in case we made an unscheduled stop in the Atlantic. In addition to my U.S. military issued inflatable life jacket, I wore my survival vest over my flight suit and my police style raid jacket. Tucked under my left arm was a nylon shoulder holster that contained my 9mm pistol and one spare thirteen round magazine.

I also carried a small five shot .38 caliber S&W revolver and a Colt CAR-15 assault rifle with two 30 round magazines tapped together. An additional 20 round M16 magazine, extra pistol magazines, revolver ammunition, handcuffs, a strobe light and other equipment was secured in my military issue survival vest. Many of us also carried canteens and food in our helmet bags, because we never knew how long we would be out on a chase, or where we would end up.

Since I had some time to spare, I decided to feast on some crackers and lukewarm water while I kicked back to watch the show. After I finished my last cheese cracker and I sipped some water from my canteen, I heard the Citation pilot ask if we would take the lead position in the chase.

As Bill P. brought Emily in behind the Aztec, the Citation pulled up and off to the side to give us plenty of room to maneuver. The coastline of South Florida was off in the distance and our arch enemy, nightfall, was approaching fast. If a smuggler had one chance in a thousand, it was at night, in a chase over a well lit city. (I am not going to explain why.) I will say, that safety was our first consideration. As you can imagine, things could get very complicated, when we pursued a smuggling aircraft over a major city, that included a sky full of legitimate air traffic. Fortunately, the FAA air traffic controllers did an amazing job in clearing paths for us, whenever we crossed over into U.S. airspace.

Shortly after getting in behind our target, we spotted all sorts of debris being thrown at us from the open pilot's side window of the smuggling aircraft. Bill P. reacted quickly, as he yanked and banked Emily to the left and right, to prevent us from getting hit by tie down ropes and other items that could have seriously damaged our aircraft.

I was literally sitting on the edge of my seat, while the crazy bastards in the Aztec continued to throw things at our aircraft. Clearly, if any of these items crashed through our windshield or got caught up in one or both of our propellers we would be in serious trouble. Our aircraft was of course unarmed except for our sidearms and my rifle. Under the circumstances, all we could do to defend ourselves was to perform some fancy flying. Then it happened! A streak of light similar to a tracer round or a flair, shot out from the pilot's side window and whistled right by us.

Once again Bill P. reacted quickly and pushed the controls forward and dove for some safe airspace. "He's firing at us," I yelled, as the flair like object rocketed past our plane just missing us. As soon as I made my comment, the radio crackled as the details of what just happened were transmitted to the other Customs aircraft.

Under the circumstances, I would have loved the opportunity to open the emergency window and pepper the drug plane with 30 rounds of ammunition from my Colt CAR 15 assault rifle. Unfortunately, our rules of engagement prevented us from defending ourselves in this fashion.

In anticipation of a possible stateside interdiction, our Black Hawk helicopter was cruising along the beach between Miami and Ft. Lauderdale. As we approached the coastline, the lights came on as night fall blanketed South

Florida in darkness. By the time we went feet dry (crossed over onto land), we were pursing the smuggling aircraft over rush hour traffic.

No matter what this drug pilot did to elude capture, we managed to stay right behind him, as if we were dog fighting with an enemy plane that just invaded the United States. With no where else to go, the smuggler pilot in the Aztec set up to land at the International Airport in Ft. Lauderdale. While our co-pilot Dennis Del G. worked with the FAA and Customs Air Traffic Controllers, Bill P. planted Emily on the Aztec's tail, as the drug smuggling pilot made his final approach to land.

A few seconds later we touched down right behind the drug plane. As we continued our pursuit, I cracked the crew door open in anticipation of jumping out to make my arrests. I knew that once I left Emily, I would be on my own until the Black Hawk arrived, or Bill P. and Dennis Del G. were able to shut the Aero Commander down and give me a hand.

While Bill P. was giving some last minute instructions to his co pilot, I spotted the cockpit door on the bad guy plane open. Bill then reminded me to run around the wing and not under it.

As soon as I acknowledged his advice, Bill called out, "Get ready!"

While I inched closer to the open cockpit door, I kept telling myself to remember to run around the wing instead of under it, to avoid being decapitated. (All Aero Commander aircraft had a high wing instead of more traditional low wing. When the engines were off you could crouch down and walk under the wing. When the engines were turning, you had to walk around the wing to avoid being hit by the propeller.) As we continued to taxi down the runway, the drug plane veered off to another taxiway toward a deserted part of the field. All I could think about was getting to the bad guys, before they were able to exit their aircraft and make a run for it.

Before Emily came to a complete stop, I jumped out and ran around the left wingtip in order to safely execute this enforcement action. As soon as the Aztec rolled to a stop, I knelt down behind the right wing and pointed my Colt CAR 15 assault rifle at the cockpit. The second the cockpit door opened, I yelled, "U.S. Customs!" Once the two smugglers exited the aircraft and they made their way down the wing, I grabbed the co-pilot/kicker by the hair and forced him down to the ground. While I covered the pilot with my rifle, I ordered him to get face down on the ground next to his friend. By the time the Customs Black Hawk landed and inserted a bust crew, the two drug smugglers were in custody.

Just as I was recovering from a massive adrenaline rush, my Aviation Group Supervisor informed me that he wanted another Air Officer to receive the credit for making these arrests. My supervisor made this decision, because the other Air Officer's monthly stats were down. (Even though we were unable to make an arrest for air dropping a drug shipment in Bahamian waters, we were able to take the two smugglers into custody for their attempts to damage our aircraft in flight and assault federal officers.) After shaking my head in disbelief, all I could do was return to my aircraft and wait for Bill P. and Dennis Del G. to take me as far away from this place as possible.

Under the circumstances, the flight back to Homestead AFB was a quite one. Everyone knew I was disappointed to put it mildly. Once we landed, I changed my clothes and used the fifty mile car ride home to cool my jets while I considered all that transpired. As far as my supervisor was concerned, he ended up making things up to me, by allowing me to run free and work in the field, when I began to conduct air smuggling investigations.

Both drug pilots were later found guilty and were sentenced to four and five years in federal prison for assaulting federal law enforcement officers. As I look back on this incident, I can not help but think of all the talented people that make up this job. Fortunately, we tended to have more laughs than disagreements.

The next time I flew with Bill P. we ended up chasing a smuggling aircraft into another South Florida Airport. The picture that hangs in my den to this day, shows me and Bill P. standing in front of the plane that we seized during another nighttime interdiction mission. For the record, Bill P. was just like the other Customs aviators mentioned in this book; a true professional who was a pleasure to work with.

THE WORM TURNS

As the Special Agent in Charge of U.S. Customs in Miami at the time, Pat O'B. was determined to find a way to enable us to be more effective in our interdiction efforts. The way to accomplish this was to extend our area of operation deep into the Caribbean. In order to legally extend our area of operation, Miami SAC Pat O'B., Stuart S., from Customs Regional Counsel and a few other officials, including the Customs Commissioner created a plan that resulted in a change in federal law. This new law dramatically expanded our ability to interdict smugglers well beyond our borders. With the U.S. Customs Service, the State Department and the Bahamian Police working together, a plan was put in motion to create a joint Bahamian-American Narcotics Drug Interdiction Team. The operation was called BANDIT and few Americans are aware that it ever existed.

Before Operation Bandit changed the rules of engagement, the islands in the Bahamas were a safe haven for smugglers; a place where smuggling aircraft and vessels operated with little or no danger of being interdicted by Bahamian or U.S. authorities. Operation BANDIT changed the rules of engagement and permitted U.S. interdiction forces to operate in the Bahamas under strict guidelines. To be more specific, Operation BANDIT authorized U.S. Customs Officers and Agents to conduct joint interdiction operations in the Bahamas, as long as a Bahamian Police Officer was on-board the American aircraft or vessel.

Operation Bandit enabled Bahamian police officers to be inserted into locations that they were unable to respond to on short notice without our assistance. In other words, with our help, the Bahamian Police were now able to capture smugglers in the act. This was often accomplished, by using our technology to acquire the targets that our aircraft and vessels interdicted on behalf of our Bahamian Allies.

Once Operation Bandit was initiated, anyone using a U.S. registered vessel or aircraft to air drop, or attempt to introduce any illegal contraband within 250 miles of the United States, could be prosecuted under Title 19 United States Code 1590. The days of smugglers having a free reign in the Bahamas with no threat of U.S. intervention were over. We would eventually end up doing our job so well, that many smugglers were forced to operate further away from their traditional Bahamian drug sanctuaries. Please keep this in mind as you read on, because this victory of sorts, proved to be one of the underlying reasons, why the undercover operation featured in this book was initiated.

Even though the Bahamian-American Narcotics Drug Interdiction Team (BANDIT) was no secret, it took a while before every drug pilot caught on. During one interdiction mission that we flew, a pilot flying a smuggling aircraft air dropped his load within sight of our coastline. When this drug smuggling pilot flew into Ft. Lauderdale International Airport, he was surprised to see that we were hot on his tail.

While one of our patrol boats picked up the contraband in international waters, my colleagues and I in the U.S. Customs Black Hawk helicopter surrounded the smuggling aircraft as it rolled to a stop. The moment we placed the confused drug pilot under arrest, he asked why he was being handcuffed. My response was for violation of 19USC1590. As soon as I informed our prisoner about the change in federal law, he remarked, "But you didn't tell us about this." Naturally, when I responded, I asked our prisoner if we should have dropped leaflets over the Bahamas and Colombia, to advise him and the other smugglers, that a new federal law allowed us to make arrests under circumstances that were previously prohibited? The worm had turned and it felt great to have the upper hand over our otherwise elusive enemy.

Until the word got out, there were a number of very shocked and surprised smugglers, who thought that they could drop a drug shipment to go fast boats then land on a Bahamian Island, or fly into the U.S. and walk away free men. As long as Bahamian cops were working with us, U.S. Customs Agents and Officers could go anywhere in the Bahamas. Once we landed in Bahamian territory, the Bahamian Constables took the lead and moved in to make the arrest. Our job was to "protect the crew and our aircraft" unless summoned by the Bahamian police to assist. When we operated in the United States, we jumped out first and usually found the eager Bahamian cops toting their British Sterling 9mm submachine guns as they followed us into action. It was pretty amazing stuff.

During the early stages of Operation BANDIT we confused the hell of a lot of people in both countries. The rules of engagement had changed in our favor and the U.S. and our Bahamian Allies started to kick-ass in plain English. In time, we would force the smugglers so far south, that the incidents of airdrops and land based deliveries on Bahamian islands by private aircraft decreased dramatically.

Even though the front line of the Drug War in South Florida and the Caribbean had shifted, there was plenty of work to be done. One of our biggest problems was that we were generally too slow to react to new smuggling trends. The solution was to remain flexible and not be afraid to be just as bold and innovative as the smugglers were. Officials like Miami SAC Pat O'B, Stuart S. and Customs Commissioner Carol H. did just that.

CHAPTER 5

PURSUING AIR SMUGGLERS ON THE GROUND

While serving as a U.S. Customs Air Officer, I was just as interested in flying drug interdiction missions as I was in learning how to conduct air smuggling investigations. Early on in my career I adopted the attitude, that if I was going to work with pilots I needed to know what made them tick. More importantly, if I was going to start arresting pilots who were smugglers, I wanted to know as much as I could about aviators, aircraft and flying. In other words, I believed in the old adage, know your enemy. Learning how to fly and flying drug interdiction missions in U.S. Customs aircraft, helped me in more ways than one in this regard.

Before I could become a successful air smuggling investigator I had a lot to learn. In addition to reading technical manuals and flying magazines, I constantly asked questions and learned how fast and how far different aircraft could fly with various amounts of fuel and cargo on board. I also had to learn which planes were best suited for air drops. This included learning how crew and cargo doors could be modified, to facilitate a successful airdrop and allow the kicker to close the door in flight, once the drug shipment was jettisoned. Some smuggling aircraft were also modified to accommodate an additional supply of fuel in rubber bladders, metal tanks, or in 55 gallon drums. The more fuel and cargo a plane carried, meant that it was limited in the number of people that could be carried on board. Smugglers also had to maintain the "proper weight and balance," in order to insure the safe operation of their aircraft.

Thanks to my network of airport contacts and sources of information, I seized a number of aircraft, that were modified in violation of federal law to facilitate acts of smuggling. Becoming familiar with different types of illegal modifications, was something that I learned in the field and not in a formal training environment.

While developing my skills as an Air Officer, I also learned, that a legitimate FAA (Federal Aviation Administration) approved extra fuel system, is available for a ONE WAY "ferry" permit. This type of permit allowed an aircraft to be transported a long distance for a legitimate reason. To make this type of fuel system an illegal installation, a smuggler would install the "ferry tanks" and not file a notice with the FAA or get a 337 certificate. Drug smugglers were also known, to keep a plane equipped with an additional fuel system and fly more than the one flight than the ferry permit allowed.

My first big break as an Air Officer came, when a U.S. Customs Agent who was getting ready to retire, introduced me to a contact of his at a local airport. The day I met the documented source of information called Airport Sam, I immediately knew that he was extremely knowledgeable about private aircraft, as well as a wide variety of air and marine smuggling activities.

Even though Airport Sam was interested in working for Customs for the money, I sensed early on in our relationship, that he liked the intrigue and also enjoyed being one of the "good guys." In addition to the fact that I personally liked Airport Sam, I also found him to be very eager to work with an agent who didn't mind putting in long hours. In fact, as you will read, Airport Sam would become one of the most active and reliable sources of information I ever had.

Initially, I focused my efforts on identifying aircraft that were being used by smugglers, to fly drug shipments into the Bahamas and the CONUS (Continental Unites States). This included locating aircraft that were fitted with illegal fuel systems, that extended the range of a plane, so it could travel farther without having to refuel.

During the first few months that we worked together, I was able to develop a reputation for being an active air smuggling investigator. This reputation, along with the experience that I developed, made it possible for me to get promoted and become a Special Agent. Best yet, I was able to get assigned to the newly formed Miami Air Smuggling Investigations Group 7.

Steve Minas was the first supervisor assigned to Group 7. Steve was the son of a well respected Retired U.S. Customs Agent and one of the most devoted special agents on the job. As a tribute to Steve, who passed away in 2016, he is the only U.S. Customs Agent who I identify in this book by using his full name.

If there's one person helping St. Peter to secure the borders that surround heaven, it's Steve Minas. Rest in peace my friend.

SAC MIAMI AIR GROUP 7-THE EARLY DAYS

Whether I was working air smuggling cases as an Air Officer or as a Special Agent, I was pretty much a one man unit. This meant that I usually worked out of the trunk of my car and dressed in comfortable clothes, while covering the northern part of our area of operation. In fact, with the exception of Steve Minas, I rarely if ever worked with any of the agents in my group. To his credit, even though Steve was the Group Supervisor, he was available 24 / 7 to assist me whenever I needed help.

The 1980s was also the end of an era, when federal agents and police detectives kicked in doors the old fashion way and made arrests without the help of a SWAT Team. As an example, Steve Minas and I went on one raid together, when we took a smuggler into custody, who was harassing a federal witness by unleashing rats in the old ladies house. Needless to say, it was our pleasure to take this demented soul into custody.

Throughout my career as a U.S. Customs Agent, I was absolutely intrigued by all aspects of smuggling, especially air smuggling. While catching someone in the act of smuggling was exhilarating, infiltrating a smuggling organization and dismantling it from the inside out, was an adventure on par with the escapades of spies.

I should also point out, that even though I was operating in a target rich environment, it still took a great deal of hard work to make a case. It was also well known at the time, that a special agent was only as good as their informants and sources of information. As I mention elsewhere in this book, the main reason why I was successful in this regard, was because I was a "people person." I developed this skill at a very young age, while spending quality time with my father and my paternal grandfather.

Whenever I spent time with my paternal grandfather, the man I was named after, I thought he was the Major of New York City. I felt this way, because everyplace we went, my grandfather seemed to know everyone we met on the street. One reason for this, was because my grandfather and I never took a subway train or a bus. Instead, we walked everywhere. As a result, we were always meeting different people, when we walked from my house on East 29th Street in Brooklyn, to my grandfather's apartment building at 609 Rogers Avenue.

My paternal grandfather was also a great story teller. One of his favorite topics was to tell me about his younger days in Italy and his time in the Italian cavalry. Listening to my grandfather tell his stories, taught me to respect the fact that other people had interesting things to say. Later on in life, I became someone who was just as interested in relaying a good story, as I was in hearing one. This became a critical attribute to have during my law enforcement career, when I interacted with others.

In addition to being very entertaining, my grandfather was also very instructive. Looking back, my grandfather seemed to be determined to pass on as many pearls of wisdom as possible, right up until the end of his life. In addition to what I learned from our time together, my paternal grandfather made me feel very special, because he spent so much of his time with me. Even though I didn't realize it at the time, later on in life, I adopted the same trait and made it a point to spend time with my informants, sources of information and contract personnel.

My father was another people person, who got along just as well with strangers, store owners and casual acquaintances, as he did with close friends and relatives. At a very young age my father and his father showed me the importance of being sociable and interacting with others. My father also showed me how you could get better treatment, better service and better deals, when you were respectful and friendly.

One story worth repeating involves my younger years, when I though every adult male in Brooklyn was named Johnny. This seemed to be the case, because whenever my father was making a purchase, he would invariably remark in a friendly fashion something to the effect of, "Hey, Johnny, you're killing me. Can't you give me a better deal than this?"

The day finally came when I asked my father why Johnny was such a popular name. He laughed and explained how he used the name Johnny as an icebreaker, or a way to be more down to earth when he dealt with a stranger. Whatever he did worked, because he usually got a better deal by being more personable. There were also times when my father became a crafty SOB, who let whoever he was dealing with know, that he would not be taken advantage of.

I probably learned the most about how to cultivate and maintain good contacts and work undercover, when I went with my father when he visited local businessmen. One of his favorite stops was a bicycle shop that was owned by two brothers. Another one of my father's favorite stops was the local Oldsmobile car dealership. He especially liked to drive one particular car salesman crazy. I'm convinced that they had a mutual respect for each other and truly enjoyed haggling over the price of a car.

Making these regular stops with my father instilled in me the importance of taking the time to visit your network of contacts. In other words, people will end up doing a lot more for you in the long run, when you spend more time with them as a friend, as opposed to only stopping by because you need something. As an example, if you need to develop information at a private airport, or in a marina, you need to make regular visits to those locations that are more social in nature than official. Buying someone lunch, or stopping by for a cup of coffee to shoot the breeze, will do more for you in the long run, than if you come across like a typical bureaucrat.

When my informants, sources of information and contract personnel gave me valuable intelligence information, or performed a particular service, I didn't get up and leave once our business was concluded. Instead, I made it a point to be sociable and spend time with them. I did so for several reasons. One reason was because I liked people. I especially liked my core group of informants, sources of information and contract personnel. Simply put, they were a colorful collection of misfits, eccentrics, "angels with dirty faces" and patriots. I also learned a great deal about air and marine smuggling, money laundering and operating private aircraft, as a direct result of spending quality time with my network of contacts.

I should also point out, that my fellow agents and I were very selective, when it came to allowing someone to become a member of our core group of sources of information and contract personnel. As an example, two people who worked for us on one particular operation never made it into the core group and were cut from the team. Another person who wanted to work for us was never recruited, when another Customs Agent told me to avoid this individual at all cost.

I also didn't think it was appropriate to treat the people who were providing valuable information and assistance like a prostitute. As a result, my fellow special agents and I maintained a friendly professional relationship with our informants and sources of information.

My father and my grandfather were "regular" guys. There was nothing pretentious about them. The example they set, as well as their mentoring, made it possible for me to recruit, direct and control some of the most successful informants, sources of information and contract personnel who ever worked for a law enforcement agency.

ESCAPE, EVASION AND SURVIVAL

For as long as I live I will never forget January 8, 1987. One this particular night, I just finished working on some paperwork at the Group 7 office and was walking to my car to go home, when I heard the air operations scramble alarm over the loudspeaker. The moment I spotted U.S. Customs Pilot John R. run to his car and grab his gear, I went over to see what was going on.

As soon as John R. said that they were "short in the back," I eagerly volunteered to go along. Once I grabbed my Colt CAR 15 rifle and my helmet bag, that contained my flight suit, survival vest, raid jacket, water, food and extra ammo from the truck of my G-ride, I ran out to the flight line to join the others. By the time I jumped in the back of the Black Hawk helicopter, U.S. Customs Pilot Gene P. and John R. were turning over the engines and preparing to take off.

As any U.S. Customs Pilot or Air Officer will tell you, whenever we scrambled, we never knew where we would end up, or what would happen during each mission. Despite being well armed with weapons and survival equipment, U.S. Customs aviators wore military flight suits, military issue flight jackets and other police and military gear, so we could operate anywhere at anytime. This included, being trained and equipped to participate in different types of enforcement actions, while operating on different types of terrain, in different weather conditions.

It was part of the adventure to buckle up and go feet wet, then race over the ocean in hot pursuit of drug smugglers. As I am sure many of my colleagues will agree, we never thought about the dangers of ditching at sea, or what might happen once we jumped out to make an arrest with little or no backup. In fact, I personally believe, that U.S. Customs aviators operated with the same level of enthusiasm, as U.S. military aircrews during a combat mission.

As soon as we lifted off, Gene P. received the clearance from the Air Force control tower to transverse the active runway. In less than eight minutes, we were feet wet and racing into the darkness, toward a target that was being tracked near Bimini Island. Because our Bahamian Police escort was off that night, we were bound by the old rules of engagement. This meant that we were prohibited from taking enforcement action in the Bahamas. Nevertheless, we went on this mission to accomplish as much as we could, while operating within the boundaries of agency policy.

While we were hauling ass over the ocean, our crew in the Citation Jet was monitoring the activities of a Cessna 210, that was making its way toward Bimini Island. During this intercept, a U.S. Coast Guard Falcon 20 Jet joined up with our Citation Jet.

When we were about eight miles away from Bimini, we were notified that the target aircraft was descending for either an air drop or a night landing. A second or so later, we were advised that "the bogey" crashed. During this particular mission, I was sitting in the starboard side door-gunners window seat behind John R. As soon as I looked over John's shoulder, I saw a huge fireball light up the night's sky off in the distance. Once again, my colleagues and I had a front row seat to the action, in a conflict that was being waged while tourists enjoyed the night life of South Florida.

Based on the size of the fireball, Gene P. and John R agreed that there was nothing more for us to do, so they turned the Black Hawk around and headed back to the barn (slang for our base). Shortly after we turned around, the U.S. Coast Guard asked us to fly over the crash site and check for survivors. Without hesitating, John R. turned the Black Hawk back around and flew straight toward the burning wreckage, that illuminated the sky above Bimimi Island.

As soon as we arrived over Bimini and we made our first low level pass over the crash site, I could not believe my eyes, as I leaned all the way out of the open door gunner's window and called out over the intercom, "We've got survivors down there!"

As soon as our Pilot in Command (John R.) remarked, "What!" he banked the Black Hawk in a tight right turn and slowed her down to a gentle hover.

After hearing my report, Gene Parker immediately radioed the U.S. Customs Citation Jet crew, to report that we had two survivors wading ashore. It was also easy to see, that the survivor wearing the white pilot's uniform shirt appeared to be in pretty bad shape.

Based on our report from the crash site, the U.S. Coast Guard notified the authorities in Nassau, Bahamas and requested authorization for us to land and conduct a rescue operation. I could not believe my ears, when we were ordered three times not to land. The U.S. Coast Guard then asked us to stay over the crash site and wait until a U.S.C.G. helicopter from Opa Locka Air Station arrived in forty-five minutes.

As soon as we received this news, the sea below became filled with go-fast boats running lights out. These "suspected" Bahamian drug smuggling vessels showed up like vultures, to recover any contraband that floated free of the burning wreckage. It was truly an amazing site to behold, as we circled above the crash site in our intimidating behemoth of a helicopter, while we waited for the U.S. Coast Guard to arrive.

At the request of the United States Coast Guard, our new mission was to keep an eye on the injured pilot and refuse to let any of the smuggling vessels pick him up. Best yet, we had to accomplish this impossible task without landing. For the next forty-five minutes, we yanked and banked, dove and climbed for one hell of a ride, as we waited for the U.S. Coast Guard helicopter to arrive on station. In the meantime, the fire from the "suspected" smuggling aircraft burned for almost forty-five full minutes, before it extinguished itself.

Because the "suspected" drug plane ditched within a stones throw of the beach, it was easy to keep the injured drug pilot and his kicker under surveillance. Every time one of the go fast boats tried to move in closer to shore, we would swoop down and scare the living shit out of the bad guys with our enormously large and loud low flying black helicopter.

After thirty minutes of playing games with the Bahamian boat crews, the pilot of the U.S. Coast Guard helicopter called us on the radio, to advise that he was ten minutes out and on the way. That was the good news. The bad news was, that after waiting all this time, the U.S.C.G. refused to land without an armed escort to protect their rescue party. U.S. Coast Guard personnel weren't stupid. They felt that the situation was too risky, to put two unarmed crew members on a Bahamian Island in the middle of an apparent drug deal. The U.S. Coast Guard then contacted us and asked if we could assign an armed U.S. Agent to provide security for their rescue party.

When a radio report advised that Bahamian cops were on the island and were ready to assist us, I sat back in my seat and wondered where these Bahamian cops had been since we arrived on station. We had been hovering over that stretch of beach for some time and had not seen anyone except for the injured pilot and his associate.

The next time John R's voice came over the intercom, he asked for a volunteer to be placed on the U.S. Coast Guard helicopter. Since our Black Hawk Helicopter was not equipped with a transporter beam, the only way that we could transfer the lucky volunteer over to the U.S. Coast Guard chopper was to land on Bimimi. This automatically posed a bit of a problem, because we were previously ordered not to land on Bahamian soil. Despite the risks involved, I eagerly volunteered to help rescue the badly injured suspected drug smuggling pilot.

Without wasting any time, the U.S. Customs Black Hawk helicopter raced back to the nearby runway to drop me off. Once the Black Hawk landed, I jumped out and handed my Colt CAR-15 rifle to an Air Officer. I did so, because this was supposed to be a "rescue" mission, not an enforcement action. As soon as the Black Hawk lifted off, the crew waved to me, as the chopper returned to the U.S. Customs Air Branch complex at Homestead Air Force Base.

While I stood on the edge of the runway, it hit me that I was all alone, on an island that was a popular location for smugglers to use as a base, before making the final 37 mile run into South Florida. As I crouched down and scanned the area around the runway, I realized how crazy I was, for volunteering to help the Coast Guard rescue a badly burned suspected drug smuggling pilot.

Eventually, a spotlight illuminated the sky off in the distance as the U.S. Coast Guard helicopter made "a B52 approach" in order to pick me up on the runway. As the searchlight got closer, I stood up and used my U.S. Navy issue flashlight to signal the crew. Once the chopper set down, I ran over, jumped inside and knelled between the two pilots.

"OK, we'll lower you down when we get over the beach," said the U.S. Coast Guard pilot as we lifted off. As I looked around, I saw the crew chief preparing the harness that I would wear as I was lowered over the side of the chopper. Under the circumstances, all I could do was roll my eyes in complete disbelief, that I could have been so stupid as to cheerfully volunteer for this mission.

In a matter of seconds we were over the beach. Unfortunately, by the time we arrived, one of the go-fast boats made its way to shore and had the badly injured pilot on board. The remaining go fast boats were also in the immediate area. This meant that not much changed, as far as the potential security problem was concerned.

"OK, we'll lower you here," said the Coast Guard pilot, as he put the chopper into a stable hover.

"No way," I said, before I quickly added, "The rules have just changed. I'm not getting lowered down on top of some druggie go-fast boat."

As the pilot sized up the situation and realized that I was not about to follow his order, he glanced back at me and said, "What's next?"

"Time to go to Plan B," I said.

When the Pilot asked, "What's that?"

I shook my head I said, "I don't know, but this isn't it."

While the Coast Guard pilot flew the helicopter back to the runway, I considered my options, as far as the best way to accomplish our mission. During the very short flight back to the runway on Bimini, the Coast Guard PIC (Pilot in Command) radioed the two jets circling overhead, to tell them that things looked hostile on the beach. (No shit!)

As soon as we landed, a voice on the radio reported that "Nassau" said it was safe to land and that the Bahamian police were standing by to turn the injured pilots over to us. All I could do was shake my head and wish that the person on the radio was going with me, since he thought it was safe to go for a walk on the beach in this neighborhood.

After hearing the last radio message, the U.S. Coast Guard PIC looked back at me and said, "Would you take my crew chief and paramedic down to the beach on foot?"

As I unbuckled the harness, I keyed the headset mic and said, "Lets get this over with." Within seconds we were out of the chopper. After we ducked down and ran out from under the rotating blades, we stood off to the side for a second to assemble. When the crew chief asked me, "Which way do we go, Sir?" I looked at the polite Crew Chief and motioned him to follow me as I remarked, "This way."

As I led the way down to the beach, all I could think about was how much I hated being called Sir. Once we entered the trail at the edge of the runway, we became enveloped in some heavy brush. This particular path looked as if it had been used many times in the past, to carry drug shipments from planes to awaiting boats on the beach. We didn't get very far, when the three of us froze, as the bushes ahead of us rustled with activity. When two Bahamians dressed in civilian "street" clothes came closer, I heard the crew chief say, "Oh shit," in a low tone of voice.

Under the circumstances, I instinctively reacted by drawing my 9mm pistol, while I glanced back at the crew chief and said, "Chief, we're about to create an international incident." As I looked back down the trail, in the direction of the beach, I yelled, "U.S. Customs! Don't move!'"

The second I relayed my command, the two Bahamians froze and called with their British accents, "Don't shoot, Mon. Come with us. We'll take you to them."

As I holstered my pistol, I approached the two Bahamians and asked if they were Bahamian Police Officers. When I got no answer, the two fairly well dressed Bahamian men turned and walked toward the beach. Once again, I shook my head and led our rescue party on our mission of mercy.

A few seconds later, we emerged on a beautiful stretch of beach that would have been a nice place to spend some time, if it was located in South Florida. From a security standpoint, the bad news was that there were several Bahamians on board the go-fast boats that were parked in shallow water along the beach. Others were standing near their vessels.

Standing on the bow of one of the boats, was the badly burned "suspected" drug smuggling pilot, who was screaming at the top of his lungs that we shot him down. Needless to say, this was pure bullshit, because those of us who were flying in the Black Hawk were some eight miles away, when the aircraft crashed in shallow water along the beach. Since it is impossible to open the door on a Citation Jet in flight, it was also impossible for our Citation crew to shoot this aircraft down.

While I provided security, the Crew Chief helped the female paramedic get the badly burned pilot down from one of the Bahamian go fast boats. As soon as the female Coast Guard paramedic escorted the badly burned pilot back to the chopper, the Crew Chief asked me to help him get the other crew member. Just about this time, a short Bahamian in a dirty blue uniform police shirt, who was carrying a Belgium FAL assault rifle and a rusted 12 gauge shotgun with a cracked stock emerged from the crowd.

When the two gun toting Bahamian in the blue police shirt asked me to follow him, I responded and said, "Where to?" as I looked around and continued to size up the situation.

"The other one is down the beach. He needs help too," said the local cop.

At this point, the U.S. Coast Guard crew chief asked if I would mind, if he left to help the female paramedic take the badly injured pilot back to their helicopter. For some reason unknown to me at the time, I stopped and turned to face the Crew Chief and said, "You better wait for me. Don't go leaving me behind."

After assuring me that they would wait for me, the Coast Guard Crew Chief quickly added, "Go get the other guy and meet us back at the chopper." A split second later, the Crew Chief ran off to catch up with the female paramedic and her badly burned patient.

Now I was getting concerned. My instincts told me that this was not a good situation to be in. As a result, my first reaction was to offer to help the local constable by carrying one of his weapons. If the shit hit the fan I figured a long gun might prove handier than my pistol. It was also at this time, that I regretted leaving my rifle in the Customs helicopter. As I said before, the only reason I did so, was because this was supposed to be a rescue mission. What a mistake that was.

After we made our way a little further down the beach, I stopped and turned to my little sidekick and remarked, "Hey, where is this guy? You said he was a few hundred yards away." When the Bahamian constable responded, he pointed into the nearby patch of brush and said that the other injured bad guy was no longer on the beach, but in the bush.

As I looked into the overgrown vegetation along the beach, all I could see was a lot of darkness. I can't explain it, but I instinctively knew that trouble was close by. "No way. This is it." I said. Then, as I looked the Constable in the face, I remarked, "If this guy is healthy enough to run away, he doesn't need to be rescued."

The little Bahamian cop persisted. "Come with me, Mon. You can help me arrest him in there," again pointing into the brush along the beach.

Without wasting any time I faced the Bahamian Constable and remarked, "Forget it, my friend. I gotta go. If you want him arrested, call DEA, 'cause I'm outta here." The second I turned to leave, I heard the distinctive sound of the U.S. Coast Guard helicopter as it streaked over my head and kept going. I'll never forget how I looked up at the orange and white U.S. Coast Guard helicopter, as it left me alone, on this God forsaken Bahamian island that catered to drug smugglers. About all I could say was, "Son of a bitch,"

When the Bahamian cop looked at me and remarked, "They left you behind, Mon," the only thing I could think to say was, "No shit."

As I began to walk away, I had no idea how I was going to get back home in one piece. To make matters worse, by the time I made my way back to the vicinity of the crash site the armada of go-fast boats were pulled up on the beach by their crews. This resulted in a rather unfriendly crowd forming, with several Bahamian go-fast boat operators making fun of my predicament.

I knew my situation was getting worse, when one of the Bahamians, who I had every reason to believe was a smuggler, called out, "Mr. Customs Mon. Why don't you let us give you a ride back to Miami?"

As soon as the crowd laughed at my expense, I did my best to sound friendly when I responded and said, "No thanks."

When another Bahamian remarked, "Come with us, Mon and we'll take you for a ride down the coast," I decided that it was time to nip this bullshit in the bud, before things got real ugly. As far as I was concerned, the only course of action that made sense was to show the "Pirates of the Caribbean," that I was not going to be taken advantage of without a fight.

As soon as I stopped walking and I turned to face the crowd, I had no idea what I could or should do, or what the crowd would do next. Fortunately, the Bahamians made the first move, when a rather large Bahamian wearing a Mr. T starter set of gold chains and a gold watch, stepped forward and squared off with me. When the obvious leader of this group spoke with a British type Bahamian accent, he sounded dead serious when he said, "Hey, Mon, your friends left you behind. Where do you think you're going, Mon? This is an island."

Before I responded, I looked up and scanned the sky hoping to see a U.S. Customs Black Hawk helicopter streak overhead, but this aircraft was no-where in sight. Neither were the two jets. This meant that I was all alone and left to fend for myself. As I felt what little control there was fading away, I remembered what the New York City Police Academy instructors said about how to react in a dirty street fight. It was time to let the Bahamians know, that I was not to be fucked with and to do so without provoking them.

I should also mention that the Bahamian cop who was armed with a FAL assault rifle and a shotgun was standing quietly off to the side of crowd. As far as I was concerned, this Bahamian Constable represented absolutely no authority on this island. If he did, he would have come to my defense early on, but that was apparently too much to ask of this particular Bahamian policeman. Even the two Bahamians who we met earlier, never showed their faces and proved to be no help at all.

After weighting my options, I drew my 9mm pistol and held it by my side as I took a step closer to the rather large Bahamian. Since I had absolutely nothing to lose, I ignored the crowd and looked their apparent leader in the eyes and said, "I'm leaving and nobody follows me, understand." When the big Bahamian asked me where I was going, I continued to look him right in the eyes when I remarked, "To make a phone call."

As soon as I finished speaking, I continued to face the unfriendly crowd, as I backed into the vegetation that ran along the beach. Once I was out of sight, I took off running and headed inland. All I could think about as I ran was the music of the song "Runin Through the Jungle" by Credance Clearwater Revival.

It's amazing what goes through your mind at a time like this. In addition to thinking about a song that fit my predicament, I also remembered the three words that were the motto of the U.S. Air Force Water Survival School that I had attended. ESCAPE, EVASION, SURVIVAL! So far I had escaped and I was evading. Now, I needed to survive.

Once I found a suitable place to hide out, I took stock of my equipment and supplies. In addition to my 9mm service pistol and four magazines, I had my five shot .38 Special Smith & Wesson revolver, some extra revolver ammunition, a USMC K Bar Knife, my Navy issue crook neck flashlight and pack of cigarettes that I didn't need, because I didn't want to give my position away. Since I wasn't taking prisoners, I forgot about my handcuffs and continued to quickly go through my pockets and came up with a pack of chewing gum and oh yes, my portable radio.

To make myself less of a target I turned my raid jacket inside out and tied it around my waist over my green Nomex flight suit. I did this, to prevent the day glow yellow letters that spelled U.S. CUSTOMS on the back and the agent's badge that was on the front from being seen from a distance. I then pulled out my radio and began to broadcast in a low but steady voice. I stopped when I realized that there was no radio repeater on Bimini Island.

At this point, I resigned myself to accept the fact, that I was trapped for a while, until someone realized that I was Missing in Action. Holy shit I thought was I in trouble. A split second later, a strange sense of calmness came over me like a protective blanket and I actually started to grin. I then thought of a U.S. Customs Pilot friend of mine, who told me what it was like when he was shot down during the Vietnam War and how he evaded the NVA for three days until he was rescued.

This was 1987 and I was only thirty-seven miles from the USA, yet I might as well have been on the other side of the world. As I took cover in the most defensible position I could find, I did my best to remain quiet and calm. In fact, I became so in tune with my surroundings, I was able to listen to the mosquito's breath.

After what seemed like an eternity, I heard the distinctive sound of the Black Hawk helicopter, as this massive jet black flying machine raced back and forth over Bimini Island looking for me. As I broke from cover, I knew that yelling would be of no use. Fortunately, I remained calm and had the presence of mind to use my U.S. Navy flashlight to signal the Black Hawk chopper crew. Luckily, Air Officer Bill H. spotted my light. Once that happened, the U.S. Customs helicopter turned around and hovered near my position.

The bad news was that I was in a location where the large helicopter could not land due to the presence of so much vegetation. Once the Black Hawk pilots spotted a suitable place to land, they flew over to this location and made wide circles, as a way to let me know where they would be able to pick me up,

With my pistol in hand, I ran toward the clearing where the Black Hawk was circling. As soon as I broke through the brush into a rather large clearing,

U.S. Customs Pilots John R. and Gene P. came in so fast, I saw the tires on the XXXL size U.S. military chopper compress, as the Black Hawk made contact with the ground.

While I ran toward the Black Hawk, someone opened the cargo door all the way, just in time for me to jump inside. The second I landed in the cargo bay, Gene P. pulled pitch and we took off as if we were leaving a hot LZ in time of war. As soon as I saw the smiling faces of the crew, I smiled back and gave them the thumbs up.

On the flight back to Homestead Air Force Base, I heard the story of how the U.S. Coast Guard Pilots took off as soon as the badly burned pilot was placed on board their aircraft. Worse yet, the U.S. Customs Service was never told of my whereabouts, until our Black Hawk crew inquired via radio about the status of the rescue mission. It was also at this time, that our Black Hawk Pilot in Command advised the Coast Guard, that a car would be sent to Miami to pick me up. The reason for this was because Black Hawk helicopters were too big to land on the helipad at Jacksonville Memorial Hospital in Miami. From what I was told, the U.S. Coast Guard response was, "Oh, we left your agent on the beach."

As soon as they heard that the U.S. Coast Guard crew left me behind, the U.S. Customs Black Hawk crew raced back to Bimini to locate yours truly. This incident was investigated and naturally nothing happened. The U.S. Coast Guard helicopter crew admitted to leaving me behind and said they did so, because the security problem for their crew ended, once the injured party was placed on board their chopper. (Unbelievable!)

To this day, I still find it hard to believe, that I was placed in jeopardy, because a U.S. Coast Guard pilot thought the life of an injured "suspected" drug smuggler was more important, than the life of a U.S. Agent. My kids deserved to be raised by their father and not by the flag that would be presented to their mother at my funeral. I risked my life for this particular U.S. Coast Guard aircrew and the least they should have done, was wait for me to return to their helicopter.

For the record, the U.S. Coast Guard is an outstanding organization. History is filled with numerous instances, when U.S. Coast Guard personnel performed countless acts of bravery in both war and peace. That said, as far as I am concerned, the U.S. Coast Guard Pilot who decided to leave me behind, made a really bad call and should have been severely disciplined for doing so.

CHAPTER 6

MAKING THE TRANSITION TO UNDERCOVER AGENT

Rather than plunge right into the primary focus of this book, I thought it would be beneficial to explain how I made the transition from criminal investigator to undercover agent. I also thought it would be beneficial to introduce you to some of the key players involved in this true story. To accomplish this, I decided to explain how I met the men I would recruit to serve in The Blade Runner Squadron.

AIRPORT SAM, THE GAMBLER, MAJOR TOM & THE COLONEL

As I stated earlier, Airport Sam proved to be incredibly knowledgeable when it came to identifying private aircraft that were configured for smuggling. Airport Sam was also the documented source of information who enabled me to initiate an investigation into one of South Florida's most successful smuggling organizations.

It was also through Airport Sam that I met The Gambler aka Mr. Lucky and Major Tom, two private pilots employed in private aviation, who were also very eager to work for me as documented sources of information. The Gambler aka

Mr. Lucky was a military veteran with a pilot's license who made a good living buying and selling planes and running various businesses. Major Tom was a highly decorated Vietnam era helicopter pilot, who flew cargo planes then went into private aviation. Major Tom also happened to be the only African American to serve in our unit. Both The Gambler and Major Tom were real characters, who enjoyed trick fucking bad guys as much as everyone else who worked with us. Personally, I'm glad they were on our side.

Once The Gambler helped me make some cases, he introduced me to another private pilot I recruited and called The Colonel aka Captain Mona. The concept of networking continued throughout my career as a U.S. Customs Agent, when my contract pilots, sources of information and confidential informants continued to introduce me to people, who were eager to work undercover for Uncle Sam.

CALLE OCHO

I had another big break in my career, when Group 7 Supervisor Steve Minas asked me to become the control agent for a confidential informant that he wanted to me to work with. Steve believed that a Cuban American informant I ended up calling Hombre de la Calle (Man of the Street) aka Gordo (Chubby, Fatso), had a great deal of potential and needed to be properly directed.

I was nominated to be Hombre's control agent, because (as I was told) another agent who didn't act quickly enough, lost out on using the information that this informant provided, to make a major drug seizure. According to Steve

Minas, instead of the U.S. Customs Service being able to make this case, another agency ended up seizing thousands of pounds of marijuana.

While on the surface this might not seem to be a big deal, the Customs Service was unable to pay Hombre de la Calle the payment that he deserved, because our agency did not receive credit for making this particular drug seizure. Steve also knew that you increased the chances of making other major cases, when your informants, sources of information and contract employees were well paid and loyal to your agency.

The day Steve took me to the Little Havana section of Miami near Calle Ocho (8th Street) and he introduced me to Hombre, I instantly knew that we would get along just fine. Knowing that Hombre was a former smuggler who never got caught didn't bother me one bit. In fact, if anything, I liked the idea that my newly documented Cuban informant was a survivor, who was smart enough to voluntarily change sides before the authorities were able to close in on him. Besides, U.S. Customs Agents tended to have the most diverse types of informants, sources of information and contract employees of any federal law enforcement agency. Our list of "human assets" included commercial and private airport workers, licensed pilots, marina owners, merchant marine captains, merchant seamen, convicted felons, defendant informants, law abiding citizens and corporate executives.

Immediately after we got acquainted, Hombre told me that two drug traffickers from California were on their way to Miami with $500,000 to pick up 20 kilos of cocaine. To be even more specific, Hombre added that these two drug traffickers would be driving a car with Wyoming license plates. Sure enough, after working a surveillance for two days with the Miami Police Department Narcotics Unit, the two subjects arrived in South Florida as expected.

After conducting a mobile surveillance from Miami to Ft. Lauderdale, a trip that involved me deputizing the Miami cops as U.S. Customs Officers, we used a police dog from the Broward County Sheriff's Office to alert on the car that the two subjects were driving. After writing a search warrant and visiting a judge in the early hours of the morning, the Miami PD narcotics cops and I opened the luggage that we found in the trunk and seized $530,011 in drug money. In addition to being a decent size money seizure, this case established the credibility of Home de la Calle, a documented source of information, who would become a major player in the undercover operation that is the main focus of this true story.

Another case that had a direct impact on the undercover air operation that I would eventually initiate, involved me being introduced to a source of information who helped me seize a private plane that was intended to be used by Colombian smugglers. During this investigation, The Gambler and Major Tom introduced me to a pilot I ended up recruiting and calling Captain Video aka Captain Cuervo.

CAPTAIN VIDEO AKA CAPTAIN CUERVO

According to The Gambler and Major Tom, a pilot friend of theirs had information about a Colombian who was looking to purchase an expensive aircraft for a smuggling venture. Just as they had described, the man I ended up calling Captain Video turned out to be another colorful character with a great sense of humor, who was extremely reliable and trustworthy.

Rather than work this case alone, I received help from FBI Agent Kenny P. and his partner Agent Rick C. While Kenny P. was the senior of the two agents, Rick C. was an experienced younger G Man. Kenny and Rick proved especially helpful, when I needed to cover Captain Video whenever he met with the Colombian subject of this investigation. In the end, we decided not to risk exposing Captain Video in order to make a more substantial case. Instead, I settled for the technical violation that enabled me to seize the plane that Captain Video identified as the aircraft that the Colombian intended to use in a smuggling venture.

Doing so enabled me to protect Captain Video's identity as a documented source of information for the U.S. Customs Service, while also paying him for the seizure of such an expensive private aircraft. This case also enabled me to establish Captain Video's reliability as a documented source of information. In the process, we became very close friends on a professional basis. As you will read, Captain Video would later join Airport Sam, The Gambler, Major Tom, the Colonel, Hombre de la Calle and others as a member of the SAC Miami Group 7 undercover air operation.

OPERATION EXCALIBUR

Every federal agent needs a major case to jump-start their career. At the time, a major investigation like Operation Excalibur was often referred to as a GS13 case. This meant, that any special agent who successfully initiated and completed an investigation of such magnitude, was usually considered a shoe in for a promotion to a GS13 (Senior Special Agent) position.

Before I go any further, I need to explain how I initiated the U.S. Customs end of this complex investigation of international significance. I first became interested in the owner of the Royal Motorcar Dealership, when I was driving home late one night and I stopped to admire the exotic cars that were on display in the showroom. Even though I had driven by 1624 E. Sunrise Boulevard on numerous occasions, something caused me to stop that night and take a closer look.

While I admired the showroom full of exotic cars, I had a premonition that this dealership was a front for a criminal enterprise. When I say I had a premonition, I mean, that there was no doubt in my mind that the day would come, when I would be able to prove, that this particular exotic car dealership was backed by drug money. As a result, there was also no doubt in my mind, that I would seize this establishment at some point in my career.

IT'S A SMALL WORLD AFTER ALL

As I mentioned before, after becoming an Air Officer I started working with a documented source of information I called Airport Sam. One night after making another seizure based on his super reliable information, I took Airport Sam out for dinner, to explain the other ways that he might be able to help me make cases. During this discussion, I explained in more detail, that U.S. Customs Agents could make money laundering cases and seize businesses and other assets, as long as we could prove that these items of value were purchased with the proceeds from criminal activity.

That night I realized that we live in a very small world, when an enlightened Airport Sam, told me about a smuggling organization that used the money they made from drug smuggling, to purchase all kinds of expensive assets, including an exotic car dealership called Royal Motorcar. As I continued to listen to Airport Sam, I couldn't believe my ears. My documented source of information knew enough about the smugglers behind the Royal Motorcar dealership, to enable me to open a criminal investigation. Was this unbelievable, or what?

After thoroughly debriefing Airport Sam, I briefed Steve Minas and opened a case on the exotic car dealership and the smugglers involved in the group called the Excalibur Organization. In addition to Airport Sam, the confidential source I called The Gambler aka Mr. Lucky had his own insight into the Excalibur smuggling organization. The Gambler was also able to provide me with some valuable intelligence information on the Excalibur Organization, that corroborated some of the information that Airport Sam provided me with. This meant, that I had two reliable sources providing the same intelligence information about a major

South Florida drug smuggling organization.

NOW THE FUN BEGINS

Shortly after I opened this investigation, I received a phone call from a high ranking DEA supervisor, who was pissed off to no end, that I had the nerve to initiate a case, that he didn't believe was within the jurisdiction of the U.S. Customs Service. Needless to say, I was right and he was wrong, because the U.S. Customs Service was 110% justified to investigate the crime of money laundering.

At that time, the term currency/narcotics was used to describe a criminal investigation that involved the laundering of money by smuggling organizations. In fact, using this term in a conversation, was often enough to make some DEA Agents turn green. Whether DEA liked it or not, U.S. Customs Agents were authorized to investigate any individual, group, criminal organization, or corporation that used the proceeds/money raised from ANY criminal activity, including DRUG SMUGGLING, for any purposes, including purchasing items of value.

It also pissed me off to no end, that this particular DEA manager, a man that I came to have a great deal of respect for, was giving me a ration of shit over what he considered a jurisdictional issue. In fact, during this rather heated telephone conversation, I told this high ranking DEA manager, that if he had a problem with me initiating this investigation, he should call the Special Agent in Charge, not me.

Eventually, a temporary cease fire was called and my request to have this investigation become an OCEDEF case was approved. This meant that Operation Excalibur would be a multi-agency task force investigation that included the U.S. Customs Service, DEA, the IRS, the U.S. Attorney's Office and the Broward County Sheriff's Office. In the end, this joint investigation led to a 57 count indictment against thirteen key figures in one of South Florida's most successful drug smuggling organizations.

In order to make this case, I worked with another U.S. Customs Agent (Dave D.), a DEA Agent, IRS Special Agent Rick K. and two detectives from the Broward County Sheriff's Office. For the record, Broward County Sheriff's Office Detectives Dan De C. and Billy B. were without question two of THE BEST cops I ever worked with in my entire law enforcement career.

While working together, we gathered the evidence necessary to prove, that the subjects of this investigation smuggled 6.9 tons of cocaine and 12,000 pounds of marijuana from Colombia through the Bahamas into South Florida. After a great deal of hard work, that was periodically interrupted by serious inter-agency conflicts between the Customs Service and DEA, my colleagues and I gathered enough evidence to make our case against the smugglers in the Excalibur Organization.

On April 13, 1987, a joint task force of U.S. Customs, DEA and IRS Agents along with members of the Broward County Sheriff's Office and the Miami Metro Dade Police Department executed a number of arrest, seizure warrants and search warrants. By the end of the day, we had completely dismantled the Excalibur smuggling organization, by arresting all thirteen major violators and seizing approximately $7 million dollars in drug assets, including six aircraft, 29 exotic cars, 46 weapons, 1000 rounds of ammunition, expensive jewelry, including gold Rolex watches, one go-fast racing boat, fur coats, coin collections, radios, mobile phones, beepers, expensive household items and a custom made pool table.

Operation Excalibur was a screaming success, especially since it wasn't an every day occurrence, that the United States Government was able to seize the contents of an exotic car dealership that was used to launder money for a drug smuggling organization. After the successful completion of Operation Excalibur, I paid Airport Sam and The Gambler AKA Mr. Lucky $250,000 for providing the original information that enabled me to initiate this case on behalf of the U.S. Customs Service.

As a result of this investigation, I was able to further establish my working relationship with Airport Sam and The Gambler; two sources of information who were directly responsible for me being able to create the undercover operation that is the primary focus of this true story. It was also as a direct result of the overwhelming success of Operation Excalibur, that I was able to enhance my reputation as a self-starter and approach my superiors for permission to establish a rather unique type of undercover air operation.

CHAPTER 7

BREAKING AWAY FROM THE PACK

In October of 1988, I took a long hard look at the resources at my disposal and decided to venture out into uncharted territory. As busy as we were in Group 7, not one agent was able "to put a load of dope on the table" (make a drug seizure) in the U.S. This was the case, because in the early days of Group 7, the U.S. Customs Agents assigned to this unit didn't have any informants or sources of information who were able to facilitate the seizure of a drug shipment. We did aggressively try to indict drug contraband by secretly installing court ordered tracking devices on suspect smuggling aircraft, but even this tactic did not prove to be very successful.

It is also important to remember, what I said about the major victory that U.S. and Bahamian interdiction forces achieved in the Caribbean in the mid to late 1980s. Once the interdiction forces became effective in driving the smugglers away from South Florida and their safe havens in the Bahamas, U.S. Customs air and marine units, as well as other agencies, became an occupation force of sorts that remained in place to prevent the return of the smugglers. Even though we did not completely stop smugglers from operating, we did manage to make them change their way of doing business.

As soon as I started working air smuggling cases, I became curious as to how individuals and criminal organizations got into the business of using planes to smuggle. Between flying drug interdiction missions, seizing approximately twenty drug smuggling aircraft, working other cases on the ground, constantly debriefing sources of information and working with veteran U.S. Customs pilots, air officers, special agents and a few local cops, I began to get a good feel for how the bad guys operated. This included, learning why the smugglers were successful and why they got caught.

Before I got promoted and I became a Special Agent, I believed that we had to change our tactics, in order to continue to ride the wave of success that our interdiction efforts brought about. As far as I was concerned, the controlled delivery process, also known as a transportation case, was the way to go. I was convinced that as long as we had the right private help and we were able to get the right introductions, we would be able to successfully infiltrate smuggling organizations. Once this happened, we would be able to seize drug shipments and assets, while arresting major violators and insuring successful prosecutions in federal court.

However, before we could mount a successful controlled delivery/transportation case, we had to seek approval from DEA to do so. This situation existed, because DEA was the federal agency that approved or denied all requests for the "country clearance," or the official permission to travel to and operate in foreign countries. This included traveling to countries like Colombia, Venezuela and Jamaica.

Like it or not, the U.S. Customs Service was a competitor of sorts and was forced to go to DEA, to ask for permission to conduct (drug smuggling) investigations and undercover operations that involved foreign travel. Forcing the U.S. Customs Service to ask DEA for permission to make a case, that could potentially make DEA look bad, was like having Macy's ask Bloomingdales for permission to have a sale.

By this time in my career, I worked for over two years with a core group of sources of information and confidential informants, who were responsible for providing me with the intelligence information that enabled me to make arrests and seize millions of dollars in drug assets. For reasons that I explain throughout this book, I believed that we were ready to take on bigger and more meaningful targets.

My plan was to create the best undercover air unit in federal service; one that could be used to transport large quantities of drug contraband over long distances, in order to execute the most successful controlled deliveries imaginable. In order to complete the types of missions that I hoped to execute, I needed to gain access to aircraft that had the fuel capacity or "legs" to travel long distances, while carrying multi-hundred and multi thousand kilogram shipments of cocaine. I say cocaine, because this was the drug of choice at this period of time. Naturally, we would gladly transport other types of contraband as well.

By having access to aircraft with long range capabilities, my colleagues and I would be able to convince our future "clients," that we were the right men for the job, because we operated the type of aircraft that were able to avoid detection, by flying long distances to the northeast or southwest U.S. This was a critical component to my plan, because the smuggling organizations were well aware of the interdiction capabilities of the U.S. Government. In other words, the bad guys wanted aircraft and crews that were capable of successfully delivering a large drug shipment to the CONUS (Continental U.S.)

Even though I was about to travel into uncharted and dangerous territory, my confidence level never wavered. I believed that my imagination would make up for whatever it was that I lacked in formal training or experience. Had there been a school or training course to attend, that would teach me how to run a covert air operation, I would have eagerly enrolled. Since that wasn't the case, I would have to learn as I went along.

Fortunately, I was brimming with confidence, because I knew how to gather intelligence information, conduct investigations and direct informants and sources of information. Between my limited flying experience, my time as an Air Officer and the knowledge that I picked up while working with U.S. Customs aviators and my sources of information, I felt that I would be able to handle the logistics of running a secret air unit of sorts. I also knew that I had an excellent core group of contract pilots, sources of information and confidential informants who were ready, willing and able to help me deal with the bad guys and handle the flying part of this operation.

Knowing how to smuggle without getting caught was just as important as being able to transport contraband in an undercover operation. In order for us to be convincing, the bad guys that I intended to deal with, had to believe that my colleagues and I were concerned about the same things that real smugglers were worried about. For this to happen, we had to know what worked and what didn't work.

We also had to know what made smugglers tick. In other words, once we started meeting with real smugglers/violators, we had to "walk the walk and talk the talk" as they did, or we would be immediately suspected of being undercover agents. If the mistake was big enough and it was made while meeting with the wrong group of bad guys, in the wrong place, some of us could get hurt. This meant that once we infiltrated a real smuggling organization, we had to be prepared to act like real smugglers during the execution of every phase of a controlled delivery, including the part that involved operating undercover aircraft under potentially dangerous and adverse conditions.

Once the pickup was made and our crew returned safely to the United States with a shipment of drug contraband, there would be very little time to celebrate once we started negotiating our way through the delivery phase. If everything went according to plan, we would survive the final phase of the controlled delivery and live and fight another day.

OPERATION LONG HAUL AKA "LOADS R US"

Before I approached the Special Agent in Charge (SAC) in Miami, I had a long talk with my sources of information and contacts in the private aircraft community and asked for their help. Fortunately, my private airport contacts and sources of information were well paid assets, who welcomed the chance to get more involved, even if it meant taking additional risks.

Once I presented my sources of information with my plan, I was given immediate access to a small fleet of private aircraft, that could be used to get us off the ground and into the air to start flying some missions. Since two of my documented sources of information were aircraft brokers, I was also able to rent aircraft that were suitable for undercover air operations. I was also given access to airport offices and hangar space at two different South Florida airports. In addition, The Gambler located an insurance broker, who would provide the War Risk insurance coverage for the aircraft and crews that we used in an undercover capacity. This special insurance coverage was required whenever you operated in a "war zone," or in any location that was deemed to be a high threat area. Needless to say, none of this was included in any of the formal training that I received from the U.S. Customs Service.

Eventually, the day came when I asked Senior Special Agent Pat R, who was serving as my acting Group Supervisor, if I could pitch my idea to form a Group 7 undercover air operation to the Special Agent in Charge (SAC). Timing is everything in life and thanks to Pat R. I was in the right place at the right time to pitch my plan to the SAC. Fortunately, the success of Operation Excalibur put me in good standing with my superiors and made it possible for me to be taken seriously, when I pitched the idea to form this undercover operation.

The day I presented my proposal to SAC Miami Mr. Pat O'B., I pitched my plan like a screenwriter presents an idea for a movie to a famous Hollywood film producer. As I laid out a set of blueprints of the private airport office where I intended to operate from, I told the SAC what I had in mind. By the time Pat R. chimed in and added a few pearls of wisdom, I could see the wheels were turning in the SAC's head.

When the SAC asked what I was going to use for funding, I responded with complete confidence and said, "Bad guy money all the way." I then explained how I intended to use the money or trafficker funds, that the bad guys paid us to provide our transportation services, to fund the operation. As soon as the SAC put his pipe down, I knew he liked my plan. The second he rounded his desk and said, "Let's take this up to the Regional Commissioner," I knew we were in business.

Once I briefed the Regional Commissioner (George H.) and his assistant (Leon G.), I was given authorization to proceed. That day, I left the SAC Office as the newly appointed commanding officer of an undercover air unit that had no assigned "government" aircraft, or crews, other than the contract pilots and planes that I recruited through my contacts in South Florida. What I did have was permission to proceed and in federal law enforcement circles, authorization to take action was more important than anything else.

Ironically, the idea to form the SAC Miami Group 7 undercover air operation, that unofficially became known as The Blade Runner Squadron, did not come from a group of high ranking government officials whose job it was find ways to win The Drug War. Instead, this plan was proposed by an eccentric U.S. Customs Agent with an over active imagination who loved to fly. It also helped a great deal, that the Special Agent in Charge of Miami at that time (Pat O'B) saw the potential of my proposal, for had he not done so, The Blade Runner Squadron would have never gotten off the ground.

CHAPTER 8

OPERATION WHITE CHRISTMAS

Shortly after I was given authorization to establish an undercover air operation in Miami, I was assigned to a temporary detail (TDY) in Boston in the early winter of 1988. As you will read, this TDY couldn't have come at a more opportune time.

In the late 1980s, the U.S. Customs SAC office in Boston was comprised of about forty special agents. These agents were responsible for investigating acts of smuggling in Massachusetts and other parts of New England. They also conducted collateral investigations in support of other Customs offices and participated in joint investigations with other agencies.

During my temporary detail (TDY) in Boston, I was assigned to work with Special Agent Jimmy S., the most colorful and famous U.S. Customs Agent in all of New England. Everyone who reads this true story needs to know, that Agent Jimmy S. was the central figure in every record setting controlled delivery that was successfully executed in New England. The four Boston controlled deliveries that I received authorization to write about, are stories about team work and by all accounts, Jimmy S. was the Captain of the Boston team. Each and every controlled delivery that we successfully executed in New England and elsewhere, were major engagements during The Drug War, that were fought by a relatively small number of U.S. Customs Agents and other law enforcement officers, as well as by our contract personnel, sources of information and confidential informants.

Whether you call it fate, destiny, or Divine Intervention, I found myself in Boston at just the right time, because Jimmy S. had an informant who recently infiltrated a Colombian smuggling organization, that wanted to transport over 500 kilos of cocaine from Colombia to New York via New England. Unfortunately for Jimmy S. and his hard working CI, their case wasn't going any further, because the Colombians promised to provide the necessary front money, after they saw the plane that would be used to make the pickup in Colombia.

Like most special agents in the Customs Service, Jimmy S. did not have the wherewithal to complete this controlled delivery on his own. Unfortunately, a special agent could not pick up the phone and request headquarters to provide an undercover crew and a suitable plane out of inventory. As big as the U.S. Customs Service was, it did not have a fleet of undercover aircraft standing by, all fueled up and ready to go at a moment's notice. Another way of putting this, is to say that our Uncle Sam was an old guy on a recruiting poster and not an executive in the rent a plane business.

The moment I saw Jimmy wondering how he was going to complete this case, I assured him that his transportation problems were solved. Now that I had Jimmy's undivided attention, I explained that I was recently given authorization to establish an undercover air unit, that was designed to provide undercover transportation services in cases such as this. As Jimmy stood up, I could see the expression on his face change to one of relief. I don't know who was more excited me or Jimmy S.

There I was, with my untested undercover airline looking for our first mission to fly and Jimmy had a case that would never be made, unless he found a suitable plane and crew, that could fly to Colombia to pick up over 500 kilos of cocaine and return to Massachusetts in the dead of winter. Naturally, Jimmy was full of questions and I was full of answers.

In order to answer some of his questions, I picked up the phone on his desk and dialed The Gambler's airport office in South Florida. After dispensing with the usual jokes, I got down to business and said, "I need a crew and a plane that can fly 2000 miles non-stop and carry 1100 pounds of cargo."

After hearing The Gamblers first question, I told him to hold on, as I looked over to Jimmy and his partner Special Agent Richard (Dick). O'C and asked, "What kind of strip are we going into?" Jimmy was quick to give me the answer. As I turned my attentions back to The Gambler, I answered his question in a matter of fact tone of voice and said, "Unimproved, in the jungle."

As I continued my conversation, The Gambler agreed to provide us with a former military aircraft that carried enough fuel to fly from Colombia to New England. When Major Tom picked up the extension I had my first volunteer. Then Captain Video agreed to go along and was recruited to fly as the Contract

Pilot in Command, because he had more experience than Major Tom, in the aircraft that The Gambler was willing to rent us for this mission.

After we discussed the case, I hung up and promised to get back to The Gambler, Captain Video and Major Tom when I knew more. As I sat on the other side of his desk, I told Jimmy that he had a plane and a crew that could make his case a reality, once we received front money from the bad guys and country clearance from DEA.

As soon as Jimmy briefed his Assistant Special Agent in Charge (ASAC) and the Special Agent in Charge (SAC) about our plan, the New England based agents wanted to know if the Boston office would lose the "stat" (statistic) to the Miami office. This was a valid concern, because my permanent duty station (Miami Group 7) was providing the contract pilots and the plane to make the pickup.

Under the circumstances, I assured the Boston agents that my contract pilots would fly for them and that I would do everything possible to help them make this case in their area of operation. I said this, because as far as I was concerned, the gold badge that I carried in my pocket was issued by the U.S. Customs Service, not by the Miami Customs Service. Once our superiors blessed the plan, I was told to get everything ready on my end.

The first order of business was for me to call my contract pilots in Miami and give them the good news that we had our first mission to fly. Once I got them on the line, I put Jimmy on the speaker phone and introduced him to my contract pilots and The Gambler. Now that we had the green light to launch, we solidified our arrangement with my contacts in South Florida. Since we anticipated receiving an ample amount of front money from the Colombian subjects of this investigation, we agreed to pay The Gambler $10,000 as a deposit for the rental of the undercover aircraft. The remaining balance would be paid at a later date.

That night Jimmy and I left the federal building on Causeway Street in Boston in great spirits. As far as I was concerned, I was fulfilling my destiny and doing exactly what I was put on this earth to do, as far as my federal law enforcement career was concerned. I also believed that too many things were happening for all of this to be one big coincidence.

As I drove the 85 miles to the motel on Cape Cod where my family and I were staying, I thought about all that had transpired to bring me this far in my journey. I never once thought that I bit off more than I could chew. It was also at this time, that I affectionately became known as the Air Czar by the agents in the Boston Office.

THE BAPTISM OF FIRE

In order to accomplish our goal and put a load of dope on the table, we used every minute of every day to carefully orchestrate this controlled delivery from beginning to end. For several weeks, Jimmy S., Dick O'C. and I, along with other agents, spent our days and nights meeting with the Boston informant, recording phone calls and updating our contract pilots, while doing more paperwork than a school teacher at test time. After the Thanksgiving holiday, it was time to pick up some front money from our Colombian "clients."

Once we arrived in South Florida to take the next step in this case, Jimmy S. led the Boston agents on the surveillance in Miami. At the end of a sumptuous meal at a first class restaurant, the Boston Source of Information was paid $40,000 in front money to seal this deal. Once our undercover operative was back in his car, the agents made sure that they weren't being followed, when they escorted the CI back to his hotel room for the debriefing.

As you can imagine, we were all happy campers when the $40,000 in "front money" was presented to Jimmy S. Now that we had a descent amount of expense money, we made arrangements to conduct a "show and tell" of the undercover aircraft the next day. Just to make sure that we covered all the bases, we contacted the U.S. Customs RAC Office in Ft. Lauderdale, to let them know that we were moving the undercover aircraft to an airport in their area of operation. A call was then placed to the Colombians, who were ecstatic that we were working so fast to accommodate their request to examine the plane.

After conferring with my contract pilots and making the arrangements to show the Colombians our plane, Jimmy and I stopped at the Pelican Bar next to Cafe 66 in Ft. Lauderdale. While we sat and watched the boats pass by under the 17th Street Causeway Bridge, we had a drink and did our best to relax, because once the Colombians checked out our plane, our crew would be heading south.

THE SHOW AND TELL

Even though we always seemed to get along, it wasn't easy for a "Miami" Agent to operate in Ft. Lauderdale's area of operation, without being suspected of poaching or invading their territory. To his credit, the RAC Ft. Lauderdale (Greg J.) always treated me well and let me explain myself, whenever my presence in his jurisdiction was a disturbance in The Force.

That evening we found Greg in his office. Just as I introduced the Boston agents to him, our conversation was interrupted by a phone call from one of Greg's agents, who just seized an airplane displaying a false tail number at a local airport. As soon as Greg repeated the description of the plane and its phony tail number, I began to die a slow and painful death. When Greg saw my reaction, he immediately covered the phone and asked what was wrong.

After quickly explaining the purpose of our visit, that included giving Greg J. an update on our case that involved conducting a "show and tell" in his area of operation, Greg realized that one of his agents seized our undercover aircraft. Even though it wasn't easy to do, Greg had no choice but to tell his otherwise hardworking agent to un-seize the undercover aircraft and immediately leave the area. Fortunately, everything worked out as planned and the Colombian broker was satisfied, that our plane was capable of flying from Colombia to the New England without having to refuel along the way.

After completing this part of our operation, we returned to Boston with the $40,000 in front money and the involvement of the subjects of this investigation well documented. The good news was, even if we never picked up their cocaine shipment, the Boston agents had enough evidence to prosecute the Colombians on conspiracy charges.

Every day before we launched, Jimmy, Dick and I prepared for the departure of our UC aircraft and crew. While the undercover plane was being prepared for the mission in Miami, the Boston CI made some last minute delivery arrangements with the Colombians. Once I drafted the op (operational) plan, copies were distributed through the chain of command to U.S. Customs Air Operations. This was done because U.S. Customs surveillance aircraft, along with other government assets, would be providing direct support to this headquarters approved UC operation.

After working this case for eleven weeks, it was hard to believe that we were within a few days of making history. By mid December final arrangements were made with our Colombian clients to have the cocaine shipment ready for us to pick up. Once we received country clearance, we were cleared to execute the flying stage of the operation. While Jimmy S. and Dick O'C. went to Florida to see our crew take off, I remained behind to set up the command post and plan their reception.

Despite the fact that we had $40,000 dollars in front money, we came up short when it came time to pay certain expenses, which including giving The Gamble a deposit for his plane. While Jimmy S. paced back and forth in our undercover office in Miami, we had no hope of proceeding any further, unless we raised the capital to proceed. Fortunately, for us, The Gambler saw the potential in our operation and accepted an IOU for $10,000 dollars. Doing so, allowed our contract pilots and a contract pilot from the Boston Office, to use his plane to fly our first covert air operation. All I could do was shake my head and be grateful that The Gambler was on our side.

In my opinion, there was something very seriously wrong with our Uncle Sam, for not adopting the attitude that money was no object when it came to funding undercover operations. If I were king, I would have given the poor slob I put in charge of an undercover air unit, a hangar or two filled with suitable aircraft, as well as some help and a reasonable amount of expense money, when additional funds were needed to further a worthwhile investigation. Obviously, that was asking for too much.

I should also mention, that some of the aircraft that I seized from smugglers were perfect for our mission. Sadly, when Special Agent in Charge Pat O'B. asked the powers to be to assign ONE of the planes that I seized to our undercover operation, his request was denied. I guess only time would tell if my idea had merit. In the meantime, we had a mission to fly.

CHAPTER 9

OUR FIRST MISSION

Once Jimmy and Dick got the green light to launch from DEA, Captain Video, Major Tom and another contract pilot, who was well known to the Colombians, boarded the undercover aircraft in preparation of departing South Florida. After taking their positions in the cockpit, Captain Video leaned out the pilot's side window and yelled, "CLEAR!" while he and Major Tom started the radial engines. Moments later, the undercover plane rumbled down the runway until she picked up enough speed to get airborne. As the former Vietnam vintage military aircraft climbed into the night's sky, she vanished from sight. The ball was now in play.

Even though I was up in Cape Cod, Massachusetts when our crew took off, I said a prayer on their behalf. With nothing else to do I went to bed to get some sleep. At 4 AM I was wide awake and getting ready for a very long day. After stopping for a container of coffee and a pack of orange Hostess cup cakes, I drove my government issued Chevrolet IROC Camaro to the command post in Boston.

At exactly 0800 hours (8 AM) The Gambler called me in Boston to see if I had heard anything yet. After I called the U.S. Customs radar center known as C3I, to get an update on the whereabouts of our undercover aircraft, I called

The Gambler back and told him that so far no one had any contact with the undercover aircraft.

WELCOME TO THE JUNGLE

While I began to worry about our crew, the undercover aircraft went feet dry over the Colombian coast and was heading inland toward its intended destination. Later on when I debriefed the crew, Major Tom said that flying over the Colombian jungle reminded him a lot of Vietnam. As everyone on board scanned the ground below, they started to spot the various landmarks that the Colombians told them to look for, when they arrived in the vicinity of the clandestine airstrip. After making a few circling passes, Captain Video and Major Tom were confident they found the right place to land.

As soon as our crew made contact with the Colombians on a hand held radio and they were cleared to land, Captain Video and Major Tom reduced power and lowered the flaps. Even though it looked like it would a tight fit, our experienced cockpit crew landed the former Vietnam vintage U.S. Air Force aircraft on the clandestine runway that was cut out of the jungle.

Once the undercover aircraft landed and came to a complete stop, a contingent of heavily armed Colombians secured the area. While our cockpit crew shut down the engines, a group of Colombians armed with assault rifles stood ready to deal with any deviation in the plan. As soon as the incredibly brave contract pilot from Boston opened the cargo door and acted like he belonged there, the Colombian in charge of the airstrip emerged from the crowd and welcomed our crew.

While the undercover plane was refueled, an array of weapons and hand-grenades were tossed in piles on the ground all around the aircraft. Being the gracious host that he was, the Colombian cartel rep had food and cold drinks available and made our crew as comfortable as possible. Once the plane was re-fueled and the aircraft was made ready for takeoff, the Colombian in charge waved to some of his men, who were waiting by the edge of the nearby jungle. Suddenly two old jeeps carrying the cargo of cocaine emerged from the bush and raced up to the plane. In less than a minute, 1264 pounds of cocaine was placed on board the undercover aircraft, under the watchful eyes of our undercover crew and the Colombian in charge.

Once the aircraft was loaded, the gunmen retrieved their weapons and pulled back away from the plane in a more casual but protective semi-circle. After saying good-bye to the man in charge, our three man crew climbed on board and secured the cargo door. As soon as they assumed their positions in the cockpit, Captain Video and Major Tom started the first engine then the second. After conducting a quick run up, Captain Video began to taxi the plane towards the narrow runway.

Even though the undercover aircraft that we used for this mission was capable of getting airborne on a relatively short field, it didn't hurt to give the old girl more time to build up speed. This was done as a precaution, to prevent from placing an unnecessary strain on her twenty year old radial engines. Remember, it was approximately 1890 miles as the crow flies back to New England. The good news was, the UC plane had plenty of power and was by no means fully loaded with cargo, even though it had a full bag of fuel on board. The bad news was, the presence of obstructions at the end of the jungle runway meant sure disaster, if our plane lost an engine on take off.

The lack of a real hard packed airstrip also made it more difficult for our plane to operate on a portion of the clandestine airfield. This became a bit of a problem when Captain Video tried to turn the plane around at the end of the runway, so he could line up with the imaginary center-line. When the soft dirt started to crumble under the weight of the aircraft, our crew was faced with the possibility of becoming stranded in Colombia. To prevent this from happening, Captain Video applied more power to the engines in order to free the plane.

As soon as the UC aircraft was rolling, Captain Video and Major Tom applied full power. The moment the plane picked up enough airspeed, the undercover aircraft was rotated into the air. Once they were wheels in the well (with the landing gear retracted), our crew felt relieved that they successfully completed the first half of their mission.

Just because they left Colombia in one piece, didn't mean that our undercover crew was in the clear. They had a perilous journey ahead of them, as they flew the unheated cargo plane toward the frigid New England coastline in the dead of winter. (The heavy winter clothing that they brought along, was the only protection that our crew had, to cope with the frigid conditions once they flew further north.) In addition to having to buck some very serious head winds, our crew would also have to fly through some very bad weather as they made their way to Cape Cod.

I was also getting a bit concerned, that the winter storm that was coming our way, would make it much harder for our crew to land safely at Otis Air Force Base. To make a potentially bad situation worse, we expected our crew to be exhausted and our plane to be very low on fuel by the time the UC aircraft reached Cape Cod. The good news was, we had a very experienced U.S. Customs Citation Jet crew assigned to support our operation. If anyone could help our undercover crew make it back it one piece, it was Customs Pilot Martin V. and his crew from the Miami Air Branch.

By 12 noon, Jimmy S. and Dick O'C. returned to Boston and joined me in our makeshift command post at the Boston SAC Office on Causeway Street. By now, all three of us were worried because we hadn't heard from our crew since they departed the U.S. Navy Base at Guantanamo Bay, Cuba. (At this time in the operation the undercover crew was overdue by two hours.)

While Jimmy S. paced back and forth in the Boston office, it seemed as if he asked me every five minutes about the status of our plane and crew. I reassured Jimmy that it wasn't time to panic. I did my best to retrace their steps on a giant map on the office wall. I also made periodic calls to Sector Communications (Customs 911) and C3I (The U.S. Customs Radar Tracking Center).

While Jimmy and I chain smoked cigarettes and waited to hear the some news about our crew, I looked out the Boston SAC office window and watched the snow start to fall. All my life I loved the snow. Nothing made me happier as a kid, or as an adult, than to be in a snowstorm.

Even blizzards made my day. Now things were different, because the lives of three men were at stake. As a result, the last thing we needed was a snow storm to blanket the area, because flying an undercover air operation was risky enough, without adding bad weather to the equation. Last but not least, was the fact, that the undercover aircraft was not equipped to handle frigid weather and could easily ice up and crash, especially if the weather conditions over the ocean deteriorated any further.

Despite all of these concerns, I knew that our crew would make it through the storm. At the risk of sounding corny, even though I didn't know where they were, I believed that our crew was protected by a higher authority; after all, Almighty God would never be on the side of the drug cartels during The Drug War.

After waiting hours to hear from our crew, Jimmy, Dick and I were at a loss for words. Every time the phone rang, we lost years off the tail end of our lives, when we received updates from C3I and the Miami Air Branch, about the efforts that were being made to locate our plane and crew. Good news came a little after one o'clock. According to a C3I Radar Detection Specialist, a U.S. Customs Citation Jet crew from Miami just intercepted the undercover aircraft as it passed by Haiti.

Jimmy and Dick could tell by the look on my face that all was well, as I excitedly relayed the good news. When I asked if I could speak to the crew, the C3I operator patched me through to the U.S. Customs Citation Jet. After hours of pacing and worrying, I felt a tremendous sense of relief, the moment I heard Captain Video's voice over the radio, as he relayed the size of the load and the fact that all three were returning with no bad guys on board as passengers. As I quickly passed the news to Jimmy and Dick, I could see the weight of the world lift from their shoulders. The boys were alive, victorious and on their way back to Massachusetts.

While Customs Pilot Martin V. and his crew escorted the UC plane on its long and arduous journey back to New England, I thanked the Customs Citation Jet crew and the C3I Detection System Specialists for their help. After I hung up the phone, I smiled wide as I walked over to Jimmy S. and extended my hand and said, "Congratulations, Jimmy, you just made the largest seizure of cocaine in New England since the Pilgrims landed." Even though the UC plane was a long way from Massachusetts, Jimmy, Dick and I exchanged handshakes and enjoyed the moment.

As soon as the sweet taste of victory wore off, I stood by the wall map and remarked in a more serious tone, "Now all they have to do is make it back." While Jimmy looked like he didn't want anything to spoil the good news that we just received, I explained the problems that our crew faced, as they flew north over the Atlantic Ocean in the dead of winter. Simply put, if the weather got any worse, it might not be possible for our crew to land at Otis Air Force Base on Cape Cod.

At this point in the story, I need to mention how credit for any seizure of contraband was assigned at that time. In order for the Boston SAC Office to receive credit for this substantial drug seizure, the undercover aircraft had to land in the jurisdiction of Region One. (At that time, Region One was the operational area that included the Boston office and stretched from the Canadian Border to Baltimore, Maryland.)

You could be a special agent in Timbuktu and work a year of your life on the biggest case of your career and due to events beyond your control, the credit for the seizure could be assigned to another office in another region. This meant that even though a particular case would reflect the success of the seizure, another Customs office in another region would claim the statistic, if the seizure was made in their territory.

After all the hospitality that I was shown in Boston, I couldn't let this happen. This was one time when I was routing for the Boston team and they knew it. Besides, as I said before, I was one of those Special Agents who maintained the attitude that my badge said U.S. Customs, not New York Customs, or Boston Customs, or Miami Customs. As a result, in order for this case to get credited to the Boston SAC Office, my crew would have to carry the ball all the way into Region One, regardless of the weather conditions.

Like it or not, these were the rules that we had no choice but to follow. Had our system been more flexible and accommodating, our crew could have flown a much shorter distance under much safer flying conditions directly to Homestead Air Force Base. Once they landed in South Florida, the drug shipment could have been transferred to a military C130 for the rest of the trip to Massachusetts.

For the rest of the day I kept in almost constant phone contact with our air ops people in Miami. While the Boston agents and I prepared to meet our plane, various interdiction aircraft and C3I kept the undercover aircraft under constant surveillance and directed our crew around as much of the exceptionally bad weather as possible.

Once we knew there wasn't anything more we could do on our end, the Boston Agents and I grabbed lunch at the Bull Finch Restaurant. While we ate, the weather in Massachusetts got worse. (Little did I know at the time how bad things were getting for our crew, as they flew closer to the U.S. coastline and the head winds kicked up. Freezing rain and snow also threatened to ice up the undercover aircraft that had no heater.)

After we returned to the office, Jimmy and the other agents gathered around, while I talked to a C3I Detection Specialist on the phone and relayed information about the position of our crew and their estimated time of arrival at Otis Air Force Base. By midnight it was time to travel to Cape Cod and set up our command post. Well over a dozen agents from the U.S. Customs Service and other agencies set up shop in a hotel near the airport in Hyannis.

In order to enable our contract crew to celebrate their victory, Jimmy S. and I chipped in and bought two cases of beer, a bottle of Cuervo Tequila and a bottle of Johnny Walker Black. We also had one of the Boston based Customs Agents rent two hotel rooms for my contract pilots, so they could get some badly needed sleep after they were debriefed. Unfortunately, the snow was falling harder than before and the most recent weather report predicted that the storm would get a lot worse before conditions improved.

The fatigue factor of flying over 3400 miles from our base in Miami, to the jungle airstrip in Colombia, then back to Cape Cod, Massachusetts in the dead of winter was incredible. Clearly, this mission was no milk run, to use an old World War II U.S. Army Air Forces expression.

Anything could happen at any time, especially since our crew was flying in a rented leftover from the Vietnam War.

After all the work that was put into this case, the last thing Jimmy Scott wanted to hear, was that our undercover plane had to divert from the operational plan and land south of Boston. The concern I expressed earlier, about the impact that the worsening weather could have on the UC aircraft's fuel supply was coming to fruition. Rather than tempt fate, our crew decided it was best to land to top off their tanks, before they continued on their journey to Cape Cod.

As the UC plane headed inland, Jimmy and I stayed on the phones to coordinate the receiving of our plane by U.S. Customs Agents in another part of the country. Fortunately, my contract pilots were able to make it to Baltimore, Maryland, the southern most post of duty in Region One.

While Jimmy and I waited in Boston, our crew landed and had the undercover plane refueled under the watchful eyes of U.S. Customs Agents from the SAC Office in Baltimore. Even the Customs Citation Jet chase plane landed to refuel and give the crew a chance to make a pit stop.

After taking care of business, the UC plane followed by the U.S. Customs Citation Jet lifted off and headed north as the snow continued to fall on Massachusetts.

CAPE COD HERE WE COME

After battling heavy winds and freezing temperatures, Captain Video and Major Tom were exhausted as the undercover plane neared its final destination. To complicate the situation even more, we were notified that Otis Air Force Base was being shut down because of the storm. This meant that our crew would have to land in a blinding snow storm, at a municipal airport that was closed and had no one cleaning the runway, or working in the control tower.

While dressed in heavy ski suits, our two contract pilots and the passenger from Boston had one chance to shoot their approach at Hyannis Airport, as the storm produced white out conditions and almost no ceiling over the runway. In order to conserve their energy and prevent from nodding out from exhaustion, Captain Video and Major Tom took turns flying and resting as they flew the UC plane toward Cape Cod.

The fact that almost nothing worked on our plane, except the engines, flaps and landing gear, made it even more difficult for our crew to fly this particular mission in the dead of winter. Even the avionics on board were frozen solid and were not registering with any degree of accuracy. Under the circumstances, only a very experienced bush pilot and a combat tested aviator, could keep an antique warbird like our undercover aircraft flying under such conditions.

With the temperature inside the undercover aircraft well below freezing, our crew used rolls of duct tape to reseal the windshield when snow started blowing inside the cockpit of the plane. The headwinds were so strong the plane bucked from one altitude to the next and appeared at times to be on a collision course with disaster. While working as a team, the U.S. Customs Citation Jet crew continued to relay course heading changes and other critical information to our undercover crew, as they flew blind toward the airport in Hyannis.

While slow flying behind our lumbering propeller driven cargo plane, Customs Pilot Martin V. and his Citation Jet crew acted like a mini AWAC aircraft, as they directed our contract pilots to their final destination. This was made possible, because U.S. Customs "sensor" aircraft are used to conduct a variety of surveillance and airborne tracking missions. Military AWAC aircraft and sensor aircraft, like the Customs Citation Jet, can also serve as an airborne control tower and direct other aircraft to their destination through any weather or combat conditions. In this case, the U.S. Customs Citation Jet used its FLAIR (Forward Looking Infrared Radar) to direct the undercover aircraft as it made its descent through the storm. When the undercover plane reached Cape Cod, the flight crew aimed straight for the airport in Hyannis.

From inside the cockpit of the undercover aircraft, the ground below was totally obstructed by whiteout conditions. With the airport only a few miles away, Captain Video and Major Tom worked together to fly the plane and prepare for a landing with frozen instruments. While Captain Video concentrated on easing the plane closer to the ground, he asked his co-pilot for an update on their rate of decent. When Major Tom responded, he reported that according to his side of the control panel they were descending at 80 knots. (80 knots is below stall speed for this particular type of aircraft.) After checking his side of the control panel, Captain Video informed his co-pilot, that according to his frozen air speed indicator, they were descending at zero (0) knots.

When U.S. Customs crew told our contract pilots, that according to the FLAIR on the Citation Jet, the undercover aircraft was already on the ground, Captain Video and Major Tom knew otherwise. Without wasting another second, Captain Video requested that someone turn up the runway lights, while he continued to fly blind through whiteout conditions. (Runway lights could be activated by radio if you needed to land on a controlled field where the tower had restricted operating hours.)

Meanwhile, down on the ground, while I was huddled under the wing of private plane with Jimmy S. and Jimmy B., I decided to break the tension by saying, "It's snowing out and I'm wearing boat shoes." As Jimmy cracked a smile and said something about me being a Miami Agent at heart, I felt ice cold flakes of snow pelting my face, as I scanned the sky for any signs of our plane and crew.

With the undercover plane already over the edge of the field, Captain Video flew by Braille, as he used every ounce of his experience and training to land the aircraft with absolutely no assistance from any of the instruments. Shooting an ILS (Instrument Landing) approach in a raging snowstorm, with no help from a control tower and no instruments, is a credit to many things, including the belief that there is a higher authority watching over us.

As the undercover aircraft descended lower and lower over the runway, Jimmy S., Jimmy B. and I heard the distinctive roar of the undercover aircraft's radial engines. "There she is," Jimmy. S yelled, as he pointed into the snow filled sky. Sure enough, the old warbird that we rented from The Gambler, broke through the incredibly low ceiling and finally settled down on the snow covered runway, followed by the U.S. Customs Citation Jet from the Miami Air Branch.

I'll never forget the feeling that came over me, when the undercover aircraft touched down and taxied over to the exact spot where I was standing. "They did it!" In fact, as crazy as this sounds, I never doubted that we would be able to pull this off. That didn't mean that I didn't have concerns. It means that overall, I was 110% convinced that my colleagues and I were doing exactly what we were meant to do.

While Jimmy used his portable radio to call for the van, I started to climb on board the plane, but had to stand aside, when the passenger from Boston left the aircraft in a huff and remarked something about letting him off this piece of shit. In keeping with my reputation for having a sarcastically irreverent sense of humor, I smiled and said, "Thanks for flying with us," as I climbed on board the UC aircraft, followed by Jimmy S.

After congratulating my crew, I looked around in total amazement. The interior of the undercover aircraft was frozen solid, to the point where melted snow covered the controls. However, the presence of over 1100 pounds of frozen kilos of cocaine in the cargo bay was a crystal clear indication that this operation was a screaming success. Without wasting any time, we formed a human chain and off-loaded the aircraft. Once the coke load was placed in the van, we locked the plane and left it parked where it was. Within a matter of minutes we were on our way back to a nearby hotel to debrief our crew.

Now it was time to celebrate. After a long hard day, my two contract pilots and the Boston contract pilot were looking forward to having a few drinks, when we arrived back at the hotel to conduct the debriefing. Unfortunately, as soon as we arrived, we received some bad news.

You had to be there to appreciate the situation, when Agent "Ralph Lauren" reported, that some kids climbed up the balcony of our hotel room and looted the beer and liquor that "Ralph" left outside to keep cold. (I called this particular Boston agent Ralph Lauren because he liked to wear Polo brand clothing.)

Here we were protecting over 500 kilos of cocaine in a van outside the hotel room and we were going crazy over missing a few beers and two bottles of hard liquor. What's even more ironic, is how a bunch of U.S. Customs Agents could covertly off-load all that cocaine in a sleepy little New England town, but we were unable to secure two cases of beer and two bottles of booze. Naturally, since Agent "Ralph Lauren" was slated to drive the van with the cocaine back to Boston, everyone teased him about whether or not he would lose the coke load like he did our refreshments. After a few laughs, a very resourceful Boston agent located a six pack of beer for our crew. Providing this beer enabled us to keep our word and provide beverages during the debriefing.

By 6:30 AM Cape Cod was blanketed by a heavy snowfall. Even though everyone else left to go home, I took Captain Video and Major Tom out for a well deserved breakfast of steak and eggs. All I could think about, as I sat in a virtually empty restaurant in Hyannis, Massachusetts, in the middle of a raging snow storm, was all that had transpired in the last eleven weeks.

My childhood dream of becoming a federal agent and having some type of involvement in a law enforcement aviation unit initially came to fruition when I became a U.S. Customs Air Officer. Now that I was running a successful undercover air operation, I realized the other half of the vision of my future that I had when I was a kid.

The undercover air operation that I initiated successfully completed its first mission and helped our agents in Boston make history in the process. Even though my family had to do without me for almost three months, it seemed worth it, because we achieved a major victory against a New York based Colombian smuggling organization. I felt this way, because victories of any kind are only achieved after some level of sacrifice is made.

At the risk of sounding melodramatic, I viewed The Drug War as my war. As far as I was concerned, we made this case happen because none of us were prepared to live with any other outcome. I also believed that if more people had a positive attitude about The Drug War, more cases like this could have been made, because the bad guys were no match for us when we worked together. I also believed that God was our co-pilot. I say this repeatedly throughout this true story, because it would be impossible to fly in harm's way, in some of the vintage planes that we used and return safely, without Divine Intervention on your side. You can disagree with me if you want, but that's how I felt, when I was directing and participating in these exceptionally high risk undercover operations.

OUR FIRST CONTROLLED DELIVERY

The final phase of our first controlled delivery involved the arrest of the four Colombians, who recruited our undercover services to smuggle 1264 pounds of cocaine into New England. A storage facility on Pleasant Street in the Town of Methuen was selected as the location where the arrests would be made. This particular storage facility was located next to a Mc Donald's fast food restaurant. Participating in the final phase of this controlled delivery were a number of U.S. Customs Agents from the SAC Office in Boston, a U.S. Customs Air Branch helicopter crew, DEA Agents and local police.

According to the SAC Boston operational plan, the Colombians would get the chance to inspect "their" cocaine shipment and be allowed to think that they could take half the $20 million dollar load and leave the balance behind until we received payment. Naturally, once they went to take possession of any contraband, an army of U.S. Customs Agents, DEA Agents and other law enforcement officers would move in and take the bad guys into custody. (We were very conservative in the beginning. We eventually changed our tactics in the future and started demanding payment, when we became more sophisticated and more deeply involved in mounting undercover air and marine operations.)

The final phase of this controlled delivery went off like clockwork. Once the signal was given, federal agents and local police officers converged on the unsuspecting smugglers. French fries were flying all over the Mc Donald's parking lot when we moved in. To add to the drama, the U.S. Customs Service helicopter made "gun runs" or low passes over the take down site. While this enforcement action was taking place, a number of customers left Mikey Ds to get a closer look at what was going on next door. Before anyone knew what was taking place, the real smugglers were in custody.

After this Controlled Delivery was completed, Captain Video and Major Tom spent one more night in Massachusetts, before they left in the morning to ferry the undercover aircraft back to Florida. Even though it took a few months, I was eventually authorized to pay The Gambler for the use of his plane and pay my two contract pilots for their flying services. Several months later, three of the four smugglers were convicted and sentenced to federal prison. Operation White Christmas was a success in more ways than one.

CHAPTER 10

OPEN FOR BUSINESS IN MIAMI

After completing a temporary detail in Los Angeles, I returned to Miami and got lucky, when Special Agent Chuck W. was assigned to work with me in the Group 7 undercover air operation. Chuck was a hard working younger agent with a great sense of humor, who was fun to be around. Chuck also happened to be the only federal agent I ever met, who was a card carrying member of the Three Stooges Fan Club.

Mike R. was another special agent from Group 7, who eagerly volunteered to work with me and Chuck W. in the Group 7 UC operation. Because he was a few years older than me and a lot older than Chuck, Mike was the old timer in our rather unorthodox unit. Even though Mike could have finagled his way into a much softer duty, he opted to get involved in the most dangerous aspects of federal drug enforcement work because he was a true professional. The fact that Mike was a former U.S. Marine who served in Vietnam, also meant that he would never walk away from a good fight.

PRACTICE MAKES PERFECT

While there was a clear cut element of risk in every mission we flew, some of our operations were more complicated and hazardous than others. Mission # 2 and Mission # 3 were extremely important to our development as undercover operatives, because these operations enabled us to get to know our enemy better. These early missions also enabled us to hone our skills as covert aviators and learn more about managing the logistics of mounting transportation cases using private aircraft. In addition, these early missions helped to further establish our reputation as a "can do" group of highly specialized undercover agents. Both aircraft for these missions were rented from Airport Sam.

Mission # 2 involved providing a plane and a crew to support a joint FBI/DEA transportation case that involved the retrieval of 350 kilos of cocaine from Colombia. Since our relationship with DEA was a bit strained to put it mildly, I welcomed the opportunity to instill a favorable working relationship with DEA, the agency that we affectionately called Brand X.

During Mission # 2, the undercover aircraft was damaged while taking off on an unimproved airstrip in Colombia. The damage to the landing gear caused the UC aircraft to fly at a slower speed. In addition, the undercover aircraft also sustained damage to its antennas. Since we didn't know that our plane was damaged on takeoff, we had no way of knowing why the undercover aircraft was overdue.

While I sat at a desk in the Ft. Lauderdale Executive Airport Police Sub

Station and waited patiently with a police detective and FBI Agent Kenny P., I received a call from a Radar Detection Specialist from C31. (FBI Agent Kenny P. and his partner Agent Rick C. were two of THE BEST Federal Agents I ever worked with.) U.S. Customs Radar Detection Specialists were also true professionals, who kept us updated about the status of our undercover aircraft whenever they went operational.

The minute the phone rang, one of our Detection Specialists wasted no time in reporting, that two Cuban MIGs just launched from their base and were on a direct course to intercept our twin engine Aero Commander undercover aircraft. This was happening because our undercover aircraft flew dangerously close to Cuban airspace on their way to South Florida.

The second I heard this exceptionally bad news, my vivid imagination pictured a pair of Cuban MIG fighter jets taking some type of aggressive action to bring our plane down. After what our pilots later described as an act of aerial harassment, the MIGs broke off their intercept and returned to base.

Even though our plane was behind schedule, we were happy to hear that the rented UC aircraft landed without incident in Key West. In order to prevent our contract pilots from being arrested by Customs Inspectors, our agents in Key West intervened and waited with our crew until they got refueled and took off.

As soon as the UC aircraft landed in Ft. Lauderdale, it was brought into a hangar and off loaded. When our contract pilots were debriefed, we learned that the UC aircraft hit a hole on the runway, that damaged the undercarriage and the radio antennas while taking off from an unimproved field in Colombia. The crew also explained what it was like to be in the cockpit, when a pair of Cuban MIGs intentionally flew a tad too close to their plane. As a result of this mission, DEA and the FBI were able to successfully complete their controlled delivery.

In Mission # 3 we provided a plane and one contract pilot (Major Tom) to assist an FBI investigation by transporting 300 kilos from Colombia. During this covert air operation, Major Tom was paired up with a Colombian pilot I dubbed Captain Kilo. Captain Kilo was an experienced pilot for a Colombian drug cartel, who saw the errors of his ways and decided to work for the Bureau (FBI).

While preparing to execute this operation, I had several meetings with Captain Kilo. Even though he was the enemy in the not so distant past, now that he was working for the FBI, Captain Kilo was accepted as one of us. Becoming a Blade Runner was like going to confession and having all of your sins forgiven. The fact that Captain Kilo had a family grounded him and gave him a personal reason to play by our rules.

Even though Captain Kilo spoke almost no English and Major Tom spoke almost no Spanish, they got along quite well and ended up successfully completing this mission and becoming friends. All total, Mission 2 & 3 resulted in the seizure of over 600 kilos of cocaine and several arrests. (DEA and the FBI made the arrests in these cases.)

THE NUTS & BOLTS OF THE GROUP 7 UNDERCOVER OPERATION

Even though we continued to maintain a desk at Group 7, Mike R, Chuck W. and I generally worked out of an undercover office on a daily basis. Our arrangement with our sources of information and contract pilots was very simple. The special agents called the shots and would direct every controlled delivery with input from our informants, sources of information and contract personnel. The special agents would also work undercover with our informants and contract crews, when it was necessary and appropriate to do so. While the contract pilots and sources of information flew the missions, the special agents would pace the floors and worry until their safe return. The agents also handled the paper work, paid the expenses and worked every aspect of each and every controlled delivery. In other words, we were a "soup to nuts" operation.

Early on I learned that pilots are truly a special breed. Anyone who is familiar with pilots knows that it doesn't take long to realize the difference between a "licensed" pilot and an aviator or a flier. In other words, just because you had a pilot's license didn't make you Blade Runner material.

Because our operations had some of the elements of a combat mission, we needed contract pilots who could do more than just safely operate an airplane. We needed fliers, barnstormers, bush pilots and aviators, who were also capable of effectively working in an undercover capacity. This was especially the case when they operated in a source country like Colombia.

While I admired the way in which the airline types and the former military pilots carried themselves, there was something very endearing about the barnstormers and bush pilots, who would generally kick the tires, bash the dashboard with a ball peen hammer and go for it. The majority of the contract pilots who flew for us were outstanding aviators, who were capable of flying a variety of different types of aircraft. Only two of them were less versatile. The trick for me and the other agents I worked with was to know the capabilities and personality of every member of our unit, so we could put the right mix of people together whenever we went operational.

Ever since this operation began, my partners and I wrestled with our personal feelings, of whether or not we would get too close to the people who worked for us, especially since they could be killed during one of our operations. Regardless of whether they were informants, sources of information, contract pilots, or mechanics, they were real people with real families. The men who few for us did so for a variety of reasons, including for the adventure, for the money and because it was the right thing to do. Three of the men who flew for us did so to stay out of jail, or to obtain a lesser sentence. One of those men remained with us after he paid his debt to society.

While the bulk of our sources of information and contract personnel had clean records, a few worked for us to clear a tarnished reputation. Regardless, none of our sources of information, informants or contract personnel were expendable, at least not to me and the other special agents who ran this operation.

Generally speaking, the system loved reliable sources of information and contract personnel and had no problem rewarding them in the most generous fashion possible, when they provided a valuable service to Uncle Sam. This was the case, because the U.S. Customs Service knew how much we could accomplish with their assistance.

Personally, I believed that we had no choice but to become very familiar and professionally friendly with our contract personnel, sources of information and informants, in order to know their strong and weak points. I also believed that our sources of information and contract personnel went the extra mile for us, because they knew how hard my fellow agents and I worked, to insure their personal safety and make every case a success.

As I referenced earlier in this book, all of our sources of information and contract personnel were eligible for the standard POI/POE (Payment of Information/Payment of Evidence) Payment and a MOIETY Payment that enabled any documented source of information to receive varying amounts of money for providing reliable information that resulted in seizures and arrests. Sources of information and contract personnel were also paid for providing services such as flying in undercover aircraft and working undercover.

Believe it or not, there was no sliding scale for agents to go by, when it came time to pay a documented source of information or a contract pilot. In other words, we didn't pay a certain amount for the weight of the drug shipments that we seized. To be more specific, there was no sliding scale that directed agents to pay X number of dollars for every pound or kilo of contraband that we seized. The simple truth is that we basically made the amounts up as we went along.

As far as flying was concerned, we decided early on, that the minimum we would pay a contract pilot was $40,000 to $50,000 dollars per mission. Even though all of our missions were considered high risk operations, we increased the payments for services rendered, when our crews participated in more complex and exceptionally dangerous cases. As far as I recall, the most we paid a contract pilot was $125,000 for one mission. Contract Co-Pilots and other crewmen received payments that were slightly less, than the amounts that were paid to the Contract Pilot in Command. Bear in mind, that our sources of information and contract personnel often did a lot more than just sit in a cockpit and fly a specific mission. In the largest majority of cases, our hired hands were actively involved in our operations on a daily and regular basis. This means that their contribution to our success went beyond just providing a specific service at a specific time.

When we seized assets of value, including drug money, we were able to make our payments based on a formula that did not exceed 25% of the value of any assets seized, providing that the payment(s) made did not exceed $250,000 per case. As I mention throughout this true story, Group 7 contract pilots and confidential sources of information were very highly paid, because they provided reliable information and assistance that enabled us to make a succession of major cases, significant seizures and numerous arrests. Even in the less significant cases that we worked, we still made arrests and or seized assets that had value.

CHAPTER 11

THE VERY THIN BLUE LINE

Working in the drug enforcement field is dangerous, demanding and exciting work. Despite improvements in pay and benefits, law enforcement officers in the U.S. are not paid Hollywood salaries and stunt men are not called in to take our place when the going gets rough. Very few of us are well versed in Oriental marital arts and most of us can go a career without ever pulling the trigger except at the firing range. Unlike television cops, we didn't have an hour with commercials to solve a crime or put a case together. At different times in our respective careers, many of us are called upon to place ourselves in harm's way. While the majority of law enforcement officers manage to survive their careers without getting seriously injured or killed, others are not so lucky.

Ever since 1789 the U.S. Customs Service has protected the revenue and the national security of the United States. This mission was accomplished by preventing acts of smuggling and protecting our borders. In the process, the U.S. Customs Service has had a number of its sworn personnel injured, disabled and killed in the line of duty. One casualty of America's Drug War was U.S. Customs Pilot George Saenz.

U.S. Customs Pilot George Saenz was killed in action on November 2, 1989 while assisting special agents from Group 7. At the time of his death, George was pursuing a go fast boat that was involved in an air drop operation along the South Florida coastline. Disaster struck when the U.S. Customs Black Hawk helicopter that was involved in this pursuit, shuddered, then crashed into the ocean while flying at a high rate of speed.

Imagine flying just above the ocean, at night, in a light rain, while in hot pursuit of a fast moving vessel, when suddenly your helicopter abruptly crashes into the sea and you end up gasping for air as you spiral down into the darkness. For those who were on board that night, the noise of the crash was deafening, as the rotor blades disintegrated, when the Black Hawk helicopter hit the water before it rolled over and sank. Inside the cargo compartment in the rear of the aircraft, the crew began to unbuckle their seat belts and shoulder straps, as they held their breath in the pitch black darkness below the surface of the ocean. As each crew member scrambled out of the sinking helicopter, they inflated their PFDs (Personal Flotation Device) and floated to the surface.

Up front in the cockpit, U.S. Customs Pilot Ralph G., a champion weight lifter, used brute strength to force the co-pilot's door open so he could escape. Customs Pilot George Saenz was not so lucky. As the U.S. Customs Black Hawk continued to spiral down into the abyss, George was unable to egress from the sinking helicopter.

When George could no longer hold his breath, he left this world to go to a better place. Clearly, it was a miracle that five other crewmen survived this unpredictable crash at sea. Even though it took about thirty minutes or so for the crew to be rescued, the survivors were eventually picked up by a U.S. Navy Hydrofoil that was operating in the area. Unfortunately, George Saenz's body was never recovered.

There are no words that can accurately describe the horror that was experienced by the crew members who survived this terrible accident. Likewise, there are no words to describe what it must have been like for George, when he died a horrible death in the line of duty. George's family and friends remind us by their grief, of how rich his contribution to our existence really was. His loss touched us all in many ways. His devotion to duty also inspired the people he left behind, to go on and do the best we can, for our time on this earth is short.

George Saenz's death should serve as a constant reminder to every human being who walks this earth, that there will always be casualties in the violent struggle between good and evil. Like the rest of us, George Saenz was not deterred by the fact that he might have to pay the ultimate sacrifice in order to do his job. To his credit, George bravely entered the valley of the shadow of death and feared no evil, while giving an exceptionally good account of himself, in a conflict that goes on to this day.

Does it matter whether the case that George was killed on was a big one or a small one? Is it important whether he died making history? No, not at all. George took a stand and gave his life for his country, while fighting as a frontline combatant in a very dangerous conflict, that would go on with no end in sight long after his death. He is survived by a loving family and will always hold the admiration of every member of the United States Customs Service. U.S. Customs Pilot George Saenz is a hero of The Drug War and it is my honor to introduce you to him in this fashion.

PREMONITIONS

Just before the operation that cost the life of Customs Pilot George Saenz, I sat at a desk and watched, as several of my colleagues discussed who would be going along, as part of the bust crew in the back of the Black Hawk. While I listened to this exchange, I heard a voice deep inside of me say, "Don't do it."

Now you have to understand, that I volunteered for every assignment or detail, regardless of the risks involved. This time was different. When I was asked if I wanted to go along, I responded without hesitation and said no. In fact, while I was saying no to the offer to participate in this mission, I didn't understand why I was doing so, especially since I loved flying in the back of Black Hawk helicopters. All I can say is that I had a premonition that prevented me from participating. I believe that premonition saved my life. As I mention in different parts of this story, this was not the first, or the last time that I experienced a premonition.

CHAPTER 12

NECESSITY IS THE MOTHER OF INVENTION

The day Special Agent Chuck W. received a call from Special Agent James S. from our New Mexico office we had another mission to fly. At first, the operation called for us to fly into Colombia and pick up 10,000 pounds of marijuana and a few hundred keys of coke. As we geared up to mount this operation, we had our request for country clearance denied then approved. While I am not at liberty to divulge the exact reason why our request was initially denied, I can say that there were some serious concerns for the safety of our contract pilots.

The delay, as legitimate as it may have been, threw a monkey wrench into our plans. We had a schedule worked out, that would allow a certain undercover crew to fly this mission. One of our pilots almost lost his regular flying job, due to the two weeks off that he spent with us, while we geared up for this particular controlled delivery. To make matters worse, we had a fuel leak in our UC aircraft and had already spent $9,000 in undercover funds making repairs.

Under the circumstances, we decided to blame the Colombians for the delays that they caused, even though nothing they did actually prevented us from being able to make the pickup. After we had a strategy session with Special Agent Jim

S. (from the RAC Albuquerque), he directed his Confidential Informant (CI) to tell the bad guys, that they better not call us again, unless they were prepared to pay us a sizable amount of front money. (When you have nothing to lose, you have nothing to lose by being bold.)

By late November, we weren't surprised when Special Agent James S. called and gave us the good news, that the Colombians delivered $25,000 to his CI in New Mexico. Fortunately, this amount of front money was just enough to get this deal off the ground, as long as we watched the way we spent these funds. According to our Albuquerque based case agent, the Colombians had several hundred kilos of cocaine in Colombia that they wanted us to fly to New Mexico, via "a window" or safe route, that enabled us to avoid being detected by U.S. interdiction assets.

While I can't go into detail about the plan that we proposed to our "clients" in Colombia, I can say that we used our knowledge of the radar and interdiction capabilities of the U.S. Government to present a plan that was very plausible. Whether the bad guys were too trusting, over confident, or they actually had a working knowledge of our interdiction capabilities was anyone's guess. All that mattered was that our bullshit story convinced our Colombian "clients" that we knew exactly what we were talking about.

Once we had the green light to proceed, Chuck, Mike and I picked our undercover crew and selected a plane from The Gambler's inventory of suitable aircraft. To make sure that our plane was properly sanitized, we had the tail number changed and the aircraft gone over with a fine tooth comb. Doing so insured that we removed anything that could trace this aircraft to its legitimate owner.

When it looked like we should be able to launch, we had the confidential informant from New Mexico, a guy we ended up calling The Salesman, call his contact in Colombia to make the final arrangements for the pickup. (We called the New Mexico CI/Contract Pilot The Salesman, because he was a smooth talking undercover operative, who could sell snowballs in hell to the devil. I also called the New Mexico CI who served as one of our contract pilots The Preacher.) In the meantime, we filed another request for country clearance, while we prepared our plane to fly the mission.

Even though Customs Headquarters approved this operation, we were grounded until we received country clearance from DEA. I say this over and over again throughout this book, to let you get a feel for the level of frustration that we had to endure, in order to successfully complete a transportation case, also known as, a controlled delivery. While country clearance would eventually become relatively easy to secure, the early days were difficult times. In fact, with rare exception, we usually prepared to fly a mission, without knowing if we would ever get the green light to launch.

When DEA denied our request again, Chuck and I drove Agent James S. and The Salesman to Miami International Airport to catch a flight home. After putting up with a week of delays, our colleagues from New Mexico were on their way home, when we received an important message. Just about the time that their plane left Miami, DEA reversed their decision and said that we could go. With Agent James S. and The Salesman heading home, Chuck and I looked at each other in total amazement. It was then, that we decided to let things ride and try to get the bad guys to give us a decent amount of front money.

When The Salesman was contacted again by the same group and offered more front money, we figured for sure that we would be able to launch. Once again, Agent James S. and The Salesman traveled to Miami and teamed up with me, Chuck and Mike, to try one more time to execute this operation. Unfortunately, as our crew sat in the cockpit ready to take off, the phone rang in our undercover airport office. When I answered the phone, I was told that our request for country clearance was once again denied.

This case had more stumbling blocks, than any other investigation that I worked during my entire law enforcement career. Despite these setbacks I believed that we would successfully complete this particular controlled delivery. Until then, all we could do was work on other cases and keep the Albuquerque deal on the back burner.

CHAPTER 13

THE GREED FACTOR

One of the biggest concerns that a smuggling organization has to deal with is being infiltrated by undercover agents. In order to try and prevent this from happening, smuggling organizations will usually rely on the services of a trustworthy broker, who can vouch for the people who are capable of providing a particular service. This meant, that my colleagues and I had to initially convince the bad guy who acted as a broker, that we were real smugglers. Once that happened, we were able to further infiltrate the enemy camp.

I'm convinced that my colleagues and I were successful in infiltrating smuggling organizations, because we were very good actors and we knew how the enemy operated. I also believe that we were successful because of The Greed Factor.

The fact that there was a large number of criminals involved in drug trafficking and drug smuggling activities, also made it possible for us to operate without coming under suspicion. Even though we operated in a "target rich" environment, we were always concerned about the number of times, that we would be able to repeat the undercover process that we specialized in. Fortunately, "The Greed Factor" saved our bacon each and every time that we went operational. Simply put, greed blinded the bad guys that we dealt with. This happened because greed is a very powerfully destructive force, that clouds judgment and consumes criminals from the inside out. Another way to look at this, is to consider the lyrics from famous Eagles song that says, "it's the lure of easy money that gives a smuggler the blues."

When criminals plot and plan their nefarious activities, they focus so much on making huge sums of money, they often lose sight of reality. (Hate can also be just as destructive as Greed.) I am convinced that it's the Greed Factor, that enables undercover agents to infiltrate the hearts and minds of violators, who are obsessed with making their fortune through illegal means.

Being able to game the system, or get over on the system in some "crafty" fashion, is also linked to The Greed Factor. In other words, it is the lust for riches, along with the ability to get away with a crime, that makes some people unable to realize that they are being infiltrated by government agents. The seductive nature of being able to live like a king, also clouds a criminal's vision and prevents them from seeing through the bullshit story, that is being fed to them by a smooth talking undercover agent.

Each and every time we did business with drug smugglers, The Greed Factor never failed to be our best ally. We also used The Greed Factor to impress and convince our "clients" that we were real smugglers. The bad guys saw that we had all the toys that made us credible smugglers. We had the fancy cars, planes, boats, a gold Presidential Rolex watch and the free wielding spirit that enabled us to walk away from any deal that did not seem right to us.

The bad guys we dealt with also saw us cut every corner in our negotiations to get a fair but lucrative deal. Had we been uninspired undercover agents, we might have settled for the original offer that was put on the table. Even though we were not real bad guys and we would never really be able to enjoy the fruits of our labor, we had to drive hard bargains and argue over money all the time. You might say that we pitched pennies with the best of them.

We were also successful because the bad guys lied to each other. This was especially the case, when some brokers vouched for us and recommended our services as smugglers, even though we never did business with them before.

In the end, we were victorious because we were right and because we had a clear head and the smugglers didn't. The tactics that we employed took the fight to the enemy, which went beyond the typical American response, which was to try and interdict smugglers when they penetrated our borders. Rather than wait for them to come to us, we found a way to get to them. In the end, we grabbed them by the short hairs and squeezed them for every dollar we could, while we dangled "their" drug shipment as bait before their eyes. While our adversaries were mesmerized by the thought of taking possession of the drug shipment that we "smuggled" into the U.S. on their behalf, my colleagues and I announced our true identity and shut the party down.

CHAPTER 14

GENERAL PUMA

In early December of 1989, Special Agent Steve P. and Air Officer Gary P. were working on a transportation case, that involved the possible seizure of several thousand kilos of cocaine. The targets of this investigation were based in South Florida. This case was very unique, because the subjects of this investigation believed that Special Agent Steve P. was a Cuban Army General, who was willing to use Cuba as a transit point, to smuggle drug shipments into the U.S. This case also took precedence, because Customs Pilot George Saenz was killed in November of 1989, as a direct result of this investigation.

By mid December, the Colombian source of supply told our undercover agent to hold off, until the situation in the area changed. This notification was meant to prevent our crew from getting picked up by legitimate Colombian police units, that were operating where the pickup was supposed to be made. When Mike R. and I were finally asked to provide support for this controlled delivery, we decided to make the pickup along the coast to minimize the risk to our crew.

To my knowledge, there had never been a controlled delivery, where contract pilots working for a federal agency landed a former military seaplane in the ocean, to pick up a large shipment of cocaine. Certainly, no controlled delivery operation ever publicized before, involved a covert air operation, where the crew went undercover as smugglers working for a Cuban Army General.

This case became a real deal when the Colombian subjects of this investigation delivered $75,000 in front money to a Group 7 undercover operative. As anxious as we were to go operational, the bad guys decided to do the deal after the holidays. Just like the G (the U.S. Government), the Colombians generally shut down the bulk of their operations during the Christmas Holidays. With nothing else to do but wait, my colleagues and I settled into the Christmas spirit and enjoyed the holidays with our families. Unfortunately, my holiday was cut short, when I met Hombre de la Calle in a strip joint in South Florida on December 26th and ended up arresting a fugitive wanted by DEA Agents from Massachusetts, who was hiding out in Miami Beach.

HAPPY NEW YEAR 1990 THE DRUG WAR CONTINUES

After several weeks of waiting, the Colombian violators in the Agent Steve P. and Air Officer Gary P. case said they had 6000 pounds of cocaine waiting to be picked up, at a location along the coast that seemed to fit our needs perfectly. When it came time to brief our crew, they seemed genuinely surprised to hear, that they would be portraying a group of smugglers who worked for a fictional Cuban Army General by the name of Puma.

Since good seaplane pilots did not grow on trees and we did not have two Cuban American contract pilots who were capable of pulling off this particular mission, I decided to get real crazy and have The Colonel, as in Kentucky Colonel, act like an East German pilot, whose job it was to keep the American gringo pilot Captain Video in line. I made the decision to go with the East German cover story, because the contract pilot known as The (Kentucky) Colonel said that he spoke German, when I asked if anyone in our group spoke any foreign languages. I thought this cover story made sense, because Cuba was a communist country that had very close ties with the former Soviet Union. Having a former East German pilot living and working in Cuba, sounded like something that the Colombians should find believable.

Unfortunately, when I asked The Colonel to say a few words in German at the briefing session, he limited his response to saying, "Spreckanze Duetche," before he smiled and became mute. While all eyes were on me, I looked directly at The Colonel and said, "That's it? I thought you said you spoke German?"

Even though he knew the seriousness of the situation, The Colonel stuck to his guns and defended himself by saying, that when I had asked him if he could speak German he told the truth, because he knew a few words in that particular language. Needless to say, I wanted to crawl under the conference room table, after being conned in public by one of my own contract pilots.

Even though The Colonel was a great pilot and an incredibly brave man, he was a royal pain in my ass at times. Fortunately, the language issue was ignored and we moved on with the briefing. The good news was that in the cargo section of the undercover aircraft, our crew chief and a Cuban contract pilot who was not qualified to fly a former military seaplane, spoke a sprinkling of various languages and would act as a buffer between the cockpit crew and the Colombians.

The most exotic cover story that I concocted was assigned to Captain Video. According to his cover story, Captain Video was supposed to be an American drug smuggler forced down over Cuba, during a drug run and captured by the famous General Puma. Again, according to his cover story, once General Puma realized his prisoner's value, he offered the American drug pilot (Captain Video) his freedom in return for making ten runs (smuggling flights) for the General's Cuban based smuggling organization.

LET THE GAMES BEGIN

The last thing that I wanted to hear on Sunday morning January 7, 1990, was the shrilly sound of my pager going off. I was so exhausted after not falling asleep until 4:30 AM that I stayed in bed paralyzed with fatigue. When my pager went off again, I dragged my tired 36 year old body from the sheets, to see who was trying to get in touch with me at this ungodly hour. After checking my pager, I couldn't believe my eyes, when I saw the office phone number and Gary P's call sign. I was a workaholic but this was ridiculous.

As soon as I returned the call, Gary was very excited because he just received the final go order signaling that the deal was on. Now that we had the green light to launch, I put my contract pilots and mechanics to work getting the undercover seaplane ready to fly.

Our job was to make the undercover plane that we picked to fly this mission, look like some thing that a Cuban General would fly in. In order to accomplish this, we worked an entire day painting the plane in Cuban Army colors. Again, this was stuff that none of us were taught at the Federal Law Enforcement Training Center.

Once the paint was dry and our mechanics finished going over our seaplane, the aircraft was taken up for a test flight. (All of these preparations were made at the U.S. Customs Miami Air Unit ramp and tie down area on Homestead Air Force Base. I mention this to let you know, that we often operated from a military base to maintain operational security, while preparing for this and other missions.)

The undercover aircraft that we selected for this mission was a former U.S. military seaplane, that was capable of carrying different amounts of cargo and passengers depending on the operating conditions, the duration of the mission and how it was configured. While operating with drop tanks (externally mounted fuel tanks) this particular military surplus seaplane had very long legs and was able to fly 1800 plus miles non stop under ideal operating conditions. As versatile and rugged as this particular seaplane was, it had its limitations, especially when operating in the open ocean. Any sign of white caps and Captain Video would scrub the mission.

By this stage in the operation, all eyes were on me and Mike R. because we were responsible for orchestrating the actual extraction of the cocaine shipment from Colombia. The tension inside Group 7 got so bad at times, I felt as if every little problem with our plane was often magnified by a thousand percent, because of the tremendous strain that the case agents were under.   One reason for the extra stress was because the game plan kept changing. Originally, I was asked if we could fly 2000 pounds of cocaine from land, then 2000 pounds from a lake in Colombia, then another 4000 from the coast in the open ocean. After several changes in the game plan, I was told that we would be making the pickup in a lagoon/protected location close to shore.

When we provided support to other agents, my partners and I had to periodically brief case agents, undercover agents, sources of information, contract pilots and informants about the capabilities of the undercover aircraft. We did this so they could accurately represent our capabilities to our "clients." Since it took me a long time to learn about the capabilities of different aircraft, I couldn't blame my fellow agents, or their sources of information, for not always grasping every tidbit of technical information that I threw at them in a relatively short period of time.

I should also mention, that each and every time there was a change in plans, Mike R. and I had to get together with our contract pilots and go over the maps and air charts of the area in Colombia, where the bad guys were proposing that we land to make the pick up. One of us then had to call the case agent, the co case agent and our group supervisor to go over our findings and recommendations. In addition, as far as I know, the documented Source of Information who worked on this case with U.S. Customs, as well as with the FBI, also had to be briefed whenever any changes needed to be made to the proposed operational plan. When all this was done, the appropriate UC operative then had to contact the Colombian violators.

This cycle of constant communication continued until the deal was finally consummated and the plane departed the U.S. to make the pick up in Colombia. Naturally, the constant flurry of phone calls and think tank sessions didn't always happen between normal working hours and involved a great deal of running around at all hours of the day and night.

When word finally came that we would be landing along the Colombian coast, we liked the arrangement because it was generally safer to land a seaplane in a lagoon of sorts than in the open ocean. To make sure that there was no confusion, I asked the case agents to verify that the Colombians knew the importance of our previous instructions. When I asked for confirmation that the lagoon along the coast was six feet deep and had no obstructions that would impair the landing of a seaplane, I was told not to worry because the "lagoon" was deep enough. (If I'm not mistaken I was told the lagoon was 6 feet deep.)

Even with all we that had done to prepare for this mission, we had some nagging problems to deal with. One annoying problem had to do with the need to install a High Frequency (HF) radio in the undercover seaplane that we selected for this mission. While our crew intended to use a hand held radio to communicate with the bad guys on the ground in Colombia, we hoped to be able to communicate with our plane from our command post in Miami. In order to do so, we needed to use a High Frequency or HF radio. Otherwise, we had to relay messages through the U.S. Customs and U.S. Air Force aircraft that were expected to provide air support for this operation.

Prior to launching this mission, it was also determined that one of the two compasses in the undercover seaplane was off by 30 degrees and the number two engine was burning oil. Even though we were unable to repair the compass, we were able to place some extra oil on board the aircraft, to replenish the amount that our crew anticipated they would burn during the mission.

After saying good-bye to the team that was heading south, I waited as our crew of contract pilots and confidential informants led by Mike R., climbed into the undercover seaplane and prepared to take off. Once again, our contract pilots and confidential informants would be going in harms way, with an unofficial IOU that they would be paid an unknown amount of money at some point in the future. Fortunately, the contract pilots and CIs who worked for us liked the intrigue as much as we did. They also liked the idea of helping to avenge the death of a U.S. Customs Pilot.

As I watched the UC plane taxi to the active runway, I felt bad that I had to stay behind and monitor the situation from the command post with Pat R., Steve P. and Gary P. While I watched the undercover seaplane take off, I said a silent prayer for their safe return. Once again, the ball was now in play.

PROBLEMS AND MORE PROBLEMS-WHAT ELSE IS NEW

When my home phone rang at 1 AM on January 11, 1990 my wife woke me up to tell me that Air Officer Gary P. was on the line. I had two hours of sack time the night before and wasn't sleeping very long when Gary called me at home. Even though I was bone tired when I answered the phone, I could tell by the tone in Gary's voice that we had big problems.

Due to the presence of Colombian military patrols in the area along the Colombian coast, we were expected to arrive at the pickup point no later than 0600 hours or 6 AM. We were also expected to depart the area by 0700 hrs or 7AM. This meant that our undercover crew had to leave GITMO no later than 1 AM.

When the UC aircraft landed at GITMO at 2145 hours or 9:45 PM., our crew determined that they needed a heavier engine oil to replenish the reserve tank. To make matters worse, the High Frequency radio was not working properly after being repaired and tested twice. Even though I knew this wasn't a big problem, some people were still concerned and upset that one of the two compasses in the UC aircraft was still off by 30 degrees. (I'll explain why this didn't both me under the circumstances later on in this story.)

The good news was, the U.S. Navy had the right type of engine oil for us. The bad news was, this oil was on the other side of GITMO and could not be moved to the Leeward Side, in time for our crew to service the plane and launch on schedule. This meant, that our crew would not be able to fly this mission, until we fixed the HF radio and provided them with heavier engine oil. (A landing craft was used by the U.S. Navy to shuttle vehicles and people back and forth from the Leeward and Windward Side of GITMO. Unless we had a helicopter at our disposal, we had to wait until this combination ferry boat/landing craft began operating.)

After making several phone calls, I was in the Group 7 office bright and early to get everything that was needed to make our plane mission ready. Throughout the day I had all sorts of people asking me questions about the mission at hand. While the telephones rang off the hook and pagers never stopped beeping, our trailer complex at Homestead Air Force Base looked more like the war room in the Pentagon than a U.S. Customs office.

Because one engine was burning oil we resorted to an old trick and decided to mix STP with the regular engine oil. As an additive, STP would slow the breakdown of the thinner engine oil and hopefully solve the problem, even if only on a temporary basis.

While Special Agent Jim Z. picked up two cases of STP, I picked up 55 gallons of engine oil and a new HF radio, along with 75 feet of 20/40 meter radio antenna wire, at The Gambler's airport office. Since it would be impossible for me to move a 55 gallon drum of oil in my undercover car and transport a heavy drum of oil all the way to GITMO in a U.S. Customs aircraft, we had to pump the oil into eleven 5 gallon plastic pales, that had secure tops to prevent spillage.

Once this was done, I raced back to Homestead Air Force Base, where two U.S. Custom's Pilots were standing by to take possession of this badly needed equipment. At 4:30 PM or 1630 hours, a U.S. Customs aircraft departed South Florida for our forward operating base at GITMO, Cuba. On board was all of the equipment and supplies that were required to put our controlled delivery back on track.

By 2200 hours or 10 PM. on January 11[th,] U.S. Navy technicians had the new HF radio and antenna installed on the undercover aircraft. Unfortunately, even when this radio was installed by U.S. Navy technicians, it didn't work properly. In my opinion, this wasn't the problem that some people made it out to be, because our crew could still use the UC aircraft's radio to communicate with the armada of U.S. Government chase planes. As I said earlier, our contract pilots and crew would also be able to use a hand held two meter radio to contact the Colombians on the ground, once they arrived over the LZ. With the engine oil situation temporarily under control, our plane was ready to fly, even though it still had one compass that was off by 30 degrees. OK, so the Wright Brothers flew this plane at Kitty Hawk.

As if I didn't have enough to worry about, one agent started giving me a hard time about the piece of crap that my flying circus had the nerve to call an airplane. Remember, with all the money the federal government allocated to fight the so called Drug War, none of this cash was sent to Group 7, to enable me and my colleagues to have access to a fleet of undercover aircraft, that were on par with the planes that were flown by the U.S. Government. It is also important to keep in mind, that we used certain planes because they made terrific smuggling aircraft.

As I mentioned before, even though I seized a number of private aircraft that could have been put in service as undercover aircraft, the official request to do so was DENIED. In fact, one of the private planes that I seized, was a former Vietnam vintage U.S. Air Force seaplane, that was virtually identical to the aircraft that I rented from The Gambler for this mission. Had our Uncle Sam assigned this aircraft to our undercover operation, we could have had our ace crew chief and mechanic Johnny Walker make this plane as good as new. When we needed to use this plane for other missions, we could have easily changed its appearance by applying a fresh coat of paint, a new set of tail numbers and by adding or removing different size drop tanks.

We could have also saved money, by having access to our own surplus military seaplane, instead of having to rent various models from different owners. Since we paid a lot of money to rent these planes, the owners had no problem handing us the keys. There was also some travel involved, when we had to rent planes from different owners, who were based in different locations. The fact that we purchased expensive War Risk Insurance, also made it easy for the owners to let us rent their aircraft. Had we used seized aircraft, it would not have been necessary to purchase special insurance coverage, because the U.S. Government is self insured.

Lord only knows how many suitable aircraft were seized by other agents, that we could have also put to good use. Again, as I said before, when my original proposal was approved, I was basically left to fend for myself. Even though I ended up having one or two special agents assigned to work with me on this project, we worked insane hours and never had enough help. We couldn't even get one experienced U.S. Customs Pilot assigned to work with us on a permanent basis.

Even though the so called system didn't do much to support our efforts, our colleagues in Customs Air Operations did everything possible to assist us as needed, on a case by case basis. Our Customs Air Branch contacts also hooked us up with U.S. Air Force Major Howard B; an outstanding military officer who proved to be another major supporter of our covert operations. This guy literally moved mountains for us. In other words, networking, not any official dictates or memorandums of understanding, enabled us to get whatever "specialized" assistance that we needed.

If we suffered anywhere, it was when it came to running the day to day operation. This was the case, because those of us who ran this operation on a daily basis, were basically responsible to DO EVERYTHING. On those occasions when we did receive "help," we usually spent more time explaining why we had to do X,Y, or Z than it was worth. This meant that on any average day, the one or two special agents that I worked with on a regular basis, were responsible to direct every aspect of this undercover operation. This included, directing the informants, sources of information and contract personnel who were involved in a number of on going investigations and undercover operations. It is also important to remember, that we usually pursued several leads and worked a number of cases at the same time, never knowing which ones would result in a successful controlled delivery/transportation case.

While all this was going on, my colleagues and I (generally two or three of us) recruited new informants, new sources of information and new contract personnel. In addition, we conducted surveillance operations, worked undercover when necessary, participated in various enforcement actions, wrote reams of reports, drafted monetary payments for sources of information/informants and contract personnel, made payments when the money arrived at the bank, received and made numerous phone calls at all hours of the day and night, conducted briefings, conducted joint investigations with other Customs Agents and other law enforcement officers and coordinated all of our undercover air operations with U.S. Customs air operations, as well as with military assets.

My colleagues and I also had to rent the appropriate undercover aircraft and recruit the right contract personnel for each mission. We also had to check the weather conditions, write the operational plan for every mission and re-write the operational (ops) plan every time changes were made. Oh, I forgot. In addition, there was a period of time, when I received unannounced visits from two Central Intelligence Agency employees, who periodically "dropped by" to say hi and chit chat about the Drug War and what the smugglers were up to in Colombia. We were also visited by a representative from a foreign Customs Service. In whatever time my colleagues and I had left, we were allowed to have a personal life. When we finally went operational, we were often away from home for a few days to a few weeks, only to return to the same intense level of activity.

AN EXCEPTIONALLY LONG NIGHT IN THE GROUP 7 TRAILER

Because I knew that we were all under a lot of pressure, I tried my best to ignore the negative remarks that were made by an agent, who was clearly under a great deal of pressure. When the hazing continued, I left the Group 7 trailer to get some air before things got really ugly. Fortunately, Senior Special Agent Pat R. came to the rescue and restored a sense of order.

Just about the time that Pat intervened and played referee, Mike R. called from GITMO to report that the U.S. Air Force E3 AWAC aircraft went tits up on the runway and was unable to take off on schedule. Under the circumstances, I couldn't resist and had to remind General Puma, that at least my piece of shit of an airplane was able to get off the fucking ground and fly the fucking mission, even if the HF radio didn't work any better than some of its navigation equipment. In fact, I was pissed off to no end, when the agent portraying General Puma didn't bad mouth the U.S. Air Force, when their multi-million dollar AWAC surveillance aircraft, that was supported by a first class maintenance crew, was unable to take off, but the antique that my guys were flying was ready to get airborne.

It also pissed me off to no end, when I caught flak when the HF radio that was installed on the undercover aircraft didn't work properly. My attitude was, if highly skilled U.S. Navy technicians were unable to make this particular piece of communications equipment function as designed, what the hell was my contract pilots supposed to do to make this situation any better? Once again, Pat R. came to the rescue and got everyone to cool off and get back on track.

I can't emphasize enough, that in addition to the fact that my contract pilots had one operational compass on board, they were also being escorted to and from the pickup point in Colombia, by specially equipped U.S. Customs and U.S. Air Force surveillance aircraft. At any time, all my contract pilots had to do to check their course heading, was use the proper call sign and the assigned primary or secondary radio frequency to contact one of the government escort planes. Even without the escort aircraft, my contract pilots had one fully operational compass and knew how to find Colombia. In addition, the undercover aircraft was also equipped with a special tracking device, that enabled U.S. government interdiction and surveillance assets to track their whereabouts.

The fact that the contract pilots who were flying the undercover aircraft had well over 10,000 hours of flight time under their belts, also meant that I had the utmost faith in their ability to find the designated LZ (landing zone) in Colombia. I mention all this, to reinforce the fact, that ALL of the necessary bases were covered, period, end of story!

GENERAL PUMA'S PLANE GOES TO COLOMBIA

Fortunately, when the time came to launch the undercover seaplane, the U.S. Air Force E3 AWAC aircraft was put back on line in time to provide support for this mission. After all sorts of delays, the aircraft involved in this covert air operation finally took off under the watchful eyes of Senior Special Agent Mike R..

By 2:27 AM or 0227 hours, the U.S. Air Force and U.S. Customs aircrews were providing our contract pilots in the undercover seaplane with the best possible course headings to the pick up point along the coast of Colombia. While the surveillance aircraft escorted the undercover seaplane to the LZ, teams of U.S. Customs and FBI agents in Miami were monitoring the activities of the subjects of the investigation.

While I paced back and forth in the Group 7 trailer complex, I thought about the war movies that depicted the commanding officer of a fighter squadron, or a bomber squadron waiting in the control tower for the return of his crews. As a kid who loved to watch these movies, there was no way that I could truly appreciate, what that poor slob in the control tower went through, each and every time he sent combat planes and crews in harms way. Call it my fate, or my destiny, but now I was the guy in the control tower, who was waiting for one of my planes to return from a dangerous mission behind enemy lines.

While I did my best to hide my concerns, all I could think about was how the military often sent large numbers of aircraft into combat and how when some failed to return, the generals called the men who were killed, missing in action, or taken prisoner "an acceptable loss" in time of war. During The Drug War, my colleagues and I sent one plane out and one just had to come back, because in our war, we had no such thing as an acceptable loss.

By 4 AM or 0400 hours our undercover aircraft had gained twenty minutes and was only ten minutes behind schedule. Special Agent Steve P. had thought ahead and told the Colombians that we might be ten minutes late. Based on what I documented at the time, the U.S. surveillance aircraft also continued to maintain communications with the undercover seaplane.

By 0530 hours or 5:30 AM the undercover seaplane was directed by the escort/surveillance aircraft to descend to an altitude of 500 feet. The UC plane would travel at this altitude for almost sixty miles, before it descended to 200 feet above the ocean. When you're cruising at 150 knots at 200 feet over the ocean, the pucker power is intense, especially when you're flying at night. The difference between life and death was literally measured in split seconds. When the time was right, the undercover aircraft descended even further and flew just above the dark ocean, as it headed for the LZ inside Colombian territory. (This was done to evade Colombian radar.)

At 0604 hours or 6:04 AM, the undercover seaplane climbed to a slightly higher altitude and flew directly over the pick up point. Needless to say, our crew was looking forward to getting into and out of Colombian airspace as quickly as possible.

As they flew over the intended pickup point, all eyes were looking for the Colombian vessel that would guide our crew into the landing zone along the coast. (Our contract pilots knew from the last briefing session, that the Colombians were instructed to have the crew on their vessel, flash a white light as soon as they spotted our plane.) While they circled the watery landing zone, one of the Spanish speaking confidential informants on board the undercover aircraft raised the Colombians on the two meter radio. After making contact with the bad guys, a Group 7 Cuban CI advised Captain Video and The Colonel to land in between the reef line and the beach.

Back at Homestead Air Force Base, those of us in the command post were anxiously waiting for an update from the U.S. Customs and U.S. Air Force escort/surveillance aircraft that were monitoring this operation from a safe distance. When one of the surveillance aircraft reported that the undercover seaplane was descending over the pickup point, I remarked, "Go, Team, Go," before I quickened my pace across the floor to burn off some nervous energy.

Even though there was no Colombian boat in sight, our crew decided to fly the mission as planned and land in the water along the coast to make the pickup. As the undercover seaplane skimmed the water, Captain Video held the controls with his left hand and gently reduced the power settings with his right hand, as he executed what initially appeared to be a text book water landing. Unfortunately, disaster struck the moment the undercover seaplane started to settle into the otherwise calm water along the beach. The expected smooth landing turned into a very rough ride, when the boat-like hull of the undercover seaplane landed in less than the required amount of water (four feet) and scrapped across the bottom of a sandbar.

As the undercover aircraft came to a complete stop, a huge wave of muddy sand filled water cascaded over the front of the seaplane. Our undercover crew was literally stranded between the rock and the hard place, with the angry ocean to their left, while a rather large number of surprised Colombian Indians stood on the beach to their right. Our crew was pissed and for good reason. Everyone had been told not to worry. The Colombians were either assholes or ignorant to believe that a seaplane this big, could land in two feet of water and four feet of mud.

Unable to budge, our undercover crew faced immediate disaster, when the owner of the cocaine shipment sent an emissary out to speak to the crew of the stranded seaplane. When two of the crewmen in the back of the seaplane opened the cargo door, an angry Colombian immediately questioned them in Spanish and asked if there were any gringos on board? To his credit, CI # 3 did his best to defend Captain Video, especially when the Colombian emissary said that he wanted to kill the gringo pilot. Luckily, our crew stuck to their cover story and convinced the cartel rep to help them free the plane so they could keep to the original plan.

While I continued to pace the floor of the command post, the clock ticked past the 30 minutes that the undercover seaplane was expected to be on the water in Colombian territory. Even though we had three surveillance aircraft providing overlapping coverage of the area, no one on our side could tell us what was going on, as far as our undercover crew was concerned.

After an hour passed, the High Frequency radio in the Group 7 office, which was supposed to be the Command Post of the famous General Puma, came to life as a Colombian radioman relayed messages to General Puma about his plane. According to the Colombian radio operator, the general's plane was stuck on a sandbar and was in the process of being freed. Moments later the Colombian manning a land based HF radio contacted General Puma, to report that one of the Colombians on the beach wanted to kill the gringo pilot of the seaplane.

There are no words to describe how I felt when I heard that one of the Colombians wanted to execute Captain Video. With no time to spare, I thought fast and realized that our only hope was to have General Puma (Agent Steve P.) use Captain Video's wacky cover story to try and save his life. After a quick think tank session, we all agreed that it was time for General Puma to put his foot down and find out what the hell was going on with his plane and his crew.

In one of the best undercover performances I ever witnessed in my entire career, Special Agent Steve P. got on the HF radio in the back office of Group 7 and acted like a very distinguished and pissed off Cuban Army General, when he contacted the Colombians he was dealing with. If I had any connections in Hollywood, I would have given Special Agent Steve P. an Oscar, for the performance that he put on that night and throughout this particular UC operation. Again, they simply can't teach you stuff like this in any training academy.

With dignity, poise and firmness in his tone, General Puma demanded that he be told what was going on with HIS airplane and crew. Since timing was everything in these calls, Special Agent Steve P. waited for the right moment to explain how he captured the gringo pilot (Captain Video) and agreed to give him his freedom after he flew ten missions for him. Fortunately, Steve P. got his point across and the voice on the other end seemed cooperative and sounded convincing, when he said that he would take care of everything. Best yet, the Colombians never doubted the authenticity of General Puma and for that I am eternally grateful.

Back in Colombia, the main Colombian on the beach waved his hand and ordered everyone into the water to help free the plane from the sandbar. The serious faced Colombian Indians turned into a friendly group of helpers, that used brute force and some applied physics to pull the plane free.

Obviously, the Colombians had either lied to Undercover Agent Steve P. or screwed up, but that was to be expected when dealing with Colombian drug traffickers. Instead of the boat that they promised, the only vessel in the vicinity of the watery landing zone was a dilapidated wooden rowboat that rested on the beach. The Colombians also disregarded the requirements that we relayed to them, that involved the need for our seaplane to operate in a minimum of four feet of water. Perhaps the Colombians lacked the sophistication to pay proper attention to detail. Either way, our crew would not be transporting any cocaine or flying home, unless they managed to break free from the grip, that this shallow sandbar had on the undercover seaplane.

There are no words to describe how a person can feel, when you are responsible for the lives of others, especially when things are not going as planned and you are powerless to do much more than pray. I also learned early on, that there are factors that cannot be put into an Ops Plan, that can influence the outcome of an operation. In this case, the unknown was a shallow sandbar.

Back in Colombia the local natives managed to free the plane from the sandbar and stood back as Captain Video started the engines. By this time, our crew had spent almost two and one half hours stuck on a sandbar along the coast in Colombia. After a short run up of the engines, to make sure all systems were working as designed, Captain Video and The Colonel applied full power and pressed forward with the crowd cheering him on.

As far as the cocaine was concerned, the Colombians told our crew to fly ten miles inland and land on a dirt road to pick up the load. Naturally, you can imagine what was going through the minds of our crew, when they were told that the cocaine shipment was waiting to be picked up ON A ROAD 10 MILES INLAND FROM THE BEACH! Was this some kind of cruel hoax, a set up, or what? What happened to the original plan, to land along the coast, get loaded and go?

With only two choices at their disposal, our crew opted to play along and go for the brass ring. As the seaplane picked up more and more speed and was about to get up on step, the undercover aircraft struck another sandbar and the takeoff had to be aborted.

The second Captain Video chopped the power, another wave of muddy seawater cascaded over the cockpit, the engines and the fuselage as the plane came to a screeching halt. Once again, there are very few words to describe how we all felt, when this distressing news was passed our way. Our seaplane crew was in an even worse predicament, because unless their situation improved, they would be stranded in Colombia.

Clearly, things did not look good for our crew and I was running out of prayers. Once again, the local natives pitched in and began to pull the undercover aircraft free from the second sandbar. While the crowd on the beach used long ropes and an old rusted out jeep to pull the plane free, our cockpit crew worked the engines and relayed their instructions to one of the Customs informants in the back of the cargo bay, who in turn relayed the instructions to the people on the beach. All that stood between our crew and freedom was 1000 miles of ocean and Lord knows how much sand, mud and rocks.

While armed with his tremendous sense of humor, The Colonel kept telling everyone on board the stricken aircraft that everything was going to be just fine. Even when the plane got stuck on a sandbar for a second time and things were far from okay, The Colonel kept telling everyone in a very factious tone of voice that everything was under control. I guess you had to be there to appreciate his sense of humor.

While I waited by the radio for an update, I knew I had gotten too close to my contract pilots and sources of information and was paying a price for it now. As crazy as this may sound, I actually felt as if I had carved years off the tail end of my life, by investing so much in my concerns. I kept saying to myself, just one more controlled delivery and I'll move on, but I never did. I had experienced some ecstatic moments in the past, but this was the hard part of what I did for a living.

BACK IN COLOMBIA

One again, the undercover seaplane was towed into position to make another run at getting airborne. No one said much when Captain Video and The Colonel started the engines and applied full power. During this attempt to take off, the 28,000 pound former military seaplane picked up more and more speed without meeting any obstructions.

While using every ounce of experience at his disposal, Captain Video waited for the right time to pull back on the controls and ease the former military air sea rescue plane into the air. Instead of heading back to GITMO or the CONUS, Captain Video banked the undercover aircraft in the opposite direction and flew over the cheering crowd that stood on the beach below.

When the lead U.S. Air Force E3 AWAC plane observed the UC aircraft take off, they contacted the U.S. Customs Air Unit at Homestead AFB, to relay the news that our plane was airborne. My sense of relief was short lived, when a crew member on board the U.S. Air Force AWAC plane quickly added that the undercover aircraft was heading inland.

Once again all eyes were on me. By the way some people were looking at me, I got the distinct impression that they thought my contract pilots were traitors, who changed sides in the middle of a battle. Senior Special Agent Pat R. was the only calm person in the room, who didn't look at me as if I had three heads. When Air Officer Gary P. asked me to explain why my contract pilots were flying inland, I looked at my concerned colleague and remarked something to the effect of, "How the hell am I supposed to know? I am here with you."

SO MUCH FOR THE OPERATIONAL PLAN

After flying a relatively short distance, The Colonel spotted a Colombian on the ground waving frantically, as the seaplane approached the location on the road where he was serving as a lookout. Once again, The Colonel proved that he had a great sense of humor, when he asked Captain Video if they would get paid if they returned to the States without any cocaine. When Captain Video responded, "No," one of our most colorful contract pilots remarked something to the effect of, "There's got to be some coke down there. After all, this is Colombia. Even ten keys will do." Clearly, the tension needed to be broken and everyone had a good laugh, thanks to the Contract Pilot called The Colonel aka Captain Mona.

As our contract pilots sized up the makeshift runway, they were grateful that the "rush hour" traffic had died down. Their landing spot was a dirt road located in the middle of no mans land, in the Colombian territory known as La Guajira Peninsula. This time Captain Video wasn't taking any chances. Rather than go straight in, he executed a maneuver known as dragging the strip, before he landed to make sure the road was suitable to set the plane down on. Once he was certain that the undercover plane would not sink into soft sand or muddy clay, Captain Video came back around and set up to land on the makeshift runway.

As soon as the undercover seaplane landed and came to a stop, the UC aircraft was surrounded by Colombians who were armed with an assortment of assault rifles and submachine guns. As the U.S. Customs confidential informants in the back of the undercover aircraft opened the cargo door, a truck pulled up and parked by the rear of the plane.

Rather than over heat the engines, that were already a bit strained after playing tug of war with a sandbar, Captain Video shut the motors down, while the plane was loaded with 520 kilos of cocaine. Once they were loaded and ready to go, The Colonel thought he was being funny, when he joked around about how the engines had started flawlessly each and every time they needed them to. Captain Video immediately felt jinxed and could not believe it when the # 2 engine would not turn over.

By now the Colombians were waving rifles and cheering them on. Unless the number two engine started, our crew wasn't going anywhere. The tension inside the cockpit grew as the next minute passed. Fortunately, when Captain Video cranked the #2 engine over again, she started right up. With a thousand pounds of fuel in her tanks and the 520 kilos of cocaine in the cargo bay, the undercover plane took off and headed back to the Group 7 office at Homestead AFB.

At 9:04 AM or 0904 hours the lead U.S. Air Force E3 AWAC aircraft reported that the UC plane was airborne and feet wet (over the ocean) and had resumed radio communications with the surveillance aircraft. According to the message that was relayed to us by the U.S. Air Force, we had a count of four on board, which meant that everyone who went on this mission was coming back. We were also told how much our crew picked up. Regardless of whether we had 50 kilos, 500, or 5000, we had a prosecutable case against those who were responsible for the death of a U.S. Customs Pilot.

As the undercover plane flew further and further away from Colombia, I imagined hearing cannons firing in the background as the 1812 Overture played very loud in my mind. The Blade Runner Squadron had done it again.

THE DRUG WAR - THE ONLY ONE WE GOT

Once we passed the initial test by picking up the 520 kilos, the Colombians invited General Puma to pick up 2500 more. Compared to Phase 1, Phase 2 looked like a walk in the park. After taking the beating that she did, in the shallow water along the coast, our undercover seaplane had more holes in her than a duck on opening day. In fact, due to her "battle damage," she was out of the seaplane business for a while. This meant that we had to reach out to our contacts and come up with another airworthy undercover aircraft for the second part of this operation. Thinking ahead we pre-positioned another suitable plane on our most forward operating base in the Caribbean (GITMO).

While Mike R. was doing the advance work on GITMO, I got our crew together in Miami and arranged to hitch a ride on a Customs plane, that was willing to take us to the U.S. Navy Base in Cuba, before heading on to the Customs Air Unit in Borinquen, Puerto Rico. Long before the U.S. Navy Base at Guantanamo Bay, Cuba became a POW Camp during The Global War on Terrorism, GITMO, was an American military outpost that served to protect our national interests. To be specific, during The Cold War, GITMO was a thorn in the side of the Soviets and their Cuban Allies. During The Drug War, GITMO served as a base for U.S. interdiction aircraft that needed to operate farther from U.S. shores. GITMO was also ideally suited to serve as a "secret" location, to launch covert air and marine operations.

The U.S. Navy Base at Guantanamo Bay, Cuba is divided into a windward and leeward side that is separated by a rather wide harbor entrance. Vessels that are designed to serve as "landing craft" are used to ferry people and vehicles across the inlet. Learning the ferry system schedule is perhaps the first item on your agenda, especially if you intend to travel from one side of the base to the other and be anywhere on time.

Just as you would expect, the U.S. military personnel on GITMO always treated us with the utmost respect. As I mention elsewhere in this book, the U.S. Navy Base Police, as well as the U.S. Naval aviation and marine maintenance personnel were especially helpful to us during our visits to GITMO.

In addition to a small Jamaican style restaurant where you could buy food near the leeward side airport, there was a standard military mess hall, as well as an Officer's Club called Danny's Hideaway where we used to eat. Federal agents passing through are generally billeted at the BOQ or Bachelor Officers Quarters on the leeward side of the island. Another BOQ is located on the windward side. On different occasions we were billeted in the BOQ facilities on both sides of GITMO. As a result, we spent time on both sides of the base at various times for various reasons.

In order to get around on GITMO, the U.S. Customs Service placed a fleet of dilapidated vehicles, that look like leftovers from a Mad Max movie, on the leeward side by the airport. Since looks aren't important on GITMO, the government vehicles stashed there for our use served the purpose of providing basic transportation and nothing more.

Generally speaking, spending time at GITMO was a very relaxing and peaceful experience. In addition to the pleasant climate, there are facilities to work out in and an outrageous pool to go swimming in. If you liked to swim in the ocean, GITMO has some excellent places to go snorkeling. During my first trip to GITMO as an Air Officer, I was so relaxed I only smoked 8 or 9 cigarettes the whole time I was there. This time things were different.

As soon as I stepped off the Customs plane, Mike R. pulled up driving one of our old trucks. As Mike was passing cold sodas to our pilots, I overheard him tell our undercover crew that the second mission we were expected to fly was scrubbed aka canceled. Initially, I figured Mike was joking, but once I walked over to meet with him, I realized that he was quite serious.

There we were standing on the tarmac next to the runway with no mission to fly. Since the Customs plane that ferried us to GITMO had to leave for a run to Puerto Rico, we had no choice but to stay put until we serviced the undercover plane.

With phase two of the case involving Agent Steve P. and Air Officer Gary P. being handled a different way, the decision was made to have us remain on GITMO with a plane and a crew, while our agents back in the states tried to get one of the other pending transportation cases off the ground.

From an operational security standpoint, being based on GITMO posed certain problems, because we normally didn't have access to a secure phone. This meant, that we had to watch what we said, when we made calls back to the states on a pay phone from GITMO. Even though we usually talked in code and watched what we said when we spoke on any phone, it wasn't difficult for us to relay brief messages, when we called our supervisor or other agents from GITMO. Since a lot more needed to be said to discuss the potential cases that were pending, we relied on Group 7 Agent Chuck W., who was back in Florida, to do his best to set up a deal for us.

Based on what we knew so far, one group had 700 kilos for us to pick up and had asked us to pick their load up near Port Estrella, Colombia. Since we had received an additional $25,000 in front money on the Jim S. (New Mexico) case, all we needed was someone to pass us the coordinates via a secure radio and relay the green light to launch.

When a snowstorm hit New Mexico the weather kept everyone from flying out to meet us. More important than anything else, was having our New Mexico office send the $25,000 in front money to Miami so Chuck could start paying our expenses. In addition to paying for gas and oil, we needed some front money to pay the war risk insurance coverage on the plane before we went operational. In addition, we also had to give our undercover crew some money for the time they were spending with us. To keep this deal on track, the Southeast Region laid out $10,000 during the early stages of this investigation. Unfortunately, that wasn't enough.

When Chuck called us at GITMO, to tell us that our New Mexico office had seized the trafficker funds, Mike and I knew that it was futile to remain in Cuba. There we were, four hours away from picking up 700 kilos of cocaine and a fugitive, but we had to stand down because someone seized the money that was earmarked to pay some of our basic operating expenses.

Before I go on, perhaps I should explain the difference between seizing and recovering money. Once an agent seizes drug money, the cash is put into a general fund or is considered evidence and can not be tampered with or spent until the case is prosecuted. You can only "recover" drug money or trafficker funds under certain situations.

When a subject of an investigation gives an informant or an undercover agent expense money to further a smuggling venture, that money can be used accordingly and does not have to be "seized." Once you seize what is known as trafficker funds, you have no choice but to apply for traditional agency appropriated funds to pay legitimate operating expenses. Therefore, seizing money that was considered trafficker funds, when it could be recovered and used to pay legitimate undercover expenses, made absolutely NO SENSE and actually impeded our operations.

Even though our contract pilots were ready to fly for free and wait months to get paid, we still needed $6000-8000 to cover some basic expenses like aviation fuel. Once again, we were fighting The Drug War with one had tied behind our backs and the other gripping our private parts to put it politely. By January 20th we were so disgusted and tired of trying to make things happen, we gassed up the undercover plane and left GITMO for Miami. So far we had done everything humanly possible to make this case work for our agents in New Mexico.

The six hour flight from GITMO in the Vietnam era seaplane was quite an experience for a buff pilot like me. In fact, I often regretted not logging all of the hours that I actually had behind the controls, after the initial dozen or so hours of flight training that I had in a single engine Cessna. After getting some additional flight time in twin engine aircraft, I should have had the discipline to pursue a pilot's rating of some kind. Regardless, whenever our contract pilots asked me if I wanted to take the controls, I always smiled wide from ear to ear and got in some "stick time."

Sitting behind the controls of this particular former U.S. military seaplane reinforced the fact that my childhood dreams had come true. Best yet, I actually got paid pretty decent money to have this much fun at work. As I cruised along at a whopping 150 knots, at an altitude of 6500 feet, I kicked back and enjoyed the view. From where I was sitting, I didn't have a care in the world.

Once we landed at Homestead Air Force Base, we transferred our gear into our G-rides and stopped in the office to see what was going on. Even though our pilots were promised $1000 before they left the states, they ended up receiving about $200 each because we were short on funds. Naturally, we covered all of their meal expenses and paid the BOQ room rate of $6.00 each per day. Even though the Customs Service would pay our contract crews and confidential sources of information down the road, we needed the seed money that we were promised to take care of our basic obligations in order to make this case a reality. When that didn't happen, we had no choice but to put the New Mexico deal on hold.

Within days of returning to Miami, Mike Ricciardo drafted one hell of a POI/POE payment request. Once I put in my two cents, the very detailed memo was signed off by our group supervisor and sent on its way through the chain of command.

Whenever, we wrote one of these payment requests, my fellow agents and I felt like we were putting our contract pilots, sources of information and confidential informants in for a Distinguished Flying Cross. Because of the contributions made on each case and the extremely high element of risk involved, our source payments generally required the approval of the highest ranking managers in Washington D.C.

ROUND TWO

Despite all that we endured in the form of long hours and some very tense moments, the second phase of Operation Nightmare was a screaming success. Between the performance by Agent Steve P. and the fact that the Colombians trusted us enough to load our seaplane with 520 kilos, the bad guys were convinced that they were dealing with a Cuban Army General, who was running a first class smuggling operation.

In order to make the second delivery, the Colombians decided to use their own plane to air drop the rest of the cocaine shipment to a vessel that belonged to the famous General Puma. To make the air drop convincing, the Colombians were told to make the drop very close to Cuban waters.

With a U.S. Navy vessel stationed off in the distance to provide security, the Colombian aircraft air dropped the rest of the cocaine shipment near the undercover vessel. Once the last bundle was dropped into the open ocean, our undercover boat crew recovered the floating evidence and rendezvoused with the U.S. Navy crew. To their credit, undercover U.S. Customs and FBI Agents battled 12 foot seas, in order to pick up 2500 kilos that the Colombians air dropped dangerously close to Cuban territory in the Windward Passage.

GENERAL PUMA

When Orson Wells went live over the radio with his famous War of the Worlds broadcast, he convinced a number of Americans that aliens in UFO's had invaded the country. In the history of live radio, no other broadcast was ever so bold or effective in fooling so many people.

Earlier, I mentioned the contribution made by Special Agent Steve P. in directing the operation that led to the record seizure of 6000 pounds of cocaine in January of 1990. Because this joint investigation was so incredibly successful, I feel compelled to go into some additional detail, about a case that was one of the most daring undercover operations executed during our nation's Drug War.

This case was the success that it was, because it offered the Colombian targets of this investigation, the ability to transport thousands of kilos of cocaine into South Florida with an increased measure of success and security. Also, keep in mind, that all of this was happening during an intense effort by the U.S. and even some Colombian officials to interdict drug shipments. For reasons that I cannot explain, Special Agent Steve P. was put in direct radio contact with certain high level Colombian based smugglers. To facilitate this infiltration, Agent Steve P. and Air Officer Gary P. built a high frequency radio tower next to the Group 7 trailer and installed a powerful HF radio in Steve's corner office. This enabled Agent Steve P. aka General Puma to give the Colombians the distinct impression that he was broadcasting from his army base in Cuba.

Once the right amount of bullshit was passed through underground channels and the introduction was made via radio, Agent Steve P. aka General Puma was able to broadcast regularly and develop a rapport with the Colombians. Bear in mind, that Steve accomplished this while transmitting over a High Frequency radio. In other words, throughout the bulk of this infiltration, Undercover Customs Agent Steve P. and the Colombian violators never met face to face.

While acting like a Cuban Army General named Puma, Steve P. formed an alliance with the subjects of this investigation and negotiated the smuggling venture described in the preceding chapter. Naturally, as I have already mentioned, the Colombian violators loved the idea of operating under the protection of a Cuban Army General, who was in a position to insure that their cocaine shipments would be successfully smuggled into South Florida.

The success of this operation, rested in Steve P's. ability to carry himself as a Cuban Army General and make believers out of the unsuspecting Colombians. One must admire his capabilities, especially when you consider that Steve would sometimes broadcast several times a day, in order to negotiate the terms of the deal and discuss the smuggling venture with the subjects of the investigation. One slip of the tongue or one mistake and the case would be lost.

Before he would broadcast from the back room of the Group 7 trailer complex on Homestead Air Force Base, Steve would compose himself for a second then go on the air. As soon as Steve sat behind his desk and he flipped the switch, he transformed himself into General Puma.

To watch Steve in action was quite a treat. The manner in which he spoke and the inflections in his tone of voice, made the Colombians believe that they were speaking to a distinguished Cuban General, who was ally in the drug trade. Steve had no props or uniform, nor did he broadcast from a makeshift bunker for effect. To his credit, as an outstanding undercover agent and consummate actor, Steve P. went in and out of role with the flick of a radio switch.

Clearly, no one lived with more pressure during this undercover operation than Customs Agent Steve P. Throughout this operation, many of us had a chance to make a contribution, but none of us could take the place of General Puma. As I said before, if an undercover federal agent was ever entitled to receive an Oscar for his command performance, it's Steve P.

In February of 1990, the Colombians wanted to meet the General. This meeting was necessary, because as far as they knew, General Puma had stockpiled "their" cocaine, but had not delivered one ounce to South Florida. As a result, it was time for General Puma to meet with his Colombian business associates.

Since Agent Steve P. was supposed to be a Cuban General, it was imperative that he travel with his immediate staff. A decision was made to meet on neutral turf in the Cayman Islands. Since U.S. Customs Agents and FBI Special Agents had no authority in the Cayman Islands, our undercover agents and backup team would be going in unarmed. Pat R. and Mike C. from Group 7 were assigned to lead the backup and technical team during this phase of the operation.

The day that Steve P. traveled to the Cayman Islands, he immediately transformed himself into the famous General Puma. Accompanied by his bodyguards, who were Cuban American U.S. Customs Agents, General Puma checked into a resort hotel and waited to receive his guests.

As a result of this undercover meeting, four hours of video recordings were obtained. This meant that the case agents and the federal prosecutor now had faces to match up to the voices from all those months of radio transmissions. Steve, or should I say General Puma, had done it again!

In February of 1990, the Miami Air Smuggling Investigations Group 7 in conjunction with the FBI, arrested a total of 9 major violators, recovered $400,000 in drug money and seized a total of 6000 pounds of cocaine on this case.

As you will read in this two part book series, there were times when certain factions hated the involvement of other agencies in a particular investigation. In other instances, law enforcement officers from different agencies got along unbelievably well. In fact, the DEA manager who gave me more crap than anyone I ever met in my entire law enforcement career, was actually someone I respected a great deal and wished I worked for. This guy was a touch son of a bitch, who defended DEA's jurisdiction with a vengeance.

While some of our bosses were tough SOBs, others were more laid back and were nowhere near as aggressive as DEA supervisors. Since they say that "nice guys finish last," I preferred working for a boss who knew how to aggressively defend their agents and their jurisdiction, when it was appropriate to do so. Overall, I was pretty lucky in that regard and generally worked for supervisors and managers who were worth respecting.

The author behind the controls of a rented undercover aircraft

Flying in formation with a New Mexico based U.S. Customs Beechcraft King Air C12

One of our smaller 350 Kilo cocaine loads.

Operating on the open ocean - Undercover Seaplanes - Our Secret Weapon

A Miami based U.S. Customs Citation Jet provided critical support to the first and fourth CD that we executed for the U.S. Customs Boston SAC Office

Nighttime take off from GITMO.

New Mexico CD 750 kilos inside UC Vessel

New Mexico CD 750 kilos wrapped in plastic on deck of UC vessel

Using former military seaplanes enabled us to conduct certain CD air operations that would never have been conducted if we lacked access to these types of aircraft.

The author in one of the 29 exotic cars seized in a money laundering case.

The View of The Windward Passage on a relatively calm day

The Cessna 150 that the author used to learn how to fly.

U.S. Navy comes to the rescue

Long before the U.S. Navy Base at Guantanamo Bay, Cuba was used to house prisoners during The Global War on Terrorism, GITMO was used as a forward operating base to launch undercover air and marine operations during The Drug War

The author inspects a red Chevrolet Corvette that he and other U.S. Customs, DEA and Broward Sheriff's Office personnel seized with over two dozen other exotic cars from a South Florida drug smuggling organization.

The author (standing left) and Broward County Sheriff's Detective Danny DeC. (right) inspect a garage filled with over two dozen exotic cars that were seized from a famous South Florida drug smuggling organization.

The U.S. Coast Guard Cutter Seneca conducts an Underway Replenishing (UNREP) some 75 miles from the coast of Colombia, to supply fuel and fresh water to the undercover vessel, that was used by the author and his fellow undercover U.S. Customs Agents to pickup 750 kilos of cocaine in support of a joint controlled delivery with the U.S. Customs RAC Office in New Mexico.

A Colombian smuggler gives the author and his fellow undercover agents the thumbs up for a job well done, while being transported to New Mexico with 750 kilos of cocaine in an undercover Grumman Albatross Seaplane.

CHAPTER 15

INFORMANTS

While serving as an Investigator in the New York (Manhattan) District Attorney's Office (DANY), I worked drug cases involving ounces and grams of cocaine and heroin. In those days, my partner Ralph M. and I paid our number one informant $25 to $100 dollars for a night's work. Even though we were only involved in investigating low level domestic drug transactions, we viewed our work to be very important.

In contrast, as a U.S. Customs Agent I risked my life for hundreds and thousands of kilos of cocaine and tons of marijuana. I also paid my confidential informants, sources of information and contract pilots tens of thousands of dollars to hundreds of thousands dollars per case. Before I initiated the Group 7 undercover air operation, I paid The Gambler and Airport Sam a total of $368,000 for services rendered and had another $250,000 in the hopper waiting to get approved. After the successful execution of a controlled delivery operation that you will read about in Controlled Delivery Book II, Pat R. and I paid six documented confidential sources of information and contract personnel $1.2 million dollars for a case that took twenty-one days to make.

On April 11th, U.S. Customs Headquarters wire transferred the authorization for me to pay $336,000 to four of my documented sources of information. The highest three payments went to three of our contract pilots, with the last payment going to Hombre de la Calle. Hombre was finally getting paid in full for helping me seize $530,011 dollars in drug money back in November of 1986. Captain Video received $85,000, while The Colonel and the crew chief were paid $65,000 for their involvement in the General Puma case.

I have to admit that I always enjoyed paying my informants, sources of information and contract personnel large sums of money for a job well done. As far as I was concerned, making large payments to reliable sources of information and contract personnel was all part of The Drug War economy. You can Monday morning quarterback this aspect of The Drug War all you want, as long as you never lose sight of the results. Just think how much you would have paid a network of reliable informants and contract personnel to prevent the terrorist attacks on 9/11/01. The Drug War is no different.

One of the reasons I wrote this book, was to inform people that the U.S. Customs Service and other agencies orchestrated numerous secret offensives against the drug cartels and smuggling organizations and had numerous victories. Most of what we did was never publicized, because as I say elsewhere in CD Book I and CD Book II, the Drug War was usually fought in secret. Even though it cost money to achieve these victories, the price was well worth it when you consider the alternative. As an example, consider what would have happened, if U.S. Customs Agents failed to cultivate the intelligence information, that led to the successful interdiction of the 75 pounds of cocaine from the Colombian freighter, that I mentioned in the beginning of CD Book I. How many lives would have been negatively affected, if this particular shipment of cocaine managed to get dispersed on the streets of New York City? The same can be said for the first operation that we worked with the Boston SAC Office, or for the 6000 pounds of cocaine that was seized on the case that was initiated by Agent Steve P. and Air Officer Gary P. and every other drug shipment that we managed to get our hands on.

Anyone who provides you with assistance, or information who is not a sworn law enforcement officer, is a confidential informant, a source of information or a contract employee. As far as the people who worked for us were concerned, all of our sources of information, confidential informants and contract personnel were formally documented by their control agent. The documentation process included conducting a criminal history check.

Unlike other agencies that tend to use defendant informants, the U.S. Customs Service of my era, received and cultivated information from a cross section of society. By the very nature of our jurisdiction, we generally had contact with all sorts of legitimate people, as well as offenders and former violators, who were willing to provide us with information and assistance for various reasons. Marina owners, private pilots, airport workers, dock workers, aviation mechanics, marine mechanics, boat owners, ship captains, merchant seamen, corporate executives and a host of other legitimate people were constantly cooperating with the U.S. Customs Service to provide information and assistance. In fact, I tended to view people who weren't compelled to cooperate with us as a Source of Information, as opposed to calling them a Confidential Informant.

Any documented source of information or contractor who was not obligated to assist us was also eligible to be paid and paid well. In contrast, a defendant informant is not paid for their information or assistance. Defendant informants use their cooperation to acquire what is known as "substantial assistance." Such assistance to the government can reduce or eliminate criminal charges and or a prison sentence.

One statement that I heard early on in my career, was that one good informant or source of information is worth at least fifty agents, if not more. In fact, some informants and sources of information are so reliable and capable, they performed a mission that most law enforcement officers are unable to perform. At the very least, a good informant or source of information is a "door opener," or someone who is able to introduce an undercover agent into a criminal organization, that could never be infiltrated without "professional" help."

The important thing to remember, is that informants and sources of information are no different than anyone else. Some people are super reliable and trustworthy, some can be vengeful, some will sell themselves to the highest bidder, some are more loyal than others, some can be difficult to control, some can have serious personal problems that can interfere with their ability to function and others can be down right treacherous and should be avoided at all cost. Some people also change and I don't mean for the better.

Some are fast learners and others take some time to get with the program. As an example, one of the most difficult sources of information we worked with, was a very respectful individual, who initially proved to be a handful to direct when it came to doing things our way. In the end and to his credit, this particular individual performed a very valuable a service, that very few sources of information could provide. (I wish I could say more but I can't.) This was one of those instances, when it paid to have patience and continue to cultivate a source of information who had tremendous potential.

While a reliable documented source of information can sky rocket an agent's career, a bad one can cost you your life, your career and maybe even your freedom. Informants are a feast or famine type of situation. You either have reliable and successful human assets, or none worth dealing with. Having a hard to handle or unreliable informant can be tantamount to career suicide. In fact, one of the hardest things to do, is convince another law enforcement officer, that their useless informant is taking them for a ride.

Despite the way that they are often portrayed on TV and in the movies, not all Confidential Informants (CIs) are dirt bags and not all contract personnel and sources of information are money grubbing mercenaries. It is especially difficult to send a CI or a contract pilot on a dangerous mission when you personally like that individual, whether they have a tainted past or not. I also believe that my fellow agents and I received the level of cooperation and assistance that we did, because our core group of informants, sources of information and contract personnel knew that we truly cared about their safety more than anything else.

CHAPTER 16

THE GREATEST SHOW ON EARTH

As I report many times throughout this book, country clearance was our nemesis during many of our operations. From an official perspective, every controlled delivery was evaluated on the merits of the case and a variety of related factors, including "risk versus reward." As far as the concern that Colombia was too hostile to operate in, my attitude and the attitude of my colleagues was, that's why they call it The Drug War. In addition, I also subscribed to the famous World War II saying that, "a happy soldier is one who complains."

As frustrating as our job was, I knew that there were times when we had to put our faith in the system and trust that DEA was trying to avoid a catastrophe, when they denied our request for country clearance. There were also instances, when our intelligence clashed with the reason why DEA denied our request to travel to Colombia.

Sometimes we were told if we could move the deal to a safer area, we might be able to go. Running covert operations was difficult enough, without having to manage our affairs in such a fashion. I say this because there was no guarantee, that we would be given the clearance to launch, if we were able to get the bad guys to move the pickup to a different location.

Just imagine how frustrating it would be, to start a new business and do everything that was necessary to open a store and every time you prepared for a grand opening, the local government shut you down for some reason. How would you like to be told that you could open for business, if you moved your store to a different location and that once you relocated, you still might not be able to operate as planned?

It was during one of our more hectic days of meeting other agents, sources of information and contract personnel, that we received an unexpected phone call from U.S. Customs Agent Jim S. from the RAC Office in Albuquerque, New Mexico. According to Special Agent James S, it looked as if he and his defendant informant were finally in a position to provide the transportation services for a multi-hundred kilo shipment of cocaine from Colombia.

THE SALESMAN

The shock of being arrested on the side of the road, in the ass end of nowhere, had a profound affect on the drug smuggling pilot known as The Salesman. The Salesman didn't have to be a lawyer to know, that being caught red handed with a planeload of drugs was enough to send him to the crow bar hotel for quite a few years, unless he cooperated in a big way.

With a list of pending federal charges motivating him to work for the U.S. Customs Service, The Salesman was ready, willing and able to make the appropriate introductions and help us infiltrate another unsuspecting group of Colombian based smugglers. As an experienced drug smuggling pilot, The Salesman was well versed in the nuts and bolts of executing a drug smuggling venture from the perspective of the bad guys. While this experience proved to be invaluable, The Salesman needed to learn how we conducted a transportation case/controlled delivery from our perspective. Fortunately, The Salesman was a fast learner.

As I repeat elsewhere in CD Book I and II, The Blade Runner Squadron was the ultimate confessional; a place where a tainted soul could get a second chance and a new lease on life, as long as they followed the rules and gave a good account of themselves. From the moment The Salesman went to work with us, he did everything that he was told to do and proved to be a real charmer with the Colombians. Just watching him in action was worth the price of admission.

Once the issue of front money was resolved, the Colombian violators asked The Salesman if he and his people would take one of their associates, a fugitive wanted in Miami, back to the United States with their 700 plus kilo shipment of cocaine. Naturally, our response was, sure why not. Anything to help a friend.

MISSION PLANNING

The first problem that we had to deal with involved the 2400 mile flight from Colombia to a safe landing zone in the Southwest U.S., a good portion of which would be over water. The good news was, the Colombians liked the idea that we were able to safely deliver a shipment of cocaine to a remote airstrip in the New Mexico desert. One reason for this, was because their stateside receivers were from Los Angeles. The bad news was, that even with extra fuel tanks on board, our undercover plane could not fly from the pickup point in Colombia, to New Mexico without stopping for fuel. In essence, our problem was finding a safe place to refuel, that would not make the Colombians suspicious about our plan, or our capabilities as smugglers. We also had to refuel in a location that we had complete control over. This meant that we would not be able to operate in Mexico.

My first order of business was to work up an operational plan, that included a list of surveillance assets that could be pressed into service to support this operation. Since the use of U.S. Customs and U.S. Military AWAC aircraft had to be requested through the proper channels, I had to meet with a U.S. Air Force Liaison Officer and our contacts in U.S. Customs Air Ops, to discuss our mission requirements.

It's important to keep in mind, that before DOD or Customs air assets were assigned to one of our operations, we had to establish the date and the time when the "festivities" were expected to take place. We also had to be specific about the location where we intended to operate. Since you had to reserve DOD and Customs air assets days in advance, we were forced to estimate when these assets would be needed. This could get tricky and nerve racking, especially when you intended to go operational on a certain date and time and we were still waiting for country clearance to be approved. Since you cannot confirm the pick up date and time with the bad guys until you hear from DEA, you cannot line up the support assets with any degree of certainty.

Another problem involved our contract crews and undercover aircraft. Since most of our contract aircrews had real jobs, or businesses to attend to, it was difficult to juggle our schedule around theirs. When a contract pilot who is expected to fly our next mission is an airline pilot, we had to wait for his next set of days off before we could schedule our operation. If the Colombians wanted us to make a pickup on a Monday and the pilot we selected to fly the mission was unable to work for us until Thursday, we had to find another pilot, delay the deal, or ask our contract pilot to risk his regular employment to fly for us, on a day when he had other commitments. Fortunately, the bulk of our sources of information and contract personnel were very flexible and were generally always available.

Even though we had a fairly decent size compliment of very qualified contract pilots at our disposal, we were required to use licensed pilots who were type rated by the FAA, to fly the specific aircraft that we intended to use in every mission. This meant that we had to put the right pilots in the right positions in the right planes. Fortunately, we were able to recruit some highly qualified multi-engine commercial rated aviators, including some who were type rated to fly helicopters, jets and more specialized aircraft. Even our two crew chiefs (Johnny Walker and Mr. Goodwrench) were highly qualified aviation mechanics.

Because all of our pilots had a multi-engine commercial rating, we had no problem flying missions in less complicated aircraft. In other instances, we had more pilots who were qualified and available to fly in the right seat (co pilot's seat), than we had qualified contract pilots who were available to fly in the left seat, as the Contract Pilot in Command. When this happened, we had to recruit pilots with the proper FAA type ratings, in order to safely operate more exotic aircraft. Thanks to people like The Gambler aka Mr. Lucky, we were always able to recruit a new pilot when we needed someone with special credentials.

Since we all generally seemed to get along, we never really had any major problems putting a crew together. It also made sense for us to put a contract pilot or CI on board who was a bad guy in a former life. For obvious reasons, a Blader Runner who was an "angel with a dirty face" proved to be invaluable when it came time to interact with real drug smugglers. At the very least, it paid to put one of our more streetwise contract pilots or sources of information on some of our flights.

I also learned early on, that not every person with a pilot's license is an aviator or a flier. I wanted aviators who were comfortable being barnstormers one minute and as disciplined as a military flight crew the next. In other words, learning how to fly and getting a pilot's license did not automatically qualify you to fly for us. We needed aviators who could make a plane stand on its tail and spit nickels. I wanted pilots who could hear a problem developing before the gauges indicated that there was anything wrong. I also wanted pilots who knew what the book said on every page, but could fly without it and not panic. Last but not least, I wanted pilots who could fly by the seat of their pants; bush pilot types who were part dare devil and part space shuttle crew.

When it came to aircraft selection, we relied on private owners and aircraft brokers to provide us with every plane that we used. Because planes cost money to rent and move around, we had to be very frugal, when it came time to acquire a particular aircraft for a mission, especially when we were dealing with limited amounts of front money. Fortunately, things got better once we started recovering large amounts of trafficker funds and were able to build our war chest.

MISSION IMPOSSIBLE

From July of 1989 to April of 1990, we went through a number of frustrating attempts to carry out the controlled delivery for Special Agent Jim S. and the U.S. Customs RAC Office in Albuquerque, New Mexico. After experiencing another last minute phone call from DEA to stand down and not launch, I decided that it was time to become resourceful.

While sitting in one of favorite hangouts, I decided to devise a new operational plan, one that enabled us to operate covertly without securing country clearance. My plan was to use another former military seaplane to make the pickup in the open ocean off the coast of Colombia. The bad news was, that according to the rules of engagement, unless we received "country clearance," we had to operate a certain distance from the Colombian coastline. Unfortunately, the water this far off shore, was not always as suitable for open ocean landings. In other words, this plan might not work, if the conditions off shore were too rough for seaplane operations. (More on this later.)

My colleagues and I developed this plan, because even if our crew was unable to land and make the pick up due to rough seas, the bad guys would know that we tried and that meant a lot in the smuggling business. In fact, we knew when we planned this mission, that there was only a very slight chance, that our crew would be able to make an open ocean pickup, especially at this time of the year. That said, we went forward with this idea, because we had to keep the ball in play, to prevent our Colombian clients from losing faith in our ability as "smugglers." I felt this way, because every time we were unable to make a scheduled pickup in the past, we had to come up with a believable bullshit story why we didn't launch. Since we couldn't tell the bad guys the truth and since I was running out of bullshit, we had to fly this mission to stay in the game and buy some time, until it was possible to get country clearance to fly into Colombia. If by some miracle the ocean was calm enough for our crew to land and make the extraction, we would have something to celebrate.

My colleagues and I were also determined to make this case, to prove to the system that we could be successful, despite their idiotic rules of engagement. Going to extra lengths to make this case was also the right thing to do.

As a point of information, The Gambler and I originally developed the concept of using large former military seaplanes to enable us to execute covert air operations, when it was impossible to secure country clearance to operate in Colombian territory. We came to this decision while sitting in a bar after a long work day. Thanks to The Gambler and Captain Video, we were equipped with this very unique capability.

CHAPTER 17

STANDING BY TO STAND BY

On April 26, 1990, U.S. Customs Service headquarters approved our operational plan. For the record, this was an era when the U.S. Customs Service was not "risk adverse." Once we received the green light to proceed, we had The Salesman contact the Colombian subjects of this investigation, to see if they had the capability to deliver the coke load by boat, to our seaplane, at a set of coordinates off the coast of Colombia. Just as we expected, the bad guys were ecstatic and looked forward to seeing us soon. Once the Colombian violators notified The Salesman, that they had 1600 pounds of cocaine ready to deliver to the designated coordinates, we prepared to depart South Florida.

Before we left we had our plane checked out one more time, to insure that it was fully operational. Once the plane was fully fueled, we loaded a large cooler with ice, soda, water, food and fresh fruit into the undercover seaplane. We also purchased batteries, flashlights and several sets of phony tail numbers and a fifty-five gallon drum of engine oil, that was transferred into a number of five-gallon cans.

While we waited for our crew to arrive, we finished loading our life raft, luggage and weapons on board the UC aircraft. Once that was done, all we needed was for our cockpit crew to arrive so we could get airborne.

BOYS WILL BE BOYS

After giving our contract pilots more than enough time to get to the airport, I decided to call the hotel where The Salesman was staying to track down our crew. Knowing Captain Video the way I did, I assumed that he crashed in The Salesman's hotel room, after a night of socializing with his co pilot and the two New Mexico based U.S. Customs Pilots, who were providing support for this mission.

When the hotel operator rang the phone in their room off the hook, I assumed our two contract pilots were en route to the airport. I learned this wasn't the case, when one of the U.S. Customs Pilots from Albuquerque called the UC office to let me know that our contract pilots were just rolling out of bed and would be a tad late. Even though I rarely drank beer or hard liquor anymore, I had nothing against people who consumed alcohol on a more regular basis. I did however take our mission seriously and knew that if no one tried to adhere to a schedule, we would never get anywhere on time.

Despite his human failings, The Salesman was a loving father and husband who had done everything humanly possible to wipe the slate clean. As he once told me, when he was flying drug loads, he never saw the people he affected by his criminal activity, because everything looked so small from up in the air. Now that he was working with us, he had a much different perspective on life and The Drug War. Even Captain Video made tremendous sacrifices to fly and work with us. Considering all of the pressure that our contract pilots were under, I couldn't blame Captain Video or The Salesman for letting their hair down so to speak. The Salesman in particular had a great deal riding on this trip. If he succeeded, he would probably be a free man, but if he failed he would most likely be sentenced to ten years in federal prison.

I also knew that our contract aircrews felt the pressures that were inherent in our line of work, just as much as the case agents and undercover special agents did. As a result, I knew that many of our sources of information and contract personnel were prone to stay out late the night before an intended launch. Naturally, I was caught between the rock and the hard place, because I could neither condone their behavior when it got a bit excessive, any more than I could condemn them for it. As frustrating as things were, just once I would have loved to have had someone prodding me to get moving, after a night of having a good time. That, I assume, was the tremendous price that one paid to be in "command," if one wants to call what I did as being in "command."

Captain Video knew that he dropped the ball, when he and The Salesman raced over to the private airport where the undercover office was located. As I would later find out, the night before had been no different than other occasions, when our crews got together to unwind before a mission. Not being a big drinker, The Salesman had the lowest tolerance for alcohol of anyone I ever met. Each and every time the fun loving Salesman tried to consume alcohol, he usually ended up face down in a bowl of peanuts, while professionals like Captain Video and Johnny Walker, could drink anyone under the table and would be sober enough to function in the morning. Fortunately, even though Captain Video had a late night, he was able to negotiate the midday traffic without incident.

After feeling the side effects of a fun filled evening, The Salesman had difficulty dealing with the motion of the small pick up truck, as Captain Video drove to our undercover office. By the time Captain Video drove through the front gate, where our undercover hangar was located, The Salesman was green behind the gills.

As soon as Captain Video parked his pickup truck and shut off the engine, The Salesman grabbed a McDonald's fast food bag from the floorboards and said, "I think I'm gonna be sick." Once The Salesman threw up in the paper bag, he immediately felt much better. Unfortunately, the last thing that Captain Video wanted to see, was the bottom of the McDonald's bag explode and fill the cabin floor of his pickup truck with the contents of his co pilot's sick stomach.

Because they were running way behind schedule, Captain Video knew they had no time to clean up the mess. Instead, Captain Video simply shook his head and said, "Come on, we're late," as he got out of his truck and slammed the door. While acting as if nothing had happened, The Salesman carefully slid out of the truck's cab and closed the door, leaving the puke filled pickup truck to sit in the hot South Florida sun in desperate need of being cleaned out.

When both pilots spotted me pacing in front of our undercover seaplane, Captain Video put up his right hand and said, "Don't yell at me," as he walked right passed me and climbed up the ladder into the cargo bay of the undercover aircraft. As I stood there speechless, I watched The Salesman follow Captain Video, as he negotiated the ladder that led into the belly of the former military seaplane.

Once Mike R. and I boarded the UC aircraft and Johnny Walker (aka Otis) pulled up the ladder, The Gambler said, "Good luck," as he rolled his eyes and cracked a smile. With the cargo hatch secured, we took our seats in the cockpit behind the crew and watched as Captain Video taxied the undercover plane toward the active runway.

ON TO PUERTO RICO

As soon as the control tower cleared us for take off, Captain Video applied full power to the engines and guided our plane down the center line of the runway. At just the right time, Captain Video pulled the controls into his chest and retracted the landing gear, while we climbed to a respectable altitude. After handing Captain Video a container of orange juice, I sat in the navigator's seat and smoked a cigarette, while I thought of all that we had been through since I started this operation in October of 1988.

As a result of all the time that we spent together, I had gotten to know the men we worked with and found their faults to be most human. Our collection of eccentrics and social outcasts was starting to become a tight little unit of accomplished undercover operatives. Because of the success of the first few missions we flew, our rather unusual undercover unit was starting to acquire a reputation as a highly competent "can do" covert operation.

Whether the undercover personnel from Group 7 were sworn law enforcement officers, contract pilots, former bad guys, patriots, or mercenary types, we all identified with the concept that we belonged to something very special. I knew everything was coming together nicely, when it became an honor of sorts, for a person who worked with us to be considered a Blade Runner. Even though labeling an individual as a member of our unofficial unit was done in a lighthearted fashion, it was a subtle way to recognize someone as an accepted member of our group.

IT DOESN'T GET ANY BETTER THAN THIS

The water below was as calm as glass, as we flew over the open ocean at 7500 feet. About three-quarters of the way to the U.S. Customs Air Unit at Borinquen, Puerto Rico, the U.S. Customs King Air C12 aircraft, that was being flown by Customs Pilot Steve S. and Ben W., pulled up alongside our starboard wingtip. There we were, flying a tight formation across the Atlantic, taking pictures of each other from a distance that at times was only a few feet away. It was moments like this that made us forget about the more stressful and dangerous aspects of our job. Just being airborne, while we flew in formation to our destination, was just what the doctor ordered to relax us all.

At 9:30 PM or 2130 hours we were on final approach and preparing to land at the former Ramey Air Force Base in Borinquen, Puerto Rico. We had spent nearly 6 1/2 hours boring holes in the sky in order to reach our initial destination. As soon as we were feet dry (over land), the UC plane landed and taxied over to the U.S. Customs Service Puerto Rico Air Unit's hangar, where we were immediately greeted by Ed H., the Acting Aviation Group Supervisor.

Just like in the real estate business, the expression location, location, location also had a significant meaning to those of us who were involved in undercover air and marine operations. Whenever we needed to operate from a forward area, we preferred to launch our planes from the U.S. Navy Base at Guantanamo Bay, Cuba, or Boringuen, Puerto Rico. The main reason for doing so, was because the Puerto Rico Air Unit and GITMO were both located approximately 400 to 440 miles from Colombia. In this particular case, we picked Puerto Rico, because our base in Borinquen was the perfect location to conduct a clandestine refueling, if our seaplane crew was able to pick up the coke load and the fugitive, who was expected to make the trip to New Mexico with the contraband.

STAGING IN BORINQUEN, PUERTO RICO

When the Colombians that we were dealing with told us to hold off until the weather conditions improved, Aldo the fugitive begged The Salesman not to leave and go back to New Mexico. To keep us happy, Aldo arranged for us to receive an additional $7000 in front money to motivate us to tough it out until the weather improved.

During our stay in Puerto Rico, we used the delay to travel to Roosevelt Rhodes Naval Air Station on the other side of the island. In addition to shopping in the PX (Post Exchange) to buy essential supplies such as cigarettes and liquor, we also meet with a U.S. Navy weatherman and personally briefed the U.S. Air Force E3 AWAC crew that was scheduled to provide air surveillance support for this mission. As a side note, I should mention that because of the way we looked and were dressed, my colleagues and I stood out a bit, especially when those of us who were U.S. Customs Agents and Customs Pilots presented our federal credentials, when we traveled with our contract crew through the more secure areas on this military base.

CHAPTER 18

READY, SET, GO!

If everything went according to plan, this particular operation called for us to fly a total of about twenty-five hours. This included the flight from South Florida to Puerto Rico, to the pick up point off the coast of Colombia, then back to Puerto Rico and on to New Mexico, with an additional pit stop on the way.

Our operational plan was simple and went like this. After making the pickup in the water off the coast of Colombia, the undercover seaplane would fly back to Borinquen, Puerto Rico and taxi to a deserted part of the field. As soon as the plane was refueled, Mike R. and I would get on board and ride the rest of the way to New Mexico, to keep and eye on our two passengers and the cocaine shipment. (In addition to the fugitive who was wanted in Miami, we were also asked to take a Colombian observer along. This particular individual represented the Colombian source of supply who hired us to transport "his" cocaine shipment to the CONUS.)

Once we landed on a mining road in the desert, we would hand the fugitive over to Undercover Customs Agent Jim S. before we off loaded the plane. Naturally, we would be under constant surveillance by government surveillance aircraft, as well as by teams of U.S. Customs Agents and Air Officers at the desert off load site. Again, if everything went according to plan, we would arrest the fugitive and the stateside receivers, once we were paid for our services and they tried to take possession of the cocaine shipment.

After waiting eight miserable days in Puerto Rico, we were finally ready to launch. I say miserable, because my dingy hotel room had a serious shortage of hot water and was occupied by an army of roaches. If I could have traded one for the other, I would have gladly showered in cold water, as opposed to keeping the lights on at night, to limit the number of roaches that were crawling all over the room.

Borinquen was also not a popular resort area when we visited this section of Puerto Rico. In addition to being a bit run down, one of the first things we were told when we arrived, was to take our guns with us if we went to beach. Even the local food was nothing to write home about. In fact, as crazy as this sounds, I ate better food and had much nicer accommodations in Haiti, than I had in Puerto Rico. Despite the fact that Borinquen was not exactly a fun place to visit, we thoroughly enjoyed working with the folks from the Customs Air Unit in PR. They literally turned their offices over to us and gave us a giant hangar to store our undercover aircraft in.

GETTING READY TO LAUNCH

When the fuel truck delivered 607 gallons of 100 octane Avgas (Aviation Gas) to the U.S. Customs hangar, Mike R. and I refueled the undercover seaplane ourselves. We performed this task so our crew could get some additional sleep. In order to take care of the is critical chore, we had Captain Video give us a break down of how much fuel he wanted us to put in the different tanks. We had our work cut out for us, since the undercover aircraft that we selected for this mission had wing tanks, drop tanks, as well as fuel tanks in the two floats. (The floats held the left and right wing tips out of the water and stabilized the seaplane when it operated on the water.)

Once we accomplished this task, we checked and filled the oil receptacles that were situated on top of each side of the wing. This was one of the few times, when any of the special agents assigned to this operation refueled one of our aircraft, added oil to the engines, or assisted one of our mechanics in some way. I mention this, because it was Standard Operating Procedure, for us to have at least one FAA certified aircraft mechanic with us at all times. Since all Mike and I were doing was filling the UC aircraft with Av Gas and oil, we figured that we could handle this chore by ourselves.

When it came time to wake up our undercover crew, we served them hot coffee, then drove them to the flight line. After we sanitized the undercover aircraft, to prevent the Colombians from finding any receipts or papers that would compromise our crew in any way, we had our crew check their wallets to make sure they weren't carrying anything that might connect them to the U.S. Customs Service or the U.S. Government. This included making sure that no one had any business cards, or any other items in their possession, that could connect them to a law enforcement officer, the Post Exchange (PX), an officer's club, or the Bachelor Officers Quarters on a military base. Again, this was stuff that was not taught to us in special agent's school.

As soon as Mike R. and I handed our crew several thousand dollars in E & E (Escape & Evasion) money, we went over the ops (operational) plan again. While our crew counted the money to verify the amount, I discussed our standing orders, that dictated exactly how far off shore our crew had to operate to avoid violating our very restrictive rules of engagement.

Knowing our limitations and suspecting how the Colombians would react, I told our crew what to say, to prevent the bad guys from getting suspicious, if the Colombian violators asked them to land closer to shore to make the pickup. I did so, because I suspected the Colombians would ask our crew to land a few miles closer to shore, were we knew the water was calm enough for a seaplane to land and make the pickup.

Just about the time that I finished giving my end of the briefing, a local cop assigned to guard the Puerto Rico Air Unit entered the Customs hangar, to relay a message that C3I was on the phone and we had a problem. At twenty minutes to lift off, the last thing any of us wanted to hear was the word problem. After picking up the phone in the hangar, Ed H. asked me to get back to the office to receive a call from Customs Air Operations on the STU3 (secure) phone. As I ran out of the hangar, I yelled to Mike to hold the plane. Naturally, everyone looked at me and shook their heads as if to say, "Please, God not now."

Once I got back to the office, I spoke to a Customs Air Officer about our intended launch. I then spoke to a U.S. Air Force Captain, who wasn't sure if the Air Force would support our operation, because JTF4 (Joint Task Force 4) was never notified about our mission. When this misinformed Air Force Captain asked me about the airdrop case off the coast of Aruba, I informed this officer, that the operation was called Aruba, that there was no air drop and our crew was planning to make an open ocean pickup off the coast of Colombia.

After having a rather frustrating 4 AM telephone conversation with an uninformed Air Force Captain, another Air Force Officer, this one a Major from JTF4, contacted me and asked questions about our operation. It was moments like this that I wished that my father was George Bush (41) or that I was George Bush. If I had that kind of juice, I would have called my favorite four star Air Force General at 4 AM, to find out how many U.S. Air Force officers have to be briefed IN PERSON, before the Air Force understands what was taking place on the front lines of The Drug War. Bear in mind, that my colleagues and I personally visited and briefed the U.S. Air Force E3 AWAC crew that was assigned to support this covert air operation. This included briefing a number of U.S. Air Force officers from full Colonels on down. Why there was a problem at 0400 hours was beyond me?

By the time I ran back to the hangar, our seaplane was taxiing toward the active runway, near the hangar that housed the U.S. Customs Air Unit in Puerto Rico. Even though I would have liked to have said goodbye to our crew before they left, I couldn't blame Mike for telling our crew to take off. After all, we didn't need permission from the U.S. Air Force to fly this, or any other undercover air mission.

As I walked out of the hangar and stood on the Customs ramp, I said a silent prayer as the UC plane took off into a jet black sky and headed south. Once our crew was on its way, Mike and I went back to the roach motel to get a few hours of sleep.

As soon as we arrived in the Customs Air Unit Office, we learned that the U.S. Air Force E3 AWAC aircraft that was assigned to cover this mission had very limited contact with our undercover plane and eventually left to supposedly track a bad guy target. After all that we did to insure the full cooperation of the U.S. Air Force, our undercover crew was left to fend for themselves.

INSIDE THE UNDERCOVER SEAPLANE

After several hours of flying over a dark and very deep ocean, our undercover seaplane arrived over the pick up point. Once again, our crew braced for action and prepared to pick up a shipment of cocaine. Unfortunately, the weather was getting worse and seemed like it would seriously hamper their ability to land in the open ocean and recover the load.

As our crew would later report, conditions along the coast of Colombia were far from ideal, with an overcast sky and some rain falling throughout the immediate area. After circling off shore for a while and not spotting anything except one boat in the distance, our crew was finally able to communicate with the Colombian smugglers over the hand held two meter radio. Just as we had anticipated, because of the worsening weather conditions, the Colombians begged our crew to land closer to the coast where the conditions were more favorable.

While circling at an altitude of one thousand feet, our crew could clearly see that the water closer to shore was more suitable for seaplane operations. Our crew was also painfully aware, that if they ventured any closer to the beach, they would be violating the rules of engagement. As wacky and as seemingly undisciplined as our contract pilots and sources of information were at times, they followed their orders and refused to land where the conditions were more favorable. Our crew knew, that there would be hell to pay, if they landed one wave closer to Colombia than the location where we were authorized to make the pick up.

One of the reasons we had to agree to fly this mission under such strict operating restrictions, was because the U.S. Customs Service was in the process of receiving full Title 21 Authority, a capability that DEA objected to giving us for a long time. This new authority enabled U.S. Customs Agents to work drug cases with less oversight and involvement from DEA. The last thing that Customs management wanted to see happen, was for our agency to lose Title 21 Authority before we had a chance to use it.

Any U.S. Customs Agent who overstepped their authority and violated their orders, might cause the powers to be in "Washington" to rethink the decision to bless Customs Agents with Title 21 Authority. There was also an attempt being made, to establish a spirit of cooperation between Customs and DEA. From what we were told, both agencies were under strict internal orders to make things work or else. Since anything was better than the way we had been operating for years, many of us welcomed any positive change.

Before I go any further, I need to explain, that the constraints that were placed on us during this particular operation, were actually ludicrous and made no absolutely sense. After all, what's the difference if our seaplane crashed in the ocean twenty miles off shore, twelve miles off shore, or two miles off shore? If our seaplane landed ANYWHERE off shore and crashed, where do you think this wreckage and the survivors would have ended up? In other words, no matter what happened, the seaplane and or the wreckage and the survivors, would eventually wash up on a beach in Colombia. In fact, common sense dictated, that it was actually safer to allow our undercover aircraft to land closer to shore, where the water was calmer and more suitable for open ocean seaplane operations. Even though these issues were raised, we were given marching orders that made absolutely no sense to any of us.

By the time the Colombian smugglers made it to the location where our plane was circling, the sea state conditions became even worse. This meant that even a Top Gun seaplane pilot like Captain Video, would be crazy to attempt an open ocean landing under worsening conditions. Both The Salesman and Johnny Walker knew, that if anyone could judge the sea state and evaluate whether or not they could safely land and take off, it was Captain Video. Rather than break the rules and risk washing up on the beach in Colombia, our crew decided to live and fight another day.

In order to avoid coming under suspicion, our crew remembered what we discussed in the briefing and told the Colombians that they used up too much fuel flying around looking for their boat and had to leave without making the pickup. As soon as The Salesman spoke into the two-meter hand held radio and said, "We're low on fuel, the weathers too bad, let's delay," the Colombian smuggler on the boat below screamed into the radio and said, "OK, OK, try in two days, same place." While Captain Video banked the undercover seaplane over the Colombian vessel, The Salesman spoke into the radio again, but used a firmer tone of voice and said, "Next time get here early. Let's do it at sun up!"

While the Colombian in charge stood on the pitching deck of the cocaine laden boat, he yelled into the hand held radio as he looked up into the sky and said, "Sunup in two days, 48 hours!" Under the circumstances, the Colombians knew that our crew was telling the truth. Not only were the Colombians late in getting to the rendezvous point off shore, but by the time they did arrive, the water was too rough for our seaplane to safely land to make the pickup.

While Captain Video applied full power and the UC plane began to climb to a higher cruising altitude, The Salesman took one more look at the scene below and observed the Colombians waving goodbye. Even though our crew had to leave the area without making the pickup, the ball was still in play.

PLAY IT AGAIN SAM

As soon as our undercover seaplane landed at our base in Puerto Rico, we debriefed and fed our crew, before I called Rob K, the Group Supervisor for Group 7. After our crew got some rest and we serviced our seaplane, our crew departed Puerto Rico, to try once again to make the pickup. Even with a slight improvement in the weather, there was no way to guarantee that the conditions along the coast of Colombia would be suitable for seaplane operations.

The moment our crew arrived on station, they were in contact with the Colombian violators, who were heading to the rendezvous point, in a boat that was heavily laden with a multi-hundred kilo shipment of cocaine. Unfortunately, the conditions were far too risky to try an open ocean water landing. Once again, the Colombians begged our crew to land closer to shore, in an area along the coast where the conditions were more suitable for seaplane operations. Unfortunately, the calmer water closer to the beach was in a restricted area where we were not authorized to operate.

Just as they had done on the last trip, our crew told the bad guys that they used up too much fuel while they waited for them to arrive at the rendezvous point. Fortunately, the Colombians understood and asked our crew to return when the conditions were more favorable. Best yet, the Colombians apologized for being late again.

Due to conditions beyond our control, the undercover seaplane was forced to leave the area without making the pickup. My colleagues and I left Puerto

Rico tested as we had never been tested before. Because we followed the rules, we had to fly home empty handed. This time our success was not measured in kilos, but in our ability to follow orders. Even though we were coming home empty handed, we got to practice our trade and live to fight another day.

CHAPTER 19

SHAKEN NOT STIRRED

Two days after we returned to South Florida we decided to try it again. Our Colombian "clients" were so impressed by our two attempts to pick up the load with a seaplane, they agreed to come up with more front money to enable us to return. The day we geared up to fly into Colombia, we worked right up to the time we were scheduled to fly to GITMO. Shortly after we assembled in the Group 7 trailer at Homestead AFB the phone rang. As soon as I answered the phone, my ASAC (Assistant Special Agent in Charge) informed me that our request for country clearance was once again denied. Naturally, in layman's terms, this meant that our mission was canceled.

After I hung up the phone, I walked into the room where all hands were seated and gave everyone the bad news. Rather than sulk in the office, we decided to get something to eat. All I could think about, as I led the convoy of vehicles north on the Florida Turnpike, was that we would have to be more creative and a little more daring, if we wanted to pull this case off. As far as I was concerned, we had too much invested in this case, to be shut down by the idiotic rules of engagement of The Drug War.

After camping out at a long table in one of our favorite bar restaurants, we ordered a few buckets of chicken wings and some beverages, while we discussed the case at hand. While I consumed my fair share of chicken wings and washed my dinner down with several gallons of ice tea, I refused to accept the fact that this case was dead in the water. As best as I could remember, DEA shut this particular controlled delivery down at least six different times in the past year. Every time we geared up to do this deal with our colleagues from New Mexico, we ended up getting closer and closer to the cocaine. In fact, we got close enough on two occasions, to see a boat loaded with hundreds of kilos of cocaine, bobbing up and down on the ocean, at a location off the coast of Colombia where our seaplane was unable to land

As bad as we felt, The Salesman was on his way to federal prison, unless he put a big case together. According to the way things worked, The Salesman broke the law and needed to pay his debt to society. He could do that by giving up his freedom and staying behind bars for a few years, or by working with us for as long as it took to clear his otherwise tarnished name. Unless we got real resourceful fast, The Salesman would be going back to New Mexico to be prosecuted, with Agent Jim S. putting in a good word for him on our behalf.

While everyone else was engaged in conversation, I sat at the head of the table and considered our options in silence. Then it hit me. There was only one way for us to make this case, given the operating restrictions that were imposed on us. As I looked around the crowded table in the corner of the restaurant, I made eye contact with everyone present and said, "We'll go by boat." For a split second no one said anything. It was almost as if what I said had to sink in and be evaluated before anyone would comment. While I continued to have everyone's undivided attention, I added something to the effect of, "Just because we're in an air smuggling unit, doesn't mean that we can't utilize a vessel to execute a controlled delivery." After all, in large measure, we were making the rules up as we went along.

By now everyone was up and running. The Salesman spoke first and said, "But what about our motto, "We fly at night if the price is right, no load too great, no distance too far. I'm the man for your contraband, one plane in, one plane out, last call?"

I knew exactly what he was referring to. After looking around, to make sure that no one else was paying attention to what we were discussing, I leaned closer to my colleagues and presented a thumb nail sketch of our dilemma. For starters, we knew that we would not be able to get authorization to land in Colombia to make the pickup. We also knew that we would never be able to land one of our undercover seaplanes in the open ocean, because the water was too rough. We tried that twice and it didn't work. Even if we managed to land in the open ocean, there was no guarantee that our seaplane would be able to get up on step and take off in rough water. Since we were prohibited by the rules of engagement from venturing any closer to shore, where the water was more suitable for seaplane operations, we had to scrub the idea of using a seaplane to extract the load.

The good news was, the Colombians believed that we were very serious players. The bad news was, that we were unable to get country clearance to fly into Colombia to make the pickup. As a result, our only alternative was to go down by boat and meet a Colombian vessel in a location where U.S. Agents were legally allowed to operate, without securing country clearance. Doing so, also allowed us to operate in sea conditions that were too rough for a seaplane to operate in. The alternative was for us to collectively walk away from an otherwise doable case. After all, the Colombians we were dealing with already proved that they were capable of using a boat to deliver the load off shore. This meant, that we should be able to meet our Colombian "clients" off shore and make the transfer at sea from their vessel to ours.

As I proposed my plan, I told my colleagues that once we picked up the 700 plus kilos of cocaine and the two bad guys by boat, we would high tail it to safer waters, where the conditions were more suitable for a seaplane to land. Naturally, we would pick a location that did not require country clearance and was safe for us to operate in. The place that I envisioned, that was ideally suited for the transfer to take place, was Puerto Rico. (This was the case because Puerto Rico was U.S. territory.)

Once our seaplane landed in the water (off the coast of Puerto Rico) and taxied over to our undercover vessel, we would use a small Zodiac rubber boat, to transfer the cocaine, the two bad guys and our undercover team into the UC aircraft. We would then fly to South Florida, where we would execute an undercover refueling, then fly cross-country to deliver the cocaine shipment and the two bad guys to undercover Special Agent Jim S.. Agent Jim S. and The Salesman would complete the final phase of the controlled delivery in Albuquerque, New Mexico.

As I sat back as confident as ever, that what I proposed would work out to our satisfaction, I could see my associates begin to smile as they digested my plan. Even though I had no idea what boat we would use, or where we would get one, I didn't allow this particular detail to spoil my enthusiasm. All I knew, was that this case would never be made, unless we made chicken salad out of chicken shit and had it taste like the real Mc Coy. Once the Colombians agreed with our plan, all we needed was a seaworthy vessel, some fair weather and a healthy blast of Divine Intervention and I was sure that we could pull this off.

Rather than wait any longer, The Salesman made a few calls and pitched the plan to Agent James S., before he called his contacts in Colombia. Meanwhile, I called my group supervisor (Rob K.) to let him know what we were up to. As soon as The Salesman finished pitching the deal to the Colombian broker we were in business. According to The Salesman, the Colombians were very impressed with our determination and looked forward to seeing us make the pickup by boat, so we could transfer the load and our two passengers to our seaplane in calmer waters.

Now I had something to celebrate. I ordered a Martini, shaken not stirred of course and plenty of olives. I had only tasted one Martini in my entire life and that was many years ago. Since I was in a James Bond type of mood, I thought it was time to try another martini, even though the first one I tasted wasn't very good. My experiment with the famous "shaken not stirred," James Bond beverage was short lived and I immediately went back to drinking ice tea and Diet Coke.

The next day I was up early and on my way to the office to develop our operational plan with my group supervisor. Once I went over our plan again, Rob K. started making calls to get us the help that we needed to execute this rather daring undercover operation. When we determined that the $27,000 dollars in front money was not enough to pay all of the expenses, Rob got the Southeast and Southwest Regions of the U.S. Customs Service to come up with a total of $30,000 in additional special operations money.

In order to carry out this mission, we needed to lease another large twin engine seaplane, that was capable of carrying two pilots and as many as six passengers, along with 700 plus kilos of cocaine, luggage, extra oil, coolers full of food and water, survival equipment and our weapons, on a long range mission from the pickup point in Puerto Rico to New Mexico. Because The Salesman set the deal up, he was a natural choice to serve as Captain Video's co pilot. Since Agent Chuck W. and I were going on this boat trip as part of the undercover crew, Mike R. volunteered to serve as the crew chief on the seaplane. Because we would be going on a long sea voyage and would be picking up two bad guys with the coke load, I also asked Hombre de la Calle to go along. As far as I was concerned, it made perfect sense, to bring a former marine smuggler who never got caught with us on such a potentially perilous journey.

Unfortunately, every contact that we had, who previously rented us former military seaplanes, was unable to provide us with the same model aircraft that we used for special purpose missions. Unfortunately, the ONLY military surplus seaplane that was available for rent, was the short winged version of the aircraft that we preferred to use. The day that we inspected this surplus military aircraft, Captain Video immediately raised concerns about using a plane that was known to perform rather poorly in an engine out scenario. When I asked Captain Video what the absolute worst thing was that could happen to us, if we used this particular model seaplane, he looked at me and said, "We'll lose an engine and we'll crash." In the end, the decision was made to go with what we had available on very short notice. It was either that or scrub the mission.

GROUP 7 WAS FULL OF FIRSTS

As far as I knew at the time, no one in federal law enforcement had ever mounted an undercover operation that involved using a vessel and a seaplane, to transport a multi-hundred kilogram shipment of cocaine, a fugitive and a Colombian observer from the Colombian coast to a destination in the United States. Regardless, I had complete faith that this plan would work.

In the last few years, I spent more time flying over the ocean than riding on top of it. Even though this was the case, I was anxious to participate in this seagoing adventure. One reason for this, was because I successfully completed a very intensive month long Marine Law Enforcement Training Course (MLETC) at FLETC, that prepared me to operate undercover and interdiction vessels. However, outside of this formal training, my boating experience never amounted to much more than commuting on the Staten Island Ferry in New York and serving on U.S. Customs interdiction and undercover vessels, that never ventured farther than 12 miles or so off shore.

Unfortunately, with all of the vessels assigned to the Customs Marine Unit, not one fit the bill, as far as our needs were concerned. In order to pull this deal off, we needed a sturdy long-range vessel that was capable of making the trip from South Florida to Colombia, then to Puerto Rico, so we could rendezvous with our seaplane. This vessel then had to make it back to South Florida, with the crew that would stay behind, while some of us continued on to New Mexico in the seaplane. Fortunately for us, Senior Special Agent Joe G. of the SAC Miami Marine Group managed to get his hands on a suitable undercover boat for us to use.

THE COCAINE EXPRESS

The one hundred foot aluminum hulled work boat that Joe G. lined up for us, had all of the makings of a capable undercover vessel, even though this boat's hull design would deliver a rough ride in bad weather. (Rough ride was putting it mildly.) Rather than waste any time, SS/A Joe G., Marine Enforcement Officer (MEO) Jimmy E., Mike R. and I met with the company officials who owned this vessel and struck a deal, that allowed us to lease their work boat at a reasonable rate. Naturally, we promised to return it in one piece.

According to what we were told, the company that owned this boat had an excellent reputation and was reputed to have done some work for Uncle Sam in the past. As a result, we felt safe in approaching them. Once the rental fee was paid, we were given a set of keys and left the office to equip the vessel for our operation.

Because Senior Special Agent Joe G. was needed to work on another undercover marine operation, MEO Jimmy E. was assigned to serve as our vessel commander for the first half of the trip. The plan was for us to pick up Agent Joe G. on our way to Colombia, when we stopped to refuel at the U.S. Navy Base at GITMO Cuba.

The week before we left was spent purchasing tons of food and supplies. At our request, the Special Agent in Charge (SAC) requisitioned four Colt CAR-15's assault rifles (shorter versions of the M16 (now known as the M4) from our firearms unit. This request was made because the U.S. Customs Service traded our previously issued Colt CAR-15's for Steyr AUG's (Austrian assault rifles). One reason I decided not to use the recently issued fully automatic Steyr AUGs, was because at that time, nobody except U.S. Customs Agents and the Austrian Army used this weapon. (I also preferred the Colt CAR 15 to the AUG and still do.) Since the U.S. Customs Service usually bent over backwards to satisfy the requests that were made by undercover agents, our SAC approved our request for the previously issued but extremely reliable Colt CAR 15s.

In order to make sure that we were adequately equipped to repel unwanted boarders, we also stocked our vessel with eighteen 20 round magazines, eleven 30 round M16 magazines, two short barreled Parkerized Remington 12 gauge pump action shotguns and a carload of ammunition. In addition to my government issued 9mm S&W 6906 service pistol and plenty of spare magazines, I brought along a stainless Walther PPK .380 ACP caliber pistol as a backup handgun. I left my 9mm SIG 228 at home, to protect my personally owned pistol from being exposed to salt water. I did this because at the time, SIG pistols were made with carbon steel slides, that were more susceptible to corrosion. I also left my issued blue steel five shot Smith & Wesson .38 Special revolver home for the same reason.

SAYING GOODBYE

After a long day of preparing for our trip, I went home to pack my bag and be with my family, before I left to spend the night on the undercover vessel. As usual, I made my sons feel as if they were being made privy to "top secret" information, when I "briefed" them about our operation.

While some people might think that I was crazy for doing so, I believed that my sons better handled my going away to work undercover, because they had a very general idea of what I would be doing when I was gone. In order to help them visualize what I was telling them, I would lay a marine chart/map on the floor in one of their bedrooms, while I "briefed" them on the operational plan.

In the process, I made my sons "help" me do the math, when I calculated things like speed and distance problems, that were required to complete a particular mission. This operation was no different.

While I showed my sons where we expected to make the sea transfer along the Colombian coast, my youngest son Michael asked me if the U.S. Navy was going to help us during our mission. The moment I told my boys that the U.S. Navy and the U.S. Coast Guard were going to protect us on this mission, my sons seemed relieved and smiled wide after being given access to such "classified information."

Needless to say, what I told my sons was only partially true. I say this, because the U.S. Coast Guard cutter that was assigned to keep an eye on us, would remain some 50 miles away once we reached the pickup point. This meant, that until the Coast Guard cutter was able to reach our position, we would be on our own for a while if we needed assistance. Even so, it was comforting to know, that a U.S. Coast Guard cutter was in the general vicinity, especially during the return trip to the transfer point in Puerto Rico.

When my oldest son Nick pointed to the U.S. Navy Base at Guantanamo Bay, Cuba and identified GITMO as the secret base where we operated from, I reminded my boys that what I did for a living was top secret stuff and that they couldn't tell anyone what they knew about my job. Again, whether you agree me with me or not, I honestly believe that my sons were better able to handle my going in harms way, because they believed that they were part of the secret life that I lived. Even though I "sugar coated" everything that I said to them, the heavily sanitized briefing sessions that I held with my sons, enabled them to visualize more realistic circumstances, instead of having their young imaginations run wild.

When the time came to put my sons to bed, I tucked them both in and told them how much I loved them. The hard part came when it was time for me to leave and break the news to my wife, that I was going along on this undercover operation. As soon I walked into our bedroom, I knew that my decision to go on this mission would not go over big with my wife. In fact, I actually contemplated not telling her at all.

After skirting around the topic, I told my wife that I decided to run this operation from the deck of the undercover boat and not from the safety of a command post on GITMO, or in the Group 7 trailer. To put it bluntly, my wife went berserk. While I tried my best not to be melodramatic about it, the simple fact was, that something very bad could happen to me during this operation and I did not want my wife and I to part company with such bitterness between us. Unfortunately, nothing I said made a difference. As far as my wife was concerned, she was shocked that I would risk my life in this fashion when I had a family to provide for. Unfortunately, we argued right up until it was time for me to leave. I hate to say it, but when push came to shove, I said adios amigo and walked out the door.

Once I got on the highway, I called my wife on my cell phone and tried to get her to calm down but nothing I said made a difference. My wife wanted me to stop this foolishness immediately and become a "regular agent," or risk the rest of our marriage eroding away, until I had nothing left but visitation rights. Personally, I wasn't ready to give up my involvement in the undercover operation that I initiated several years before.

This was no way to leave and no way to go on such a potentially dangerous operation, but I felt I had no choice. Our saying goodbye to each other wasn't anything like the crap you see in the movies. There were no hugs and kisses, or supportive "off you go my darling hero stuff." The argument we had that night was down right ugly. In fact, the only thing that my wife wanted to do with a yellow ribbon, was tie one around my neck and not around an oak tree. My wife was also not impressed, when I said that I could not bring myself to ask someone else to do something that I had not done, or would not do. As far as she was concerned, I was always doing things that others didn't do. How I hated it when she was right.

It took some time, but I eventually realized that my wife was deathly afraid of me being killed during one of our controlled delivery operations. While being the wife of a law enforcement officer was bad enough, being the wife of an undercover agent was downright nerve racking. It also didn't help, that some friends of ours did not share my rather obsessive devotion to duty and thought I was crazy for leaving my family, in order to work insane house and be gone from home for long periods of time. Having my wife remind me that "so and so" thought I was nuts, for doing the things that I did for an ungrateful Customs Service, added wood to an already out of control fire. In the end, I left my wife on very bad terms, because I truly believed that it was my destiny to go on this operation. Even though I risked getting divorced, I pressed on and drove to Port Everglades in Ft. Lauderdale, to spend the night on the undercover vessel, so the crew and I could make an early morning departure.

Preparing for such an operation called for a great deal of logistical support and back breaking hard work. In addition to our weapons and luggage, it took some doing to fill our vessel with all of the food and other supplies that we purchased for this trip. (It took a van and three cars to transport the supplies that we purchased from a warehouse store for this trip.) With our operational plan and travel authorizations completed and our supplies on board, we made a last minute phone call to Colombia to tell our "clients" that we were on the way.

When Captain Video stopped by with Mike R., we discussed the part of the plan where the seaplane was expected to rendezvous with the undercover vessel in the Mona Passage (in Puerto Rico). Since it was too early to sleep, I decided to join Mike R. and Captain Video for a late night supper. The drive to one of our favorite local restaurants in Broward County was a quiet one, as everyone seemed to be reflecting on the operation that we were about to embark on.

Once we finished eating, Mike R. and Captain Video drove me back to the UC vessel, so I could get some sack time before we departed at 0600 hours. After saying goodbye to Mike R., I found myself standing on the dock with Captain Video. I'll never forget how Captain Video turned to me and said that I didn't have to do this. I was twice as surprised to hear an adventurer like Captain Video say, that he couldn't believe that we were going to Colombia on a one hundred foot aluminum hulled work boat. He expressed this concern because the Windward Passage was famous for producing all sorts of bad weather in hurricane season.

From the moment that I planned this operation, I had every intention of going along. Simply put, this was something that I just had to do. While I stood on the dock by the undercover vessel, I explained to Captain Video how much I was affected by the responsibility of sending him and the other contract personnel in harms way. As I continued, I explained how a little piece of me went along on every mission and never came back.

Ever since I initiated this operation, I was personally responsible for sending our contract crews on a number of very dangerous missions. As a result, I felt compelled to go on one myself. Even though deep down inside I knew that I had nothing to prove, there was something about participating in this high risk covert air and marine operation that seemed like a once in a lifetime opportunity.

I also wanted to go on this mission, because from a professional standpoint, this case had it all. In fact, on a scale of one to ten, this particular transportation case/controlled delivery was a twelve. I say this, because in addition to the routine aspects of this investigation, this case had some very unique qualities that separated it from all the others. To add to the intrigue, my colleagues and I would have to live with two major violators in tight quarters for several days once the pickup was made. Once that was accomplished, we had to fly cross country in a thirty year old war bird, so we could deliver our two passengers and the cocaine shipment to our counterpart in New Mexico. Forget about making history. This controlled delivery was one big adrenaline rush and anyone who failed to get excited about going on this mission, was a water cooler commando masquerading as an undercover operative. Besides, if we survived, this adventure would make a great chapter in the book that I was writing about our undercover operation.

After hearing what I had to say, Captain Video understood my position. When there was nothing else to discuss, we shook hands and wished each other well. Then, as Captain Video walked away, he stopped and reassured me that he would be on schedule to make the transfer in the Mona Passage. Since I knew that Captain Video, The Salesman and Mike R. would never let us down, I nodded my head and offered my favorite seaplane pilot a cordial smile. As Captain Video drove away, I remembered that old nautical expression, "Red sky at night sailor's delight," as I looked up to examine the condition of the star lit sky.

Just about the time that I gave up looking for any sign of red in the sky, a car pulled up to the pier where the UC vessel was tied up. It was Hombre de la Calle and his family. After the whole family got out of the car, Hombre walked over and asked if I would meet his elderly mother, his wife and his children. How could I refuse? As soon as I met his family, Hombre's mother gently held my hand and told me in Spanish that she would pray for our safe return. I was deeply touched. These were decent people and they knew enough about what we were doing to see Hombre off and wish us well.

Once Hombre said goodbye to his family and they left the port, I remained on the pier by the undercover boat and smoked a cigarette with my favorite Cuban CI. After we finished our cigarettes and talked about old times and the case at hand, Hombre and I went below to get some sleep.

As I fell asleep that night, all I could think about was how I considered myself more than just a federal agent. Because I documented what transpired during these operations as they occurred, I also considered myself to be a self appointed Drug War correspondent of sorts. Just as I had done in the past, I knew that there was a battle that was about to be waged in this conflict and I was going to be the only "correspondent" given the opportunity to cover it. I also knew, that even if it took twenty years for my dispatches to be made public, that I had the exclusive to this unusual "Drug War" story.

Because The Drug War is a conflict that was usually fought in secret, the general public rarely if ever learned how we engaged the enemy in the dark. Even many of the movies that have been made about this subject matter, usually represent The Drug War from the bad guy's perspective. My plan was to give the general public a crystal clear picture of what went on behind the lines, when U.S. Customs Agents pursued drug smugglers in a very unorthodox but effective covert fashion. I also wanted to be the one who broke the story, that American agents are capable of mounting first class high risk covert operations without creating embarrassing scandals.

In addition, I wanted to let the public know, that a team of U.S. Customs Agents, along with their sources of information and contract pilots, made history and proved that the drug smugglers could be defeated, when our side was willing to go above and beyond the call of duty and take the fight to the enemy. The writer in me was also salivating over the chance to experience an adventure, that most creative people spent careers wishing they could document from a first hand account. The U.S. Customs Agent in me wanted to go along, because this trip represented a fantastic opportunity to perform a very unique type of undercover work. By going on this adventure, I also got the chance to go into harms way, while someone else paced back and forth in the command post and wondered if I was still alive.

That night I had a difficult time trying to fall asleep, while my mind wandered between thinking about my family and the mission at hand. At times, I was more concerned with the repercussions of screwing up, not by design, but just because I knew that shit happened. I felt this way, because the U.S. Customs Service was starting to put some undue pressure on agents, that made many of us feel as if mistakes would not be tolerated. As a result, I was forced to be very concerned about losing the four specially issued Colt CAR15's assault rifles and doing everything possible to avoid creating an international incident. After that, I could worry all I wanted about our crew, my own life and our mission.

CHAPTER 20

ANCHORS AWAY

After a few hours of sleep, I was up and about with the rest of the crew as we prepared to get underway. Once we cast off all mooring lines, Marine Enforcement Officer Jimmy E. eased us away from the dock and carefully steered the undercover vessel through Port Everglades. Once we made our way through the inlet and we headed into the open ocean, the trip to Colombia seemed like it would take a long time to complete. Regardless, there was no turning back.

As luck would have it, we weren't underway for more than an hour or so when the air-conditioning unit broke down. Because of the sea conditions and the design of our hull, the undercover vessel corkscrewed through the ocean like a mini destroyer and slammed into every wave that came our way. This caused enough salt water to cascade over the wheelhouse and across the deck, to make it impossible to keep any hatches open.

The vessel we leased for this mission came equipped with one hatch on the port (left) side of the wheelhouse and one in the rear of the aft (main) compartment. I should also mentioned, that none of the windows could be opened. Being inside a boat with no air conditioning or ventilation was like riding inside an un-air-conditioned bus in South Florida with the windows closed in the month of August.

In addition to the sweltering heat, the sea conditions were nothing to write home about. By nightfall we were all exhausted and totally drained by the heat and the constant rough ride. As darkness fell and we pushed on, the conditions worsened and by midnight we were battling even rougher seas. Those of us who were not on watch, would have loved to crawl into a nice soft bed, under an ice cold air conditioning vent to grab some badly needed sleep. Between the horrible sea conditions and the intense heat, the last thing on anyone's mind was eating. With all of the food we had provisioned the boat with, about the only thing anyone wanted to do was drink fresh water.

Eventually, I managed to fall asleep on a long black vinyl couch on the port side of the aft cabin. Meanwhile, Jimmy E. skillfully performed his duties as our vessel commander and kept us on course. After waking up in a daze at 3 AM, I looked out of a port side window and saw white capped waves, salt spray and deck line waving around in the breeze. Before I knew it, I collapsed back down on my vinyl couch and drifted back and forth in a strange kind of sleep.

By daybreak, Marine Enforcement Officer Mike C. was at the helm battling more of the same miserable sea conditions. While Jimmy E. and I tried in vain to raise our command post on the radio, our Engineer asked if we could stop so he could service the engines. As Mike C. throttled back on the three Detroit diesels, our aluminum hulled undercover boat began to bob like a cork in the choppy seas.

Since it was difficult to go below while we were underway and since we hadn't eaten anything in almost thirty hours, Special Agent Chuck W. ran down below to make some peanut butter and jelly sandwiches. Just about the time we were getting ready to get back on course, we wolfed down our sandwiches, drank a few cold sodas and cleared the decks for action.

Our vessel looked like hell. Nothing that had been tied down was still secured. All of our equipment and survival gear was all over the place. The heavy pounding and constant crashing of waves over the boat had also caused some flooding inside each compartment. Worse yet, the heavy steel storm plates that were secured on the exterior of wheelhouse were loose and the deck line that was secured in the bow deck compartment was all over the deck.

Just about the time that we were ready to get underway, I spotted two long pieces of deck line hanging over the starboard side railing of our vessel. (You never use the term "rope" to describe deck line on a vessel.) Even a novice sailor like me knew, that deck line belongs secured neatly on deck or stowed in a locker and not dangling over the side of a boat.

As soon as I told our crew what I saw, Jimmy E. and Mike C. wasted no time in checking out our dangling line problem. By the time I joined Jimmy and Mike along the starboard railing, I could tell by the expressions on their faces that we were in big trouble. As the rest of the crew assembled on the stern deck, Mike C. reported that both lines were wrapped around our drive shafts, which as you can imagine is a very dangerous place for "deck line" to be on a boat.

After Jimmy thanked me for catching the problem, Mike C. said that if we had kept going we would have run the risk of losing a drive shaft or two. If a drive shaft tore from the boat, seawater would quickly begin to flood the engine room. Naturally, if this happened we would be in grave danger.

There we were, drifting in a rolling sea, out of radio contact with our command post for twenty seven hours and unable to continue on our mission, without risking the chance of sinking. Our only hope was to send someone over the side, to cut the tangled deck line from the drive shaft. Since Jimmy E. was our Vessel Commander, he volunteered to do so. Being an avid scuba diver, Jimmy put on his dive gear and borrowed a Tanto knife from Hombre de La Calle. Once Mike C. and I tied a long piece of deck line around his waist, Jimmy went over the side. We then tied a long line to a life ring (flotation device) and tossed it over the side to give Jimmy something to grab onto when he surfaced.

As I put my life jacket on, I was very impressed by Jimmy E's display of heroism when he went over the side and entered the water. While I stood on the stern deck, as our boat bobbed up and down on the rough ocean, I felt eerie and very vulnerable. A bad situation was made worse, by the presence of white capped waves in all directions for as far as the eye could see. Each and every time our boat lifted out of the water and slipped back down, the ocean reminded us that she had complete control over our destiny. The situation seemed even more ominous, because a cloudy sky hung low over the choppy ocean, as an impending storm threatened to unleash its fury at a most inopportune time.

Even though I wasn't scared, I was very concerned. I also felt responsible for our dilemma, because I didn't wake up in the middle of the night, to tell the crew when I spotted deck line blowing around in the breeze during the storm. In my defense, I can only assume that I failed to put two and two together, because I was totally exhausted and did not grasp the severity of the situation. As far as I was concerned, the fact that I wasn't on duty at the time didn't matter.

To make a bad situation worse, we were drifting into Cuban waters. Once I heard this news, all I could think about was what we would do, if a Cuban patrol boat arrived on scene and tried to board us. Would we be justified if we refused to permit a communist naval vessel to take control of our ship? We couldn't even call for help, or ask our agency for advice, because we weren't able to get through to anyone on our HF radio.

While I can't really say that I actually prayed in the traditional sense, I did have a conversation with God about our sorry state of affairs. Naturally, we were all concerned, that while Jimmy E. was under the boat cutting away at the deck line, a huge wave would lift the vessel up and slam it down on top of his head.

When Jimmy broke the surface, he called out that our problem was worse than he expected. Not one, but all three of the shafts under our vessel were entangled by deck line. After resting for a second, Jimmy dove back down under the boat and continued to use Hombre's Cold Steel Tanto Knife to hack away at the deck line. Under the circumstances, all we could do was exchange glances and wait, while our brave Captain risked his life to save us from certain disaster.

While I looked over the side of the boat, I smoked a cigarette as I waited patiently with the others for Jimmy E. to return to the surface. I was witnessing the most heroic act of bravery by a law enforcement officer that I had ever seen in my entire career. I swore to myself that even if it took a lifetime, I would do everything possible to get this book published, so the world would learn about the acts of heroism, that were performed by men like U.S. Customs Officer James E. and the other officers and agents identified in this true story. As far as I was concerned, diving under the undercover vessel in rough seas, to remove the deck line that was wrapped around our propeller shafts, was clearly above and beyond the call of duty. Even though I admire certain celebrities for their talent, none of my favorite movie actors ever did anything like this in real life, yet everyone in the world knows who they are, but no one ever heard of Jimmy E.

While Jimmy E. was under the boat, the rolling sea lifted the hundred foot undercover vessel out of the water causing it to crash down on top of our young Captain. The force of the huge vessel coming down on top of his air tank, sent Jimmy plummeting down about several feet towards the bottom of the ocean. Thank God, Jimmy managed to recover and return to the surface after carving off several sections of deck line. Although it took some doing, Jimmy finally managed to remove enough of the deck line from the drive shafts so we could get underway. Once he came to the surface, we pulled him up onto the stern deck, where he filled us in on the situation at hand.

In Jimmy's professional opinion, he felt that we could make it to GITMO for repairs, providing we took it easy. We had a schedule to keep and so far, despite this delay, we still had a good chance of being at the pickup point on time. The rest of the day was more of the same, as we plowed through a dark green ocean towards the U.S. Navy Base in Cuba.

By nightfall the sea kicked up again. After a miserable day, we were faced with more water crashing over our bow. At about 1 AM, a bright white flash woke me from another attempt to get some sleep. At first, I thought someone set off a flair, then a second flash illuminated the wheelhouse and I heard someone yell, "Fire!" In a matter of seconds, Jimmy E. reacted by cutting off power to the white running light that had just shorted out. Before this boat trip came to an end, we would experience five small electrical flash fires, including one backup radio that burned out.

At 11 PM or 2300 hours, we saw the flashing light that signaled mariners that they were approaching the entrance to the U.S. Navy Base at Guantanamo Bay, Cuba. Once we rounded the bend of the island and left the Windward Passage behind us, the sea calmed down considerably and allowed us to cruise along like a bunch of sunshine sailors out for an evening of pleasure boating. Luckily for us, I had managed to get a message to Mike R. who was monitoring the hi-frequency radio in the Group 7 trailer at Homestead Air Force Base. Mike knew we had problems and needed to get into GITMO, not only to pick up Special Agent Joe G., but to have repairs made to our vessel. Once the appropriate code word was relayed to U.S. Navy, we were authorized to enter the harbor and our base in Guantanamo Bay, Cuba.

As we made our way into the harbor entrance, Hombre de la Calle AKA Gordo stood by the rail and admired his homeland for the first time in over 30 years. For my Cuban informant this trip was special and gave him an opportunity to see the land that he loved, if only for a short period of time. Just like many other Cuban Americans, Hombre de la Calle emigrated to the U.S. to flee the oppression of the Castro regime. Like many other Cuban immigrants, Hombre also eagerly volunteered to join the resistance movement that was sponsored by the U.S. Government. (According to Hombre, he was recruited by a CIA Officer in a schoolyard in Miami when he was a young teenager.)

I should also mention that Hombre had an amazing sense of direction and seemed to be a capable navigator. While Joe G. would spend some time taking sextant readings and calculating our EXACT position, I would often ask Hombre to tell us our current location. I don't know how Hombre did it, but he always seemed to know where we were. Even though he might be a few miles off, it was impressive to have Hombre figure out our current position, or the distance to a certain objective, without using navigational aids to make his computations.

SAFE AND SOUND IN GITMO

I was never more grateful to see land, than I was the night we relayed the password to the United States Navy and we were granted permission to enter our base in Guantanamo Bay, Cuba.

Despite the fact that GITMO was located in Cuba, I always felt like I was on American soil, whenever I arrived at the U.S. Navy Base in Guantanamo Bay. I guess the fact that our flag flew over GITMO was enough to make me feel like I was home.

Once we made our way into the harbor, the Port Officer sent Agent Joe G. out to meet us in a Zodiac boat. After Joe came on board, he guided us into our berthing area. Due to the late hour we kept our briefing short and to the point. By 3:30 AM or 0330 hours we finally hit the sack and got some badly needed rest, in a bed with clean sheets that wasn't moving.

By 0900 hours our crew was busy at work on the UC vessel. Besides giving her a good cleaning, we needed to refuel the vessel and make some badly needed repairs. The SIMA office was our first stop. As usual, the United States Navy was a cordial and generous host. Once the U.S. Navy Officer in charge of the ships maintenance section learned that we needed to get underway to complete an undercover operation, we were given all the assistance that we required.

The U.S. Military units that were actively involved in supporting and carrying out LE (Law Enforcement) Missions, performed their duties as if they were engaged in a declared conventional war. Without their assistance, it would have been considerably more difficult and in some cases impossible, for us to operate as easily or as effectively as we did.

CHAPTER 21

VICTORY AT SEA

After 24 hours in GITMO it was time to get underway. We were less than 500 miles from our intended pickup point near the Colombian coast. The Colombians expected our vessel to be at a prearranged location from Point Galinas (Chicken Point), on the Guajira Peninsula on Wednesday, June 13, 1990 at 6 PM and we had every intention of being there on time. With our tanks full of fuel and fresh water and all repairs made, we steamed out of GITMO Harbor at 0700 hours on Sunday, June 10th with our destination, Colombia.

Once we ventured out into the Windward Passage, we got back on a course heading that would take us to our next stop. After all that we endured, we were not about to return home empty handed. Every one of us was eager to get to the pickup point, transfer the cocaine shipment and the two violators onto our vessel and make the rendezvous with our seaplane in Puerto Rico. At this stage in the game we weren't thinking about the trip back to the States, or how the actual controlled delivery would go down. Instead, my colleague and I focused all of our energy and attention on making the pickup along the coast of Colombia, so we had something to deliver to the seaplane crew in Puerto Rico.

Fortunately, we had a break in the sea conditions for a while, which gave us a chance to go balls to the wall and make up some time. Joe G. was the skipper now, so we gathered around the wheelhouse for a short meeting to discuss our work schedules and assignments. Even though we were U.S. Customs Agents, we had a ship to run and we were the crew.

Joe G. was one of the first Special Agents I met when I arrived in Miami, some five years before I set sail on this undercover operation. Special Agent Joe G. was an experienced field agent who served with another federal agency before he joined the U.S. Customs Service. For the record, Joe G. was one of the hardest working individuals I have had to describe in this book. For starters, Joe G. was without a doubt, one of THE BEST vessel commanders in the U.S. Customs Service. He was also one of the most intelligent special agents I ever worked with. Besides being a consummate sailor, Joe had one hell of a sense of humor and an almost unlimited source of energy.

The best way for me to describe Joe, is to say that he was thin as a rail and looked more like a track star than a federal agent. When he was not at the helm of a U.S. Customs patrol boat, or an undercover vessel, he could be found running around the deck holding up his sextant to navigate by the stars. Joe never seemed to catch more than a few minutes of sleep in a row and had to be forced to eat. As eccentric as he seemed to be, Joe G was an accomplished street agent who participated in more than his fair share of undercover marine ops.

In order to insure that things ran smoothly, Joe G organized the crew into a two-hour on, four hour off shift, where Jimmy, Mike, Chuck and Joe ran the wheelhouse. Our engineer kept the boat running and Hombre de la Calle was responsible for the galley. My primary job was to work with Joe to run the overall operation, serve as the communications officer and handle the bad guys. In addition, I was available to help out whenever needed. This included, helping out in the kitchen and steering the vessel when I relieved people on watch.

Thanks to the United States Navy, the air conditioning unit was blowing ice cold air throughout the ship. Clearly, having our AC unit repaired greatly enhanced our ability to function as opposed to our first forty hours on board.

By the early evening the sea state took a turn for the worse and we were once again faced with rather large waves that crashed all over our deck and slowed us down. Due to these conditions, that caused us to go from making 10 knots to 8, Joe had our engineer pump 800 gallons of seawater into the bow tank for ballast. Doing so, was meant to "improve" the ride a bit, as the UC vessel plowed through rough seas. Clearly, this was all very nautical stuff.

While I stood in the wheelhouse with our vessel commander, Joe G. grabbed the white bucket that was on the deck and used it as a receptacle when he got seasick and began to vomit. As I held on for dear life, I could not believe my eyes, when I watched Joe throw up, then open the port side hatch and empty the bucket, while an angry ocean unleashed its fury on our vessel. Of all people, Joe G. was the last person I thought would ever get seasick.

When I asked Joe if he got seasick often and he looked my way and said, "Every time," I was at a loss for words. Clearly, I was in the presence of greatness, even though none of the men I'm writing about would ever admit to being brave. To venture out to sea knowing that you will get seasick each and every time, is either an act of lunacy, or an indescribable act of heroism.

After watching Jimmy E. dive under the boat to free the drive shafts and observing a sea sick Joe G. steer our vessel through the perfect storm, I knew the Colombians were no match for us. After staying with Joe in the wheelhouse for a while, he suggested that I try and get some sleep. I agreed to do so, when he promised that he would lie down once he was relieved.

At 2200 hours (10 PM) I managed to brace myself and make it down below, as our vessel was thrashed around violently in another storm. After sloshing my way through the long gangway, that was covered with a half inch of seawater, I arrived in my cabin. Since Mike C. was no fool and had taken the lower bunk, I had no choice but to sleep in the upper bunk. It took some doing for a land lover like me to pull it off, but after a few tries, I was able to fling myself up and into the top bunk, while the undercover vessel pitched up and down like a bucking rodeo bull.

The accommodations on board most ships were usually cramped and our undercover vessel was no exception. Due to a shortage of storage space, I slept with two flashlights, a flashing beacon, a U.S. Marine Corps K-bar knife, two handguns, a Spydeco knife, my life jacket, a canteen of water, a short barreled Remington pump action a 12 gauge shotgun and a bandoleer of extra ammunition in my bunk. Despite the tight fit, I just starting to fall asleep, when the undercover vessel felt as if it crashed into a huge wave and reacted as if it was going in slow motion. While the undercover vessel felt like it was rebounding in the opposite direction, Joe G. called out, "All hands on deck." "Holy shit," I said as I leaned over my bunk and looked down at Mike C. "Did he say. All hands on deck?"

As soon as Mike and I jumped out of our racks onto the seawater covered deck, we left our cabin and climbed up the ladder to the main deck to join the rest of the crew. By the time we got topside, Joe G. powered the boat down to a complete stop. Once I made eye contact with our vessel commander, I knew we were in big trouble.

While we bobbed up and down on the open ocean, Joe described how a huge wave crashed over the bow and blew the forward hatch open and flooded the bow compartment with seawater. The good news was that we were still afloat. The main reason for this was because the bow compartment was sealed. The bad news was, that we weren't going anywhere, as long as the forward (bow) compartment was filled with seawater.

To keep us from being swamped, Joe had to carefully turn our vessel around. Fortunately, we had a following sea and not a confused, or a beam sea, or all might have been lost right then and there. Even when we turned around, we were unable to get underway, because the bow of our vessel was low enough in the water to actually bob up and down under the ocean. Under these circumstances, any attempt to get underway in conditions known as "a following sea," would have caused us to "pitch poll" bow first under the water and sink. With 800 gallons of water serving as ballast in the bow tanks and the forward compartment full of seawater, we were for all general purposes dead in the water. Even with the undercover vessel turned around, we were in grave danger.

As I stood on deck by the bow, I was in complete awe of the vastness of the ocean that surrounded our vessel in all directions. Nature was a powerful force to be reckoned with and we were once again at her mercy. Fortunately, undercover agents are an over confident lot. Simply put, you had to be able to look down the barrel of a cannon and climb inside without flinching.

Even though we expected to go to Colombia and come back in one piece, we all knew that going to sea on an undercover operation in hurricane season was risky business. The fact that we were well trained and were no stranger to the risks of our profession, made it possible for us to think positive about our survival. (Even though I had no idea how we were going to get out of this mess, I wasn't scared. Concerned yes, but scared no.)

Damage assessment was easy. We were still afloat, but unable to make headway, as long as the bow compartment was flooded with seawater. As a result, our first order of business was to pump the water out of the flooded compartment. To accomplish this we would need help. Without wasting time, Chuck W. broke out our one and only pump.

I must admit that I felt pretty good, the moment I imagined tons of seawater being sucked out of the forward compartment and sent over the side where it belonged. Unfortunately, this marvel of modern technology had seen better days and immediately overheated the moment it was deployed. As soon as Chuck tossed the useless pump aside, I looked out into the darkness and wondered what life would be like if we had to abandon ship. Clearly, we were in a precarious situation.

Once again, Joe G. took command and explained that we needed to hand bail the sea water out of the forward compartment, using our one and only puke bucket. When Joe continued, he said that each one of us would toss twenty buckets of seawater over the side, before we passed the empty bucket to the next man in line. There was no debate and no complaints. Instead, we acted like a crew should act, as we lined up to take our turn bailing seawater from our stricken vessel.

As I knelt down by the bow rail and I dumped bucket after bucket over the side, I wondered what the rest of the night had in store for us. Then I thought about my wife and two sons and prayed in silence, as I finished taking my turn bailing twenty buckets of seawater from the flooded bow compartment.

Once I stood up on deck and looked around, I realized how dark it was out in the middle of the ocean. This was scary shit. It was moments like this that made you realize, that you could get seriously hurt or killed in this business. Most law enforcement officers developed a thick skin over the years and tried to avoid facing their own mortality. It was hard to get motivated to do the things that law enforcement officers needed to do, if all you did when you went to work, was worry about becoming a casualty of some sort. Most of us let our spouses or family members worry about those possibilities. This was different. Out at sea you couldn't call for help and have it show up in a matter of seconds or minutes.

While it was comforting that we were still afloat and the stormy weather had died down, our situation could change at any time. If the bad weather kicked up again, we would be in serious trouble because we were no longer operating a seaworthy vessel.

Even after every member of the crew finished taking several turns bailing water, we only managed to remove enough water, to barely expose the top step of the ladder, that led down into the bow compartment. In terms of our survival, it looked as if 99.9% of the sealed forward compartment was still full of seawater. Even after our engineer drained the ballast tanks, we were still very bow heavy, although we did seem to ride the waves a little better, now that the sea state was fairly calm. Still, without a working pump, we would have to hand bail the compartment dry. The bad news was this could take a very long time to accomplish. The other bad news was that until the seawater was removed from the bow compartment, we could be forced to abandon ship if the conditions got worse again.

The second someone suggested that we put on our life jackets, I felt a lump in my throat and found it difficult to swallow. Once we had our life jackets on, we continued taking turns bailing water. In between my turn on the bucket detail, I drafted a coded message that included our coordinates and a brief statement about our situation.

After selecting the right radio frequency, I proceeded to broadcast a coded emergency message in the clear that went something like, "Bravo, Kilo, Whiskey, Lima, Bravo, Alfa, Foxtrot, Echo, Victor, 270154." If you had a code sheet, my standard message would read; "Have taken on water…bow compartment flooded….need aircraft to drop pumps…adrift at the following coordinates. N.J." After pausing briefly, I repeated this message over and over again for ten minutes.

Once I took my turn hand bailing sea water from the flooded compartment, I waited until the alternate transmission time to send the same coded message. Even though no one acknowledged my transmissions, I performed my ancillary duties as the communications officer, by continuing to broadcast coded messages in the clear, four times an hour, at ten after, twenty minutes after, twenty minutes to the hour and once again at ten minutes to the hour.

By 0400 hours we were all exhausted but still bailing water. Since this was a serious emergency, I wrote out a much longer message in code and transmitted it in the clear, before I went back to the bow and waited for my turn to bail. Because no one acknowledged my transmissions, we had no way of knowing if the U.S. Customs Agents manning our makeshift listening post, at Homestead Air Force Base, intercepted any of my messages. Worse yet, you needed a code sheet to decode my transmissions.

The fact that the code sheet was kept at the Group 7 trailer complex and at Customs Headquarters meant, that even if someone else heard my transmissions, they would be unable to decode these messages. Fortunately, we knew that Mike R. was available 24 hours a day, to field any calls that might come in about a boat crew transmitting coded messages in the clear, while they drifted at a set of coordinates somewhere between GITMO and Colombia. Naturally, all this was based on the premise, that someone out there in radio land heard my coded distress calls and had the presence of mind to call every U.S. agency under the sun, until they reached the U.S. Customs Service.

As soon as I took my turn hand bailing another twenty buckets of seawater from the flooded bow compartment, I went on the air again and transmitted another emergency message on schedule in the clear. After a while, I became possessed by my duties as the communication officer. As our position changed due to drifting, I made adjustments to my coded message. (I was able to do so because Joe G. kept checking our position.)

While I am not at liberty to disclose the name of the agency that intercepted my mayday style broadcasts, suffice it to say, that a U.S. government listening post intercepted my coded transmissions and used a radio direction finder to determine our position. Once this was done, the duty officer called various federal agencies, including the U.S. Customs Service, to see if they had any personnel out at sea. When the U.S. Customs Service answered the question with a resounding YES, my distress signal was immediately decoded and a search was initiated.

As I have said before, despite the importance of our mission, there was no course entitled Controlled Delivery 101 at the U.S. Customs Training Academy.

In many respects, we were all self taught undercover operatives, who used our combined experiences and our overactive imaginations to prepare ourselves to go into harms way.

GOD BLESS THE UNITED STATES NAVY

We knew my messages got through, when a U.S. Customs aircraft from the Jacksonville Air Branch, that happened to be on TDY status at GITMO, was immediately scrambled and sent to the coordinates that I included in my last transmission. When the U.S. Customs surveillance aircraft located us in the early morning hours, the pilot (call sign Dogman) circled our position to keep us company. While he did so, he relayed our exact position to the U.S. Customs Air Interdiction Center known as C3I. C3I then immediately notified SOUTHCOM (U.S. DOD's Southern Command) and requested that the U.S. Military provide assistance ASAP.

At 0800 hours I was dozing off on deck, when Joe G. woke me up to tell me that the cavalry in the form of a "gray hull" (U.S. Navy surface warfare vessel) was approaching our starboard quarter to provide assistance. As soon as Joe helped me up, I looked over the starboard railing and spotted a magnificent naval vessel heading our way.

Once Joe made radio contact with her skipper, the crew of the USS Blakely lowered two small rubber Zodiac boats over the side and dispatched a Damage Control Party to our vessel to make us seaworthy again. The United States Navy was coming to our rescue. You had to be there to feel the excitement in the air.

As the Damage Control Party traveled the distance between their ship and our vessel, we could see that the sailors were having a rough time of it in the choppy sea. It was at that moment that it really hit me. Despite the politics of The Drug War and everything else that we had to deal with on a regular basis, the force that we could generate once we went operational was one to be reckoned with. As I say throughout this book, when we put our resources together, the drug cartels were no match for us.

Getting the Damage Control Party and all of their equipment into our boat was not an easy task, but one that had to be completed, if we were to continue on our mission. Once this was accomplished, we labored together in the hot sun for several hours until the seawater was pumped out of the bow compartment. As soon as the bow compartment was bone dry, the Damage Control Party went to work sealing the bow hatch, so it would not open again by accident. After working a while longer, the sailors did an outstanding job of securing the hatch and making us seaworthy again.

In exchange for some soft drinks, the U.S. Navy gave us some badly needed fresh coffee, and a box of Transderm medical patches to prevent seasickness. (I must have some set of "sea legs," because I never got seasick whenever I served on any U.S. Customs vessels, including the undercover boat that was used in this operation. I realized this during this trip, when someone noticed the Transderm patch that I wore behind my ear fell off and I never put another one on.)

By 1130 hours we were ready to get underway. Due to the choppy sea conditions, it took some doing, to get the Damage Control Party over the side and into their rubber Zodiac boats. This proved to be no easy task, due to the fact that some of the equipment the sailors used to pump our boat dry was on the heavy side. It was also a bit difficult to pass this equipment over the railing of our vessel and down to the rubber zodiac boats, that were bobbing up and down in choppy seas. Somehow we managed.

Once the fully equipped U.S. Navy Damage Control Party was back in their rubber boats and on their way back to their ship, one of the sailors gave us the thumbs up sign and yelled, "Kick Ass!" As a wide smile crossed my face, I tossed the sailors a salute and screamed, "Fuckin A," before I thought to myself, "God Bless the United States Navy."

I have never felt more proud to be an American Agent than on that day. The presence of our undercover boat was dwarfed by the commanding presence of the magnificent naval vessel that came to our rescue. No matter how much we did to make this case a success, the credit for this controlled delivery deserves to be given to the United States Navy.

WE HAVE NOT YET BEGUN TO FIGHT

As we pulled away from the USS Blakely I could almost here John Paul Jones standing in the rigging and calling out for all to hear, "We have not yet begun to fight!" Thanks to the U.S. Navy it was time for us to get back in action. With a schedule to keep, we proceeded at flank speed to our UNREP, or Underway Replenishing, which was about 75 miles from our final destination. (Mike R. had arranged for us to be refueled at sea by a U.S. Coast Guard cutter, so we would have ample fuel and fresh water to linger off the Colombian coast in case we ran into any delays.)

Once again we traveled throughout the day and night, not caring as much about the sea conditions. We were all wound up and excited that we were nearing our destination. As for me, the adrenaline was pumping through my veins with the force of a New York City Fire hose at a four-alarm fire.

That night we all got some badly needed rest. As I said before, the U.S. Navy technicians did such a great job fixing our air conditioning unit, you could hang meat inside our vessel when the sun went down and the system was on full chill. Before I went to sleep that night, I went out on the stern deck to grab a smoke and think about all that we had survived to get this far. I thought about my family and hoped that my wife calmed down by now. I knew she was scared and concerned about my safety, as well as the security of our family. She had been strong for a long time but everyone had their limits. I also wondered if our marriage would stand the test of time, or if I would end up divorced and alone.

While I looked toward the direction of the Estados Unidos (the U.S.) I called my wife's name out loud and hoped that somehow she heard me. Later on, I would learn that my wife was standing by the sliding glass doors of our home, looking out into the darkness, while she tried to imagine where I was and how

I was doing. As soon as I tossed my cigarette butt over the side of the boat, I decided to hit the sack. It had been a long day and many more were ahead of us.

By 1100 hours the next day, the U.S. Coast Guard Cutter Seneca from Boston was coming up on our stern. Once again our Uncle Sam was on time and on schedule. After the Seneca pulled alongside, she moved into position with our bow facing her stern, while we prepared to receive her boarding party. In no time flat, our crew and the Coast Guard boarding party were laboring alongside each other as lines were passed between our vessels. As soon as the hoses were pulled on board and the proper fittings were secured, 800 gallons of diesel fuel and fresh water was transferred to our vessel.

In order to complete the UNREP, we rode behind the Seneca for over an hour, while we filled our tanks with fuel and fresh water from the cutters' reserves. (The U.S. Navy conducts UNREPS differently and pulls along the side the vessel they intend to refuel. The Navy way is a lot less labor intensive.) Once the refueling and replenishing was completed, a U.S. Coast Guard Lieutenant Junior Grade (JG) met with me and Joe G. to discuss our operational plan. This briefing was necessary, because Mike R. arranged for the cutter to shadow us from a distance of 50 miles once we neared the Colombian coast. Once we left the Colombian coast, the U.S.C.G. Cutter Seneca would lay back some 50 miles and follow us all the way back to Puerto Rico, where we were expected to transfer the coke load to our undercover seaplane.

With our refueling out of the way and our last briefing over, we lowered the Coast Guard Lieutenant over the side of our moving ship and timed his fall perfectly into the Coast Guard Zodiac boat, that was running along our starboard side. As the Coast Guard rubber boat pulled away from us, the entire crew waved goodbye as we steamed toward Colombia.

CHAPTER 22

WELCOME TO COLOMBIA

At 5:15 PM on June 13th, 1990, Special Agent Joe G. throttled back on our engines and turned to me with a big grin on his face. As we shook hands, Joe said something to the effect of, "Congratulations, Nicky, we made it. Welcome to Colombia." From 12 miles offshore Colombia didn't look all that menacing. With the exception of two freighters that were way off in the distance, there were no other vessels in the immediate vicinity.

As I mentioned before, we knew the U.S. Coast Guard Cutter Seneca was shadowing us from a distance of 50 miles away. Even though her presence gave us some comfort, we knew that if the shit hit the fan, we would be on our own until the Seneca was able to reach our position. Regardless, it was nice to know that a little bit of America was not all that far away.

Shortly after we arrived on station, the crew and I assembled in the wheelhouse in preparation of making contact with the Colombians. Once I tuned in the proper radio frequency, I took a deep breath and exhaled before I spoke into the microphone and said, "Pluto, Pluto this is Popeye." After receiving no answer I tried again. This time a voice responded and said, "Popeye, Popeye, Popeye." As I smiled wide, I wasn't alone. The entire crew felt the same way that I did and reacted as if it was all worth it, when I made contact with Aldo, the fugitive who would be riding back with us.

Once I made contact with Aldo, I reconfirmed our previously agreed upon plans and gave him our position. By the sound of his voice, I could tell that Aldo was just as excited to hear from us, as we were to hear from him. Once Aldo told me that he was on the way, I felt the weight of the world lift from my shoulders. So far, so good. As I clipped the microphone back on the radio that was secured to the roof of the wheelhouse, I was in very good spirits and felt as if victory was finally within reach. Come on you bastard I thought to myself. Bring your coke load out here and get on our boat. We'll take you to America, I promise!

Now that we knew that the cocaine shipment and our two passengers were on the way, we used the time to prepare for their arrival. While Mike C. stashed a 12 gauge shotgun on the stern deck in a metal deck locker, Jimmy E. put an M16 that was fitted with a scope up on the top deck near the aft steering house. Jimmy used one of our rafts to hide the rifle along with an ample supply of 30 round magazines. We also hid a loaded Colt CAR15 assault rifle and a Remington 12 gauge pump shotgun in the wheelhouse for Joe G. to use if the "you know what" hit the fan.

After I stashed my 9mm Smith & Wesson service pistol in an appropriate place, I tucked my stainless Walther PPK and three spare magazines under a Banana Republic Vest and returned to man the radio when I heard Aldo call and say, "Popeye, can you come in closer to shore?"

"You're unreadable," I answered, even though I heard his request loud and clear.

Even though it would have been very easy to move closer into shore, we would be subjected to the equivalent of a court marshal if we violated the rules of engagement. Things began to unravel when Pluto (Aldo) called out over the radio and said, "Where are you, Popeye? Do you see the freighter?"

I paused before giving my answer, "I'm right here. You picked the spot. Let's go!"

"Can you come in closer, it's all right," he said again.

"We'll wait right here, we're not moving," I answered firmly.

As darkness fell, the sea became a little calmer. This would make it easier for us to transfer the coke load and our two passengers if they ever showed up. When it became apparent that we were starting to drift closer to the forbidden zone, Joe G. had Jimmy E. crank up our engines so we did not get any closer to the Colombia than 12 miles. To complicate things even more, it was getting late. Soon it would be pitch black out and impossible to see anything.

While Aldo raced toward our position in a vessel, that was described to us as being a small open fishing boat, I continued to call him on the two-meter radio, to guide him closer to us as the clock struck 7 PM. When Aldo's voice seemed to get louder and clearer we knew that he was getting a lot closer. As it got darker, I heard panic in Aldo's voice when he said he still couldn't see us. When Also pleaded with me to come closer to shore, I turned to Joe G. for advice.

Unless we did something to help the bad guys find us in the dark, we might never pick this load up. A lot could happen if the Colombians got disgusted and went back to the beach. If they got cold feet about traveling too far off shore, they might demand that we move in a lot closer. If that happened, we would be up the proverbial creek without a paddle. As usual, Joe G. thought fast and said something like, "Tell him to aim for the light." Joe then stepped outside onto the upper deck and turned on the searchlight, that was fixed to the top of the superstructure above the wheelhouse.

As soon as Joe illuminated the area above our vessel, an excited Aldo called out over the radio and said, "I see your light."

Once again I felt a wave of relief come over me like a Tsunami hitting the beach. Thanks to a quick thinking Joe G., we were back in the game and there was hope that we might pull this off yet. All we needed now, was the Colombians to make their way to our position without sinking and we would be in business.

While Joe G. and I stood on the port side of the UC vessel, we strained our eyes as we peered into the darkness and tried to spot the approaching Colombians. It was amazing how almost out of nowhere, the small boat came into view and approached us from the east. "That's their boat?" I remarked, before I shook my head in disbelief as the Colombians pulled up along our stern.

You had to be there to appreciate what it was like, when the bad guys finally arrived. Here we were in the middle of a multi-million dollar dope deal and these characters showed up in an old lifeboat, that had a motor strapped on the back.

Clearly, their "boat captain" either had big balls and no brains, or a combination of both, to venture this far offshore loaded with over 700 plus kilos of cocaine and six passengers, in an open boat that had seen better days. Then again, we weren't exactly playing with a full deck to have done some of the stuff that we did either.

Even with our engines in neutral, the small boat rocked back and forth as the Colombians received our cargo net that was lowered from our stern deck. After yelling some instructions back and forth, the Colombians placed two packages that contained about 40 kilos on our deck. When one of the Colombians went to put a third package on the stern deck of the UC vessel, the package went KAPLUNK into the dark green ocean. No sooner did that happen did everyone, including us, go berserk. Somehow I managed to hold the beam of a flashlight on the twenty-kilo package, as it floated away in the current, while one of the Colombians went out of his mind and acted as if his firstborn had just been swept away.

After I screamed, "Calmate! Calmate," we managed to get the bad guys to retrieve the package that drifted off into the darkness. In the process of them doing so, we lost sight of the Colombians. Even though they were out there, we couldn't always see them, as they circled our boat. Clearly, we hadn't come all this way for two measly packages of cocaine, even though it was more cocaine, than 99.9% of all the cops in America would ever seize in a twenty year career. After all we had been through, we wanted the full enchilada, so I wasted no time in getting back on the radio.

"Popeye, Popeye, come in," cried Aldo in a high-pitched tone of voice.

When I responded I said, "This is Popeye, go ahead."

"They're afraid to come back. Your boat's too big," said Aldo.

What the hell was wrong with these assholes I thought to myself, as I used a firm tone of voice to respond to Aldo's last remark and said, "What did you think we were gonna come all the way down here in, a fucking bass boat? "Tell them to calm down. We're gonna try it another way!"

"They're afraid of your engines," Aldo yelled over the radio.

Thinking fast I called out over the radio and said, "Tell your Captain to come alongside. We'll do it from the starboard side."

When Aldo reported that his boat crew was reluctant to come near our boat, I knew if we didn't make these characters happy, they would never come back and we would have done all this work for almost nothing. As the seconds passed like hours, my Cuban CI, Hombre de la Calle, appeared from nowhere. While we exchanged glances, I knew Hombre could see the desperate look on my face.

As he reached out and asked for the radio mic, Hombre spoke in a very calm and friendly tone of voice (in Spanish) and assured the Colombian boat captain, that we would hang rubber fenders over the starboard side of our vessel, so his vessel would not be damaged by our boat once he came along side. When Aldo came back on the air and enthusiastically said, "OK, OK, they'll do it," Hombre smiled and handed me the radio mic. We were back in business thanks to my favorite Cuban CI. Hombre de la Calle.

You can say what you want about Hombre aka Gordo being a former drug smuggler who never got caught, but now that he was a Blade Runner, he was as valuable of an asset to our cause, as any secret weapon was in the arsenal of democracy. It was moments like this, that also made me feel, that all the time I spent cultivating and directing my sources of information and contract personnel was worth it.

While the dilapidated relic of an open boat pulled up along our starboard side, we put out the rubber fenders and prepared to transfer the rest of the coke load and our two passengers onto our vessel. As usual, Joe G. was like the TV character "Mc Giver" and designed a retrieval system using metal mountain climbing clips and long sections of very sturdy nylon deck line. While my colleagues threw the specially modified lines over the side, so the Colombians could secure packages of cocaine to the nylon line, I used a long boat hook to grab one package at a time from the Colombian vessel. In no time we were pulling "package" after "package" over the side of our boat and filling the stern deck with an impressive amount of cocaine.

We worked fast and furious to get the entire load onto our deck. At one point Aldo tried to climb on board our vessel, but I yelled at him to get back and said, "You can't come on until we get the whole load." (That guy was so fed up with the conditions in Colombia, I'm convinced that he would have walked on water to get on our vessel.)

As Aldo begrudgingly complied and sat back down on the Colombian vessel,

I could see that he was not a happy camper. Personally, I didn't care how he felt, since our survival depended on us always being in complete control. Then, one of the Colombians lost his grip and sent another twenty kilo package into the drink between our two boats! "Relaxo! Relaxo!" we yelled, then "Calmate!" Fortunately, the package of cocaine was recovered, just as Aldo yelled, "Don't get it wet."

As I looked down at Aldo and the other bad guys I thought to myself, "You fucking assholes. If you only knew that you just handed your precious drug cargo over to a group of undercover U.S. Customs Agents. Who gives a shit how wet it gets, no one will ever get the chance to put this poison up their nose. Not now."

As soon as the last few packages were pulled into our boat, Aldo ran up the line like a rat scurrying onto an old freighter in a filthy harbor. Then came the cartel representative, who was responsible to keep an eye on the merchandise and report back to the source of supply, once the shipment arrived safely in the United States. The bad guy I would end up calling Shithead looked like he was the expendable type. This poor bastard was so seasick when he got on board our vessel, I actually found myself feeling sorry for this Colombian, even though he was the enemy.

As the Colombian vessel prepared to pull away from us, I called down to the crew and asked if they wanted some beer. Once the word "cerveza" got their attention, I yelled over to Chuck W. to give them some beer. I never expected Chuck to throw them the beer like he was passing them the kitchen sink. I thought for sure that Chuck was going to send that case of Budweiser right through the bottom of their boat, by the sound it made when it landed in the bottom of the Colombian vessel.

While the Colombian boat crew headed back to shore, I greeted our guests. In order to keep the case alive and get the others who were involved, we had to play along and fulfill our roles as bad guys. As soon as Aldo approached me, he extended his hand and said, "You must be Popeye." After I introduced Aldo to "my boat captain," I was introduced to the seasick Colombian who represented the source of supply. As far as the two bad guys were concerned, my boat crew and my plane crew would provide the transportation services to deliver the cocaine shipment all the way to New Mexico. In return, Aldo also knew that my colleagues and I expected to be paid $4,500 per kilo when the cocaine was delivered to the stateside receivers.

The first order of business was to secure the coke load and inform our passengers about the rules of the boat. Everyone, including our guests, carried the cocaine into our vessel, until the entire shipment was stored below and wrapped in a plastic tarp, to prevent any additional salt water damage. (After all, we had to make it look good.)

Once we finished storing the cocaine, I handed the seasick Colombian (Shithead) a full gallon of fresh water and told him in a firm tone to drink plenty of fluid, to replace what he was losing every time he threw up. As soon as Aldo translated what I said, the young kid nodded his head and seemed to appreciate my concern for his well being. It would have been so easy to let the seasick Colombian dehydrate and suffer like a dog. Enemy or not, for some reason, I could not bring myself to let this kid get any worse off than he was.

I then let Aldo take a fast shower, while his companion continued to throw up and pass out on a couch in the main cabin behind the wheelhouse. While Aldo was drying off, he asked me if I had a cigarette. Being a gracious host, I reached into our supply locker and removed a full carton of American cigarettes. When Aldo told me that he preferred a different brand, I decided to make a point by ripping the carton out of his hand, as I remarked how I would do better the next time we passed by a fucking convenience store. Aldo realized that he would have to eat humble pie or do without cigarettes, so he changed his scumbag like disposition and graciously accepted the free carton of smokes.

Rather than have our guests stay near our cabins where we our extra weapons were hidden, we told Aldo and Shithead, that they could sleep on the long vinyl couches in the upper aft compartment behind the wheelhouse. Since Shithead was already camped out there, Aldo settled in and made himself at home. As the young Colombian puked his guts up, passed out and puked some more, Aldo was given a clean sheet and curled up across the way from his amigo. I also gave our seasick Colombian passenger a bed sheet, so he could be more comfortable while laying under the ice cold air-conditioning unit.

As our vessel cruised along with a following sea, I could not help but marvel at all that we had accomplished. Even though it took a year to get to this point, my colleagues and I were able to pick up over 700 kilos of cocaine and two bad guys from Colombia. Best yet, we did so by circumventing the rules of engagement and operating in such a fashion that did not require country clearance from DEA.

While Aldo and Shithead fell fast asleep, Joe G. was able to quietly pass a message to the U.S. Coast Guard Cutter Seneca that all was well. With the Cutter Seneca shadowing us from a safe distance, we made our way toward the Mona Passage.

Every time Hombre de la Calle walked by the small mountain of cocaine that was piled high down below, he shook his head and said, "Nicky, I see it, but I don't believe it." We were all ecstatic and had to resist the urge to scream at the mere sight of the large quantity of drug contraband and all that we had accomplished.

It would be a long and uneasy night for most of us, especially since we had to sleep with the two Colombian bad guys on board our vessel. Amazingly though, it did not take long for everyone to get into role. With the two bad guys under constant surveillance by at least one of us at all time, the rest of the undercover crew rested while we continued on our journey.

CHAPTER 23

BORN TO BE WILD

As the sun came up over the horizon, the Stepenwolf song "Born to Be Wild" was playing in the wheelhouse, while MEO Mike C. steered our undercover vessel toward the rendezvous point.

When I met Aldo in the wheelhouse, he seemed to be in an exceptionally good mood and made a comment about how impressed he was with our operation. As much as I despised this guy, I took what he said as a compliment, because it meant that whatever we were doing to act like real smugglers was working. This was made possible because our entire crew was putting on one hell of a show.

By 0800 hours on Friday, June 15th, 1990 we had the Mona Passage in sight. The small Island of Mona was about 35 miles from the main island of Puerto Rico. As I mentioned earlier, in order to avoid having to get country clearance to operate in foreign territory, we decided to make the transfer to the undercover seaplane in U.S. territory.

While we watched the movie Midnight Run on our VCR, Aldo broached the topic of having us run additional loads for him. "Get me to a phone as soon as I get back and I'll order up another 1000 kilos," he said.

"Sounds great, Aldo, but let's get paid for this one first," was my answer.

"No problem, you'll get your money in a few days," remarked Aldo.

Aldo and I got along OK on this trip, even though I continued to despise him with a passion. In addition to the fact that he had the personality of food poisoning, Aldo had a serious attitude problem. This made dealing with Aldo one big mind game. Personally, I couldn't wait to turn him over to Special Agent James. S in New Mexico.

Despite the fact that he was the enemy, Aldo was made as comfortable as possible during our journey. On the only two nights when the seas were calm enough to allow us to really cook dinner, we fed Aldo a meal that was fit for a king. We kept him in cigarettes, soda, food and warm blankets, especially when the air conditioning got exceptionally cold during the night. We ate together and slept only a few feet from each other. We even shared the one toilet and shower together. You might say that we were one big happy family.

Sometimes, no matter how much planning you put into an operation, it is impossible to prevent a disaster from occurring. The sight of a 110 foot U.S. Coast Guard Cutter heading straight for us when we entered the Mona Passage, was enough to ruin everyone's day, especially Aldo's.

"Get below now!" I yelled to Aldo, "and take that fucking loser with you!" referring to the seasick cartel representative.

I was right behind them, as they nearly fell down the aft ladder to the compartment where the coke load was stashed. I could see by the expressions on their faces that I had their undivided attention, when I reassured them that everything was still under control. "The company we rented this boat from is legit. Once they run our name, they'll realize that we're a real research vessel. We're not on any hot sheet, so there's a good chance that they'll check us out and leave. Besides, it's still a little too rough for them to board us." Once Aldo translated what I said to his very concerned traveling companion, I tried to sound as reassuring as possible, when I instructed our two passengers to stay put.

As undercover agents trying to execute a controlled delivery, we desperately needed to keep the charade going, right up until it was time to execute the delivery phase and make our arrests. Clearly, the last thing that we needed was to have a U.S. Coast Guard crew board our vessel. Whether this Coast Guard crew stumbled on our presence, were out of the loop as far as the nature of our undercover operation was concerned, or they knew who we were and got too close, didn't matter. All that mattered was preserving the covert nature of our mission. Keep in mind, that the Coast Guard was supposed to shadow us, to provide assistance in case we ran into trouble. They weren't supposed to get close enough to be seen, or God forbid attempt to board our vessel.

While Hombre de la Calle kept an eye on our guests, I ran up the ladder to see what was going on. When I got up topside I gave Joe G. the OK sign and went out on the stern deck. By this time the Coast Guard cutter was in radio contact with Joe and had been quietly tipped off to who we really were. As soon as I made my way out on the stern deck, I joined the other agents who were standing along the starboard side guardrail.

"Commence waving and smiling," I said as the U.S. Cost Guard patrol boat continued to trail alongside. I knew that they would leave eventually, or at least I hoped they would, so I hustled back inside and went below.

As I did my best to appear relieved, I looked at Aldo and said something to the effect of, "You can relax, they're leaving."

After hearing what I said, Aldo appeared equally as relieved, as he took a long drag on his cigarette, after having experienced such a close call.

I then went on to say, "Once they checked us out and we came up clean they had no reason to board us. Let's stay outta sight. The last thing we need them to see is any Hispanic guys on board." Once again, Aldo relayed my words to the representative of the source of supply, who sat frozen near the pile of cocaine that he had been sent to keep an eye on.

THE PLANE, THE PLANE

Shorty after we arrived in the Mona Passage, the undercover seaplane appeared overhead. That was the good news. The bad news was, that the conditions in the Mona Passage were too rough for our seaplane to land. Fortunately, we selected an alternate pickup point, that was some distance away inside the bay near Mayaguez, Puerto Rico. Even though the last thing that we wanted to do was take another boat ride, we had no choice but to do so. After a very rough ride, we finally arrived in the Bay of Mayaguez.

As soon as we were in position at the alternate transfer point, we started to carry the coke load out on deck. Although Aldo seemed very interested in pitching in to help us out, Shithead was inside the main cabin watching the end of a movie on the VCR. With all hands out on the stern deck and getting ready to load the Zodiac boat, I turned around to count heads. I did this throughout this voyage, to make sure that I knew where the two bad guys were at all times. When I realized that Shithead was missing I yelled out to Chuck, "Where's Shithead?"

By this point in our trip, Agent Chuck W. seemed to be just as disgusted with the lazy Colombian observer as the rest of us. When Chuck told me that Shithead was watching TV, I called out for everyone including Aldo to hear and screamed, "Tell that mother fucking loser to stop watching cartoons and get his fucking ass out here and help!"

Aldo knew that we were all pissed off at his traveling companion. "I'll get him," Aldo said as he quickly ran into the main cabin and yelled at Shithead to move his ass and get out on deck to help us.

The undercover seaplane was a sight for sore eyes, as it came in low over the bay, then banked and came in for a landing near the undercover vessel. Once again we were doing business like the bad guys. As soon as the UC plane touched down in the calm Bay of Mayaguez, we used a rubber Zodiac boat to shuttle the coke load, then our luggage over to the open cargo door. After thanking Joe G. and his crew for a job well done, I went over the side and joined Jimmy E, Chuck W., Aldo, Shithead and Hombre de la Calle in the rubber boat. Once Jimmy E. took us over to the seaplane, we climbed on board through the port side cargo hatch. Just as I was about to leave the Zodiac boat, I smiled and said goodbye to Customs Officer Jimmy E.

Once I made it into the seaplane, Mike R. secured the hatch. As I looked around, I saw that the cargo bay was filled with 700 plus kilos of cocaine, a large cooler full of food, soda and bottled water, several pieces of luggage, as well as our two passengers, Chuck W. and our Cuban CI (Hombre). Since we were carrying passengers in addition to cargo on this flight, we had our crew chief (Johnny Walker) install some airline seats in the cargo section. This enabled passengers riding in the back to buckle up during take offs and landings.

While I instructed everyone in the cargo bay to take their seats and prepare for take off, Mike R. followed me into the cockpit. After exchanging grins with Captain Video and The Salesman, I called out, "Let's Go," as I sat in the seat behind the Contract Pilot in Command and buckled up. As soon as Mike R. sat behind The Salesman, our two contract pilots applied full power to the engines of the tired old warbird that we rented for this mission.

Because we were overloaded with cargo, passengers and fuel, it took a long time after Captain Video applied full power for the radial engines to get us airborne. Initially, the seaplane picked up enough speed to lift off the water for a few seconds, before it settled back down and continued to surf the nice calm bay at flank speed. This process continued for a bit, until the undercover seaplane remained airborne and we slowly climbed higher and higher into the sky. Once we reached our cruising altitude, we leveled off and headed straight for Miami.

As I patted Captain Video on the back and exchanged glances with The Salesmen and Mike R., I felt incredibly proud of everyone who contributed to making this case possible. I then looked into the cargo bay and cracked a smile as I gave everyone in the back the thumbs up. Even though no words were spoken, Special Agent Chuck W. and Hombre knew exactly what I was thinking.

In addition to transporting the 700 plus kilos of cocaine to our agents in New Mexico, we had two major violators on board, who had no idea that they were technically in custody. It was moments like this that I would savor for the rest of my life. Best yet, for the first time in over a week, I was able to sit back and relax, while we lumbered along at 140 knots and headed for our undercover refueling site in South Florida. Naturally, Shithead was out like a light and slept for most of the trip. When Aldo finally dozed off, Mike and Chuck kept an eye on our passengers, while I closed my eyes and nodded off. (While the bad guys were asleep, we used that time to squeeze their soft luggage to see if we could feel the presence of any weapons. When none were found, we felt safer being in their presence, now that we knew that we were the only people on board our plane who were armed.)

The next five hours passed by pretty quickly, considering that I slept for almost three of them. Once I got up, Mike fell asleep on an air mattress in the back of the plane, while Aldo woke up and seemed to be enjoying the flight. Fortunately, the sun was setting in the west as we approached the Florida coastline. We hoped that this would enable us to fool our passengers into believing, that they were in Louisiana and not in South Florida; a place that no self respecting smuggler would intentionally land with a load of cocaine on board their plane.

With nightfall on our side and air cover provided by a U.S. Customs Citation Jet and the Albuquerque based U.S. Customs King Air C12 aircraft, we prepared to land at a little past 8:30 P.M. As we approached the South Florida coastline, I told Aldo to wake up Shithead and hide in the bathroom. I explained that we had our own refueling setup in the ass end of Louisiana and that we paid our people by the pound of cargo and the number of passengers on board. I also wanted to protect their identity and keep anyone from getting a good look at our two passengers.

Under the circumstances Aldo and Shithead obeyed my instructions. As I ushered them into the bathroom in the back of the plane, I handed them a gallon of fresh water and told them to be quiet and stay put, until I told them it was safe to come out. Once I closed the door, I locked it to make sure they would remain under wraps, while we refueled the plane at one of our undercover fixed base operations in South Florida. (During the planning stages for this mission, we covered the small port hole window in the head (bathroom) on the UC seaplane, to prevent the bad guys from being able to see outside during the undercover refueling.)

Light on fuel, we settled down on the long runway and taxied over to the spot where Rob K. and a several Group 7 agents were waiting with The Gambler, Johnny Walker and two fuel trucks. The second we came to a stop, Johnny

Walker pulled a fuel truck into position and began refueling the plane.

The South Florida air smelled great when Mike R. opened the cargo door on the port side of the seaplane and extended the ladder. As I stepped down onto the tarmac, The Gambler was there to meet me. After I put my right index finger up to my lips, to signal The Gambler to watch what he said, we exchanged smiles and shook hands as I remarked, "Could you check the oil and tires please and filler up."

As The Gambler shook his head and remarked, "Loads R Us," he walked over to help Johnny Walker, while I joined Rob K. and several agents from Group 7 (Pat R, Joe A., Mike C. and Frank S.) who were standing off to the side. Congratulations and handshakes came from everywhere.

While The Gambler and Johnny Walker serviced the undercover plane, I gave Rob and the other agents a quick briefing. Immediately after Senior Special Agent Pat R. gave me $5,000 dollars in expense money and a box of super large hero sandwiches to take along on the rest of our trip, I called my home to tell my wife and sons that I was OK. Fortunately, my wife was in very good spirits and glad to hear my voice.

Just about the time that I finished my phone call, the fuel truck started to pull away from the undercover aircraft. As soon as I joined the others, I heard the bad news that we had a small fuel leak in the port side float tank due to corrosion. After all we had done, the entire mission was in danger of being scrubbed, because our plane was leaking fuel. Fortunately, Captain Video and

The Gambler were not about to see us shut the operation down, because of a little corrosion on the port side wing float tank.

In order to solve this problem, Captain Video asked for a bar of soap, preferably Ivory. As soon as Pat R. returned with the biggest piece of soap he could find, Captain Video proceeded to vigorously rub the soap back and forth over the rusted area. When I remarked, "I could just see NASA using a bar of soap to plug a leak on the space shuttle," The Gambler grinned in a devilish fashion and said, "Where do you think we learned this trick?"

Once our makeshift repair was made, we said goodbye to everyone, including Hombre de la Calle. (Hombre remained behind because his services were not needed from this point on.) When Captain Video turned to me and said, "Are you ready?," I didn't know what to say. While part of me was tempted for a second to go home, the rest of me knew that going home was not an option. Rather than walk out during the intermission, I decided to go along for the ride, so I could see how the rest of this adventure unfolded.

CHAPTER 24

GO WEST YOUNG MAN GO WEST

As I climbed back into the undercover seaplane, I looked up and could hear the U.S. Customs Citation Jet running lights out and circling overhead. Once Mike R. and I secured the cargo hatch and gave the cockpit crew the signal to go, I opened the bathroom door and told Aldo and Shithead to have a seat, because we were about to take off. While the two bad guys complied, I went up front with Mike, while Chuck stayed in the back with our guests.

As soon as we took off, Captain Video told me to look to my left. As I looked out the port side cockpit window, I could see a stream of aviation fuel leaking out of the left wing float. "I guess we should have used Ivory," was all I could think to say. Fortunately, Captain Video solved the problem by immediately transferring fuel from the port side wing float to the main fuel tanks.

The weather could not have been better as we flew across the Gulf of Mexico. While Customs Pilots Steve S. and Ben W. followed us in a C12 (King Air) aircraft, we ate our "hero" sandwiches and drank a few sodas to fight off the boredom. When our two passengers finally went to sleep, Chuck, Mike and I took turns staying awake, so one of us would always be keeping an eye on the two bad guys.

The flight cross-country in a slow moving former military seaplane seemed as if it would never end. The fact that all of us had been on the go for weeks on end, made it difficult for us to stay awake, while we traveled at what seemed like a snails pace across the sky. Still, it was all part of the show.

When we landed in Texas at 0400 hours to replenish our engine oil, a U.S. Customs Citation Jet from the Houston Air Branch circled our position to cover us, while the Albuquerque based King Air C12 landed at a different location to refuel. After servicing our engines, we took off from Hobbie Field with our escort planes keeping an eye on us, while we proceeded to New Mexico. As we continued on our journey, Aldo joined us in the cockpit. I could tell by the look on his face that he was impressed. Thank God he did not stay with us long. Before we knew it, the prick was in the back sleeping on a pile of cocaine.

While I sat behind Captain Video and admired the view, we cruised along at less than four thousand feet. When the sun came up, the vastness of the American Southwest filled the cockpit windshield. Even though I always loved the ocean, there was something clean and breathtaking about the terrain in the Southwest. That included the desert, where a native New Yorker like me described an arroyo as a ditch without water. (I'm sure all the westerns I watched in my life had something to do with my infatuation with the west.)

Once we reached New Mexico, we were on the last leg of our journey. Our plan was to land on a road located smack in the middle of nowhere, under the watchful eyes of a contingent of U.S. Customs Agents and Air Officers. As our crew began to go over their checklist procedures, we began to straighten up the cargo bay of the aircraft. Besides our cache of cocaine, we had luggage, cases of food, coolers full of soda and beer, rescue equipment, a large life raft, tools, cans of oil, blankets and a large box of fresh fruit that Mike R. purchased. (I teased my partner Mike R. that the reason he filled our undercover aircraft with so much fresh fruit was to prevent scurvy.) Once we took our positions to land, Mr. Obnoxious (Aldo) stuck his face in the cockpit a few times to see what was going on.

Not including our time on the ground in Florida and Texas we had been airborne for $17\ ^{1/2}$ hours. "That's it," said The Salesman, as he pointed to a narrow stretch of road near a drilling rig that was to serve as our makeshift runway. At first, I didn't believe it. We went through all of this and we had to land on a narrow road in the middle of the desert, that was uphill to boot. If this wasn't our wildest adventure to date, I don't know what was.

The sound of the landing gear extending was enough to snap me back into reality. There it was directly ahead of us; a long narrow road that gradually went higher in elevation and ended near the crest of a small hill. With our flaps and gear down and our airspeed reduced, we flew over the scrub pine and sage brush and came straight in as if we were making a carrier landing. As soon as we touched down, Captain Video taxied the aircraft uphill to the crest of the road, where he turned the seaplane around before he shut the engines off. The time was 0800 hours or 8AM.

WELCOME TO THE MIDDLE OF NOWHERE

As soon as I opened the port side cargo door hatch, I felt a refreshing blast of cold desert air hit me in the face. When I quickly scanned the desert around the clandestine off load site, I knew that we weren't alone and were surrounded by a number of well concealed agents and air officers.

The second I started to extend the ladder, Aldo arrived by my side with his bags in hand. When I turned to face this prick, he remarked, "He'll stay with the load," referring to his useless Colombian sidekick.

There he goes again giving orders I thought. "No!" I said, "He's going with you! He's useless!" Since I had Aldo's undivided attention I continued and said, "All I want you to do is go get my money. We'll take care of the load."

For some reason Aldo didn't argue. I guess he could tell by my tone of voice and my body language, that I was in no mood for his demanding bullshit. Instead, he said, "He's coming with me," referring to the Colombian violator I called Shithead.

"Let's go!" I said with a sound of urgency in my voice. Even though I pissed on his parade, Aldo and Shithead climbed out of the plane and waited for their ride to show up. As soon as Undercover Special Agent Jim S. drove up and parked, I ushered our two passengers over to the undercover car and made the introductions before I said goodbye.

Once Aldo and Shithead were sitting in the undercover car, Jim asked me if they gave us any trouble. As I stood off to the side, I wasted no time in saying something to the effect of, "Aldo's a first class prick and all the kid does it puke and sleep. Other than that, they're the life of the party."

After shaking hands with UC Agent Jim S., he told me to sit tight while the off load crew moved into position. Since his job was done and he was needed to help Agent Jim S. orchestrate the final phase of the controlled delivery, The Salesman left the plane with his luggage in hand and said goodbye, as he joined the others in the undercover car.

When Jim S. started to drive away, Aldo glanced back and made eye contact with me. I could tell he wasn't a happy camper. It was one of those situations, when we both knew that I disturbed his big plan and he had no choice but to do things my way, because he was on my turf. Had the situation been reversed, I would've been the one with the annoyed look on my face.

As soon Jim S. and the others drove away, a second vehicle followed by a large yellow Ryder truck drove up and parked next to the undercover aircraft. While a dozen heavily armed U.S. Customs Agents and Air Officers in camouflage clothing began to swarm around the plane, I was surprised to see a local news station film crew jump out of one of the vehicles and start filming the undercover aircraft. As I held up my hands and physically blocked their access to the aircraft, Special Agent Larry F. from the local RAC Office identified himself and told me that the news crew was cleared to film our plane and the off load. Naturally, my reaction was one of complete shock when I said, "What!" before I quickly added, "But this is supposed to be an undercover operation!"

According to Larry, the U.S. Customs Commissioner authorized a local news station to film our otherwise clandestine undercover operation in the desert. Even when the head honcho from the film crew tried to reassure me that he wouldn't film our faces, I thought this was an idiotic idea. Filming the clandestine offload of our aircraft made about as much sense, as me getting this book published, while we were actively executing a succession of transportation cases/controlled deliveries. What a deal I thought to myself, as I got into a huddle with my fellow undercover operatives, to avoid being filmed by a local news crew, that was foolishly given permission to document our undercover operation in the New Mexico desert.

While I stood off to the side in complete shock, Special Agent Larry F. continued and said, "Nick, you guys have done enough. We'll off load the plane."

Under the circumstances I was too tired to argue and appreciated the gesture, besides it was nice to sit on the sidelines and watch someone else hump this load around for a change.

As soon as the off load crew moved into position and started to unload the cocaine shipment from our plane, a young U.S. Customs Agent looked up at the undercover aircraft and made a bit of a face, while he admired the miss matched colored paint scheme and remarked, "You flew all the way here in that thing?" Considering the fact that I was very proud of the latest addition to our fleet, I couldn't help but smile and comment something to the effect of, "She sure looks like shit, but boy can she fly."

SANTA FE IS THAT'A WAY

Once the plane was off loaded and the local agents prepared to leave, Agent Larry F. told us that the Resident Agent in Charge and a special agent were waiting for us in Santa Fe.

"Santa Fe?" I said.

"Yea, Nick," responded Larry, who quickly added, "We need you to stash the plane up there." When I asked Larry where the hell Santa Fe was, he pointed off into the distance and told us that our final destination was about 60 miles to the north. As I looked at our "runway" I noticed that we would be taking off downhill.

Here we were just getting used to having our feet planted firmly on the ground, when we were told that we had to fly another 60 miles before we could call it a day. With nothing else to do but fly north, I turned to Captain Video and remarked in a New England accent, "Can't get there from here."

ON TO SANTA FE

"Hi Ho, Hi Ho, it's off to work we go," was the tune I sung as we all climbed back into the aircraft we nicknamed "The Blade Runner." Once again, we started our engines and prepared for take off. As soon as Captain Video completed the engine run up and he made sure that all systems were working as required, he applied full power. As we picked up speed, I felt as if I was previewing a new ride at Universal Studios.

Once we were airborne, we began to spot the landmarks that the local agents said that we would see from the air. (We had to use landmarks because we didn't have any maps or air charts of the area.) After about 45 minutes of flying, we arrived at Santa Fe and requested permission to land.

As soon as the ramp personnel at the fixed base operation where we decided to park approached our plane, they had all sorts of questions about the colorful looking vintage seaplane that we were flying. Since I had no intention of telling the FBO Operators the true nature of our identity, or the real purpose of our visit to New Mexico, I told the curious locals that the plane was being used in a movie.

Once we unloaded our gear from the undercover aircraft, we were driven back to Albuquerque by agents from the local RAC Office and settled into a nice hotel. As soon as Agent Jim S. and The Salesman got Aldo and Shithead settled in a local motel, we met for diner at Los Quates Restaurant on Lomas Avenue. For the record, Los Quates is with a doubt the best Mexican Restaurant in the United States of America bar none.

Even though the people at a nearby table must have thought we were crazy, we celebrated our victory when we sang our theme song to the music of the Star Spangled Banner. "Ho Ho Zay (Jose) can you see... this is a controlled delivery!" It took a year for us to celebrate the success of this case and I am here to tell you that it was worth it.

THANKS FOR THE COCAINE BUT THE MIAMI AGENTS ARE NOT WANTED

Unfortunately, the next day our morale sank to an all time low, when we reported for duty and we were told, that the local Special Agent in Charge didn't want any Miami agents involved in this controlled delivery. In other words, thank you very much, but don't let the door hit you in the ass on the way out. (The SAC in El Paso, Texas covered Albuquerque.)

As pissed off as we were, we had no choice but to leave the office. Based on what we were told, after all that we did to make this case a reality for our agents in New Mexico, their SAC (Special Agent in Charge) no longer wanted us involved. Regardless of whether this order came from the SAC, or someone else, it was a bad call as far as we were concerned.

For the next eight days we monitored the progress of the case from the sidelines. In the meantime, we caught up on our sleep, had our undercover plane serviced and ate excellent Mexican food for breakfast, lunch and dinner. By the end of the week, things were heating up, as our agents in Los Angeles were asked to follow Aldo's associates around tinsel town.

Despite the fact that we were kept out of the final phase of this transportation case, I ended up learning about the progress that was being in this case, by my good friend, Senior Special Agent Steve Di C. and Alan D. the Resident Agent in Charge (RAC LAX) from Los Angeles. These agents contacted me in my hotel room in New Mexico, after they were asked to monitor the activities of the stateside receivers, who were operating on the west coast. During this conversation I briefed Steve and Alan about what we did to help make this case and they briefed me about the events as they unfolded in LA. By the way, our agents in LA did an excellent job of conducting surveillance's in support of this controlled delivery.

ARRESTING BAD GUYS-THE FINAL PHASE OF A CONTROLLED DELIVERY

Before you can really understand how the take down went, I need to backtrack a bit. As I mentioned a few pages ago, a very strange thing happened when a local news station camera crew was allowed to film the arrival of our undercover aircraft in the New Mexico desert. As I was told at the time, the deal with the local film crew was simple. They got to film this part of our undercover operation, as long as they did not air the film footage until the case was over.

At the risk of sounding melodramatic, lives were at stake, not to mention a case that many of us had worked very hard to make. I should also mention, that trusting the media did not come easy for law enforcement officers, because we were indoctrinated to say "no comment," whenever we were approached to make a statement about a case.

The last thing that Undercover Agent Jim S. or The Salesman needed to have happen, while they were meeting with the Colombians in a hotel room in Albuquerque, was to have the local TV news station play the "top secret" film footage, of 700 plus kilos of cocaine being off loaded from a very unique looking undercover seaplane in the New Mexico desert. (This was relayed to me by our undercover personnel.) This was the kind of stuff that they can't prepare you for in undercover school. Because he was an outstanding undercover agent, Jim S. was able to calmly walk right by the TV and shut if off, while Aldo was busy talking on the phone.

Fortunately, the Colombians didn't notice the film footage on the local TV news. Perhaps the Colombians had cabin fever. Either way, it was our good fortune that the two Colombians were not paying attention to the television at that time. The only other explanation that I can think of, is that God has a special team of guardian angels looking out for the best interest of undercover agents.

As soon as the Colombians delivered $400,000 dollars to Jim S and The Salesman and the bad guys went to take possession of "their" cocaine shipment, a small army of federal agents and police officers moved in to arrest every violator involved. It took a year for us to make this case and it took the blink of an eye to take the bad guys into custody once the time was right.

CHAPTER 25

MAYDAY MAYDAY WE'RE GOING DOWN

On Friday June 22, 1990, at a little before high noon, Captain Video, Mike R., Chuck W., Mr. Goodwrench (our other crew chief/contract mechanic) and I prepared to depart Santa Fe Airport in our undercover aircraft. Despite the politics, our stay in Albuquerque was OK by TDY standards. In addition to the successful completion of another controlled delivery, we made the front page in Albuquerque, New Mexico. From what I could gather, Customs management in Washington, D.C., Miami and New Mexico was very happy with our performance, especially since the hundreds of thousands of dollars the Colombians paid The Salesman and Agent Jim S. would be divided by our two offices to help fund future covert operations.

When The Salesman had to remain behind in New Mexico, I volunteered to fly right seat (co pilot) and provide some relief to Captain Video, on the long flight back to our base in Miami. Under the circumstances, I assumed that Captain Video felt comfortable with me serving as his co pilot, because I relieved our cockpit crews on previous occasions, when we flew the long winged version of the same aircraft.

I should also mention, that even though I was never formally trained to fly on instruments, I was previously left in the cockpit by myself, when I relieved our contract pilots on night flights over the Caribbean. I'm just guessing, but when U.S. Customs Pilot Bob W. taught me how to fly, he engrained in me the importance of always scanning the instruments. As a result of what I learned from Bob W., I was incredibly comfortable flying after the sunset. Besides, when our contract pilots left me alone in the cockpit, there was plenty of moonlight and stars in the sky to provide an ample amount of illumination. I mention this, because I don't want to give the impression that I had any illusions about my capabilities as a so called "pilot." As far as I was concerned, even though I was very comfortable behind the controls, I KNEW I HAD A LOT TO LEARN.

Ever since I was a kid I always admired aviators, especially the swashbuckling types who were fliers and barnstormers and not just your fair weather airplane operators. Like other young men from my generation, I loved watching military flying movies like, Air Force, 12 O'Clock High, Fighter Squadron, The Flying Tigers, God is My Co Pilot, Dawn Patrol, The Flying Leathernecks, Desperate Journey, The Blue Max, The Battle of Britain, The Bridges at Toko Ri, A Yank in the RAF, Command Decision, The Hunters and other films that included military aircraft.

I was also always drawn to the movie characters who disobeyed orders and landed behind enemy lines to pick up a downed aviator, or the enlisted man who washed out of flight school, but later got behind the controls of a shot up B17 and safely landed the plane; an act that saved the life of a wounded pilot, who was unable to bail out with the others. This particular scene is depicted in the World War II film Air Force staring John Garfield. So for various reasons, directing and participating in these high risk undercover air operations, enabled me to live one of my dreams in life. I also enjoyed movies about maritime adventures, when crews braved storms and survived the cruel sea.

While everyone took their seats, Captain Video examined an air chart, while I tried to adjust the worn out military seat belt that was resting across the co-pilot's seat. By the time Captain Video had our two engines cranked up, I gave up trying to get the worn out and unusable woven cloth military seat belts to work and sat back with no protection whatsoever holding me in place. (Since my choices were to ride up front where the action was with no seat belt protection, or sit in the back, I chose to remain in the co pilot's seat to help Captain Video as required.)

THE PRE FLIGHT BRIEFING

When it was time to taxi to the active runway, Captain Video leaned over and told me what to do in the event that we lost an engine and I had to help fly the plane. While giving me these instructions, Captain Video pointed to the extreme right hand side of the control panel and told me to wait for his command to press the black button, that would jettison our two auxiliary fuel tanks during an in flight emergency. The two externally mounted fuel tanks, that were fixed to pods under the left and right side of the (high) wing, were designed to "punch off" under certain situations, including during an engine out scenario.

Why all of the pre-flight concerns you might ask? During our operations we routinely flew planes with a full load of fuel. We were also used to flying at sea level and not in the higher elevations, or in the intense heat of the American Southwest. As I mentioned before, of the two different models of former military seaplanes that we put into service, we happened to be flying the short winged version on this particular mission. This aircraft was known to behave rather poorly in an engine out scenario, especially when it was equipped with externally mounted fuel tanks.

To compensate for the loss of power, while flying the short winged version of this particular seaplane, we would have to immediately reduce the gross weight of the aircraft and limit any drag that would cause us to stall. The best way to accomplish this was to jettison the externally mounted fuel tanks. Naturally, this could only be done if we were flying over the ocean, or an unpopulated area. Since we would be departing from a suburban airport in Santa Fe, New Mexico, we would have to wait until it was safe to drop the extra fuel tanks.

THE POINT OF NO RETURN

As strange as this may sound, I knew the moment that we began to line up on the center line of the runway that we were going to crash. I also cannot explain why I just sat there and did not share my premonition with anyone else. It wasn't as if I was frozen in fear, because I was actually quite calm. Again, as crazy as this may sound, it was almost as if this premonition popped into my head and left as if it was no big deal.

Once Captain Video received permission from the tower to take off, our Contract Pilot in Command applied full power to the UC aircraft's radial engines. With our aircraft displaying bogus tail numbers and a miss matched paint job, we lumbered down the 8300 foot runway until the undercover seaplane gently lifted off the ground and began to climb into the hot desert air. We were airborne with a full bag of fuel, a crew of five and a cargo bay full of luggage, all of our equipment, a dozen Kachina dolls, two large coolers full of Mexican food and plenty of soda and bottled water.

As soon as we reached an altitude of 9700 feet and leveled off, the air traffic controller warned us of some nearby air traffic. While Captain Video flew the plane, I kept an eye out for other aircraft. At our cruising altitude the New Mexico desert looked beautiful. While I sat in the co pilot's seat and enjoyed the view, Captain Video was busy trying to adjust the starboard propeller setting, because the propeller was surging and could not be regulated. In other words, we had a runaway propeller.

According to what I learned from working with veteran aviators, a runaway propeller is very serious business, because a propeller that cannot be adjusted or regulated, can blow off the engine and slice through the side of the fuselage like a hot knife through butter. A blown engine also creates more drag than an engine with a feathered propeller. In an effort to prevent a real disaster, Captain Video had no choice but to shut down the disabled starboard engine. This meant that in order for us to survive, we had to control our decent to the ground using our remaining engine.

As I looked out of the co-pilot's side window and observed the engine that was no longer turning, I thought I was in an old war movie. My premonition was correct. We were really going to crash. Then, I muttered under my breath, "This shit only happens to military aviators flying B17 bombers in World War II, not to U.S. Customs Agents in 1990."

Despite the seriousness of the situation, my colleagues and I were amazingly calm, cool and collected. They say that a sense of humor can be a mask for other feelings. Since I could never pass up a chance to lighten people's spirits, I turned to Captain Video and said, "Hey, she flies pretty good on one engine."

For a guy with a great sense of humor, Captain Video was very professional when he looked at me and spoke into the mouthpiece of his radio microphone and said, "We'll never make it. We're gonna have to put it down."

While I faced Captain Video, I kept my response short and to the point and said, "OK."

I can't explain it, but somehow I got the impression that Captain Video expected me to say something else.

Rather than crash land anywhere close to a populated area, Captain Video made the command decision to try and make it back to the airport that we just departed from. As soon as he reported our in-flight emergency to the control tower, the air traffic controller listened to our problem and directed us back to the field. Captain Video then asked me to take the controls, while he addressed the issue of the shut down disabled starboard engine.

As I said before, I had taken the controls in the past to relieve our crews on long flights, but this was the first time that Captain Video gave me specific instructions about flying. While the Contract Pilot in Command pointed to the airspeed indicator, he said something to the effect of, "Hold her at 110 and whatever you do don't let it stall."

With all the confidence I could muster, I said, "OK," as I temporarily assumed command of the disabled 27,000 pound undercover aircraft.

Despite the fact that we were losing altitude and heading for the ground, I continued to remain filled with confidence, while I gently gripped the controls of the undercover aircraft. It was almost as if, all the childhood fantasies that I had about becoming an aviator had somehow prepared me for this very moment. As I did my best to control our decent, I was actually flying a vintage military seaplane during a real in-flight emergency; an event that up until now, only happened to my favorite actors in old war movies.

During this part of our in flight emergency, my job was to control our rate of decent, so we could extend our duration of flight and crash land on the runway, instead of in somebody's back yard. While I remembered everything that Customs Pilot Bob W. taught me, I continued to scan the instruments, while I did my best to control our rate of decent without stalling the aircraft.

From the moment I took temporary command of the undercover aircraft, the controls felt a bit sluggish and the plane wasn't responding as smartly as usual. Had we been flying the long wing version of the same aircraft, we would have had no problem maintaining straight and level flight in an engine out scenario. Furthermore, as I was told, flying a plane that was dirty and covered with several coats of miss matched paint, degraded the performance of the aircraft by several percentage points.

The moment I felt the plane begin to stall, I reacted just like I was trained and I recovered control of the aircraft, even if only temporarily. Stalling a plane and not recovering is the kiss of death for all on board. When you fail to maintain the proper flow of air over the wings you cannot maintain flight.

The second time she started to shudder, I felt the nose go over even more. Just as I recovered control of the aircraft, Captain Video finished what he was doing and called out and said, "I got it," as he relieved me and grabbed the controls. As I recall, the plane started to shudder a third time, but Captain Video recovered quickly and kept us in the best controlled decent possible.

As I sat in the co pilot's seat, I took another look at the propeller that was no longer turning. After rolling my eyes, I spotted the look on my face in the reflection of the dirty side window and noticed that I had aged quite a bit since takeoff. From where I was sitting, it looked as if Captain Video was doing all he could to hold her steady, as we continued our decent. It also looked as if we were losing altitude, faster than we were able to cover enough ground to reach the airport in time. Clearly, this was going to be a very close call.

One problem we had involved our landing gear. This was a concern, because the landing gear on this model aircraft took some time to lower and lock into position. Extended landing gear also created drag and affected the aerodynamics of an aircraft in flight. This meant that Captain Video would have to wait for the very last minute to lower the landing gear, if he intended to use the wheels to land. The alternative was to crash land without landing gear and slide along the ground on the boat shaped hull that the seaplane had for a fuselage. Unfortunately, this meant that once we made contact with the ground, the seaplane would crash down on one side of the V shaped hull or the other. Either way, gear up or gear down, we were potentially in big trouble.

Even though we could increase our chances of survival if we jettisoned our extra fuel tanks, we had no intention of bombing Santa Fe, New Mexico. The reason this was a concern, was because we were flying over a residential area and had no safe place to drop our extra fuel tanks. Personally, I couldn't live with myself, if I did anything that caused others to die, so I could save myself. When Captain Video raised this issue, he said we would wait until the very last minute and drop the tanks over the first barren stretch of land that we could find. The decision was unanimous and the idea of dropping the fuel tanks on someone's house was never a consideration.

While Captain Video looked straight ahead, he tried to find a suitable place for us to jettison our extra fuel tanks. As soon as he found the right spot, he repeated his instructions about dropping the tanks, while I looked at the control panel on my side of the plane, to make sure I knew exactly where the little black button was located. When Captain Video finished relaying his instructions, I sat back and waited to be given the command to jettison the externally mounted fuel tanks.

With the airport in sight, Captain Video looked at me and said, "We're gonna have to go in gear up." "OK," I said. Again, after seeing the expression on Video's face, I guess he didn't expect me to be so nonchalant, but what else could I do, panic? As far as I was concerned, if this was going to be my last life experience, I had no intention of leaving this world a screaming maniac. Under the circumstances, my senses were never more alive. This was the ultimate human experience, because I thought that I might actually be witnessing my own death unfold right before my eyes. As a result, I wasn't going to miss anything by becoming a nervous wreck.

After saying a short prayer, I realized that if the fuel tanks failed to jettison from the plane, we would drill ourselves into the ground and miss the runway by what appeared to be a few feet. Even if everything worked as designed, there was no guarantee that our plan would work and we would walk away from this in flight emergency in one piece or at all. It's also important to keep in mind, that dropping bombs looked easy in the movies, but this was different.

Without saying anything, I turned to my left and looked at my good friend

Mike R. Don't ask my why, but we didn't speak. I just looked at Mike for what might be the last time, before I turned around and faced forward. Seeing the runway high above the windshield, as we flew towards the airport was an eye opening experience. Now we were getting close, much too close.

As I took a quick glance out of the co-pilot's side window, I saw that we were still flying over the very edge of a residential community. There was no going back on the decision to ride this out all the way. Seconds later, I saw that we were finally clear of the homes below. Now all we needed to do, was clear the racetrack and the highway.

The moment I believed that I might only have a few moments to live, I became extremely concerned about my wife and two sons and wondered who would care for them in my absence. When I say concerned, I mean I thought of nothing else. It also bothered me a great deal, that my wife and sons would not know that my last thoughts were of them. In fact, it frustrated me to no end, that my family would never know, that I didn't think of anything else but them, if I ended up being killed in a plane crash.

As I continued to worry about my wife and sons, I became filled with the most intense feeling of peace and tranquility that I have ever known in my entire life. A split second later, I heard Almighty God telepathically say, "Don't worry, your family will be well cared for."

When I telepathically responded and said, "But You didn't say that I would make it," God didn't say a word. Instead, I felt as if I was being spiritually physically embraced by Almighty God. During this Divine embrace, my entire body was filled with the most intense feeling of goodness that I ever experienced in my life. What was even more amazing about this experience, was that I felt every stressful moment, personal problem and concern that I ever had, instantly removed from my memory banks, as if a tremendous burden was physically lifted from my shoulders. In fact, there are no words that can possibly describe how good I felt, when I experienced what I believe was an epiphany of sorts. Clearly, what I was experiencing wasn't self generated and was not of this world.

Bear in mind, that even though I prayed for the safe return of our crews whenever we went operational, I wasn't a member of the 700 Club, or a regular practicing Catholic when this incident occurred. I certainly didn't have the sense of faith on the day of this in flight emergency that I do today. I guess what I'm trying to say, is that I wasn't an overly religious person, who was predisposed to have a religious experience of any kind, or at least that's what I thought on June 22, 1990.

After being telepathically reassured that my wife and sons would be well cared for and being comforted by the spiritual presence of Almighty God, I sat back in the co pilot's seat totally prepared to leave this world. Don't get me wrong. I wanted to live, but I was prepared to die in total peace, if that's the way that things worked out.

I should also mention, that when I tell this story and anyone asks me how I KNEW that Almighty God was really speaking to me, my response is simple.

When God speaks to you, there is ABSOLUTELY no mistaking HIS voice for anyone else! When Almighty God spiritually embraces you, there is also no mistaking who is responsible for the indescribable feeling of pure goodness, that fills your physical body from head to toe.

As I watched the ground coming up fast, I privately said goodbye to my wife and two sons for what I thought might be the last time. When I was finished, I turned to my right and saw the look of concern that the people in the vehicles on Interstate 25 had, as we raced over the tops of their cars and trucks at flank speed. A split second later, Captain Video yelled, "Now!"

As soon as I hit the black button and jettisoned the two fuel tanks, I lowered my head and covered my face with my hands rather than watch what would happen next. As a testament to the company that made this incredibly well built military seaplane, the mechanism to jettison the externally mounted fuel tanks worked as designed. While the two tanks fell to the ground and disintegrated, I sat up straight and opened my eyes, just as if a fresh gust of air put life back in our wings and kept us airborne. Rather than prematurely drill ourselves into the ground, our plane was heading over the edge of the runway. We were alive and it felt great!

When Captain Video changed his decision to go in gear up and he lowered the landing gear, the aircraft immediately began to sway back and forth like a ride at Universal Studios. The yaw effect of our plane swaying back and forth seemed so severe, I thought that we would be flung sidewise at any minute and cartwheel down the runway in a huge fireball.

My life was passing before my eyes in an explosion of split seconds. Suddenly, the peace and tranquility that I felt a few moments ago, was beginning to slip away at the most inopportune time. For the first time in during this in flight emergency, I felt a twinge of real fear, while I wondered where God went, as our plane swayed back and forth over the runway.

Just when I thought our ordeal was over, the right main landing gear failed to lock into position on the right side of the plane. Even though our one remaining engine was straining to keep us airborne, the force of gravity caused our aircraft to crash down on the runway. In doing so, the right main landing gear collapsed under my side of the plane.

The second the undercover aircraft crashed down on the runway at a high rate of speed, we began to slide along the tarmac on the leading edge of the right wing float tank. After the seaplane scrapped along the runway for a bit, the crippled aircraft pivoted to the right and went careening off into the desert in a hearty hi ho silver. The first thing that I noticed, was that the desert was by no means as smooth as it looks from the air. In fact, so much was happening so fast, that it was difficult to compute all that was taking place.

While we bounced along on uneven desert terrain, I was immediately thrown forward because I had no seat belt protection to hold me in place. As the large yoke/controls on my side of the plane smashed into my chest, I was sent flying back against the co pilot's seat. The moment I came flying forward again, Captain

Video held out his right hand and stopped me from smashing into the control panel.

As the plane changed course, I was sent flying so hard to the right, I completely twisted my upper torso around in my seat. The moment I hit the left side of my head on the right side cockpit window, my eyes bulged at the sight of the right wing float dragging along the ground and kicking up a rather large cloud of dust. Under the circumstances, I wondered if what I was seeing was dust or smoke from a fire? It was at that moment that I became consumed with the fear of being burned alive if the plane caught on fire.

The longer that we buffeted sideways across the uneven terrain, the more we began to slow down until we finally came to a complete stop. Then, as a cloud of dust rose up from the desert and engulfed our plane, I became even more concerned that the undercover aircraft would burst into flames. All I could think about was getting out of the co-pilot's seat and as far away from this aircraft as possible. Our situation became even more dire, when the distinctive smell of leaking aviation fuel, hydraulic fuel and blown brakes filled the air in the cockpit. Hearing Captain Video yell something about a "fuel leak, fire, she might blow, everybody out," just about finished me off. At that point, all I wanted to do was get the hell out of this plane.

In an effort to evacuate the aircraft as fast as possible, I slammed my left shoulder into the steel bulkhead, that separated the cockpit from the cargo bay. Even though I hit the bulkhead pretty hard, I kept going, almost as if I was in spirit form and was able to run through the steel reinforced wall of the plane's interior. To make natters worse, it was also virtually impossible to easily make our way to the escape hatch, because all of our equipment and luggage was thrown around the cargo bay.

As I waited for my turn to evacuate the undercover aircraft, I became even more concerned about being trapped inside the seaplane, if it exploded before it was my turn to jump to safety. In fact, it was at that moment, that I became overwhelmed by claustrophobia, a scary feeling that would stay with me for a very long time.

Crash landing off a runway and into the desert like a derailed freight train was bad enough, but being trapped inside a plane that might explode at any second, was not what I signed up for when I joined the U.S. Customs Service. Surviving storms at sea, getting rescued by the United States Navy and doing the Sonny Crockett shuffle with the best the drug cartels had to offer, was all of the high adventure that I ever wanted. This plane crash landing shit was pure Hollywood and not for me. Despite how I felt, I sucked it up and remained kneeling in the cargo bay, while I waited my turn to evacuate the crash landed aircraft. In fact, all of my fellow crew members were outwardly very calm and well behaved.

I mention this, because despite the fact that my colleagues and I were a seemingly unorthodox group, we took our responsibilities serious enough to remain committed to certain traditions. Naturally, I am referring to the time honored tradition among aviators and mariners, that a crew must abandon a sinking ship, or a crash landed, or ditched aircraft in the proper order. This meant, that the passengers disembarked first, followed by the crew members according to their rank. Since I assumed the duties of the "co pilot," I would have to wait until everyone else jumped from the stricken plane, with Captain Video going out behind me.

Mr. Goodwrench our mechanic jumped out first followed by Chuck W.. Mike R. was in front of me and was next to go. Because the plane was leaning on its right side on uneven terrain, it was a little more difficult to exit the aircraft through the open port side cargo hatch. The moment Mike R. started to deploy the aluminum ladder I yelled, "Fuck the ladder, Mike, jump!" Immediately after our crew chief, Chuck W. and Mike R. jumped out of the plane, so did I followed by Captain Video.

As soon as I got up, I ran a few hundred yards away and collapsed on the ground. By the grace of Almighty God, my colleagues and I survived another hair-raising adventure. While I knelt on the ground away from the crash landed undercover aircraft and I watched the fire trucks respond, the enormity of the situation hit me like a ton of bricks. All I wanted to do at that moment was to be hugged by my wife and two sons. I was physically and emotionally drained after being on full alert for so long. When I wasn't performing a variety of very stressful and demanding duties on land, I was bobbing up and down on the ocean, dealing with real bad guys and crash landing a Vietnam vintage military seaplane, that should have been on display at the National Air & Space Museum.

Fortunately, after a few minutes passed, I began to laugh to myself, as I stood up and said, "Hey that wasn't so bad, let's do it again. Yea right!"

While I walked away from the crash site, I looked back at our undercover plane just as some New Mexico Air National Guard troops were preparing to tow the stricken aircraft to a different part of the field. As I continued walking, I knew that I would have to get back inside of one these antiques, or I would never fly again.

On a more humorous note, even though he did everything by the book and prevented a real disaster from occurring, Captain Video was justifiably concerned that this crash landing would have a negative impact on his regular flying job. No matter how many times Captain Video tried to convince me that what happened was an "incident" and not a plane crash, I kept telling him that by the way things looked it was a crash all right. The minute we spotted a very serious looking FAA official coming our way, Captain Video evaporated from sight and let me handle the situation.

When the FAA official demanded to see the Pilot in Command, I produced my U.S. Customs Service badge and credentials and managed to keep Captain Video out of the limelight. Fortunately, when I told the FAA Inspector that I was in the right seat (the co pilot's position) during this in flight emergency, he didn't ask to see my pilot's license. Personally, I think this particular FAA official would have had a heart attack, if he found out that all I had was an expired student pilot's license and not a multi-engine rated commercial pilot's license, when I assisted the Contract Pilot in Command during this in flight emergency. Instead, the FAA official told me to make sure the Pilot in Command reported to the FAA FISDO Office in Albuquerque.

Fortunately, I was the only person who was permanently injured as a result of this crash landing incident. I can only assume that I sustained permanent disc damage in the lower back and neck because I had no seat belt protection during the crash landing.

UNDERSTANDING THE MEANING OF IT ALL

The day we crash landed in Santa Fe, New Mexico will always have a very special meaning for me. To come so close to the end and survive is truly an amazing experience. I was also very proud of my crew. For such a collection of misfits and eccentrics, we had the right stuff at just the right time. What more can anyone ask?

After a great deal of soul searching, I have tried to understand why I had such a profound religious experience during this in flight emergency. All I could think of was that throughout my life, Almighty God tried to get my attention on a number of occasions, but nothing seemed to work. All that changed, when our starboard engine stopped turning and my colleagues and I started to fall from the sky like a rock. Like many people, I had taken so many things in life for granted. Even though I knew that my life lacked balance, I never did anything to improve the situation. You might say that I was going along for the ride, until the ride stopped and the reality of life got my undivided attention. Whether you call what I went though an incident, an accident, a crash, or a close call, this event gave me a new lease on life and a chance to make some changes.

There was also something about the experience of being consumed with concerns about my family, as the plane was going down, that made me appreciate how good it felt to be so unselfish. I can't emphasize this enough, but it felt great to know, that I was more worried about my wife and two sons, than I was concerned about the fact, that I might be living my last few moments on this earth.

If I can be so bold, I also suspect that God embraced me as He did, not only to comfort me, but because He was happy that I was finally thinking the right thoughts and was on my way home. Last, but not least, there is the issue of the other lives that were spared in the air and on the ground. Naturally, it's human nature to wonder, whether God spared us to save the people on the ground, or because it was not our time to go. As far as I'm concerned, we were all spared for a reason.

Clearly, surviving this particular close call got my attention and rattled my cage. Even though I had the same free will that I had before, I felt different. The fact that I could be so introspective meant that there was hope for me yet.

Even though I wonder how some people will react when they read this chapter, I feel compelled to describe this experience as it happened, because it didn't seem right to leave anything out. After all, how could I face God in the afterlife, knowing that He provided us with safe passage, but I intentionally failed to mention what actually happened in this book, because I was embarrassed to tell people that I had a "religious" experience. I would also like to add, that it's amazing how brave you can be when God is your Co Pilot.

In the end, my colleagues and I managed to successfully complete this controlled delivery and achieve victory. Based on what I was told, a certain DEA official was quite disturbed, that U.S. Customs Agents had the audacity to circumvent the rules of engagement and make a transportation case without receiving country clearance. Had things been different, this could have been a joint investigation. Then again, if a frog had wings it could fly.

Seven U.S. Customs undercover operatives risked their lives to travel to the coast of Colombia by boat, to pick up 700 plus kilos of cocaine and two bad guys, in order to execute one of the most daring controlled deliveries of The Drug War. All this was done in order to complete an undercover operation, that was ten times more complicated and significantly more dangerous than it had to be. I feel this way, because had we been allowed to land one of our seaplanes in calmer water closer to shore, we could have pulled this operation off while risking fewer lives.

When country clearance was repeatedly denied, the choice was to walk away from a perfectly good case or become resourceful. Since we were a "can do" operation, we decided to become resourceful. The rest is now history.

This controlled delivery represented everything that was right and wrong with

The Drug War. The fact that we were our own worst enemy is quite evident, when you examine what really took place during this conflict. This particular case also proves beyond a shadow of a doubt, that U.S. Agents are capable of doing some amazing things, when given the opportunity to take on the enemy in an unconventional fashion. It is also quite clear, that Americans can be a determined lot, especially when the cause is both noble and necessary. I also believe that it's important to keep in mind, that while the bad guys are motivated by greed, my colleagues and I were motivated by things that money can't buy.

DECISIONS, DECISIONS

After taking a second to consider renting a car to make the drive back to Florida, I returned home with the rest of our crew on a commercial flight. While I stood at the ticket counter on Saturday June 23, 1990, we noticed that some of the airline employees were reading about the controlled delivery that we just completed in the local newspaper.

As soon as Mike R. and I produced our federal credentials, so we could board our flight home while carrying our firearms, one of the ticket agents asked if we were involved in the case that was featured on the front page of the local newspaper. As we smiled and looked at each other, I commented something like, "We're just passing through."

Even though I was permanently disabled in the line of duty as a result of my participation in undercover operations, I am very grateful that I had the opportunity to serve in this fashion. My colleagues and I could not predict that our journey through a stormy sea would result in our getting rescued by the U.S. Navy, any more than we knew that we would crash land our undercover plane on the way home, after successfully completing our mission. Simply put, shit happens.

ON A MORE PERSONAL NOTE

As soon as I returned to Miami after the plane crash landing incident, I volunteered to participate in two additional undercover marine operations to the Colombian coast. One reason I decided to go on these seafaring adventures, was because I loved being involved in cutting edge covert operations.

While some people will say that I was an adrenaline junkie, who loved the rush of being as far out on a limb as often as possible, I defined myself as someone who took my job very seriously and was living my dreams in life. My attitude was, if I was going to be a U.S. Customs Agent, then I was going to be involved in the most exciting aspects of the job, or I would find someplace else to work.

Another reason I went operational again, was because my injuries were initially misdiagnosed. Originally, I thought that I was just very sore and badly bruised. In fact, it wasn't until some time passed and I never got better, that I had an MRI and was diagnosed with multiple disc injuries. Years later, government doctors would add a total of eight line of duty physical injuries to my medical file, including permanent and degenerative injuries to my spine and both hips. I also refused to take "trauma leave" when I saw how my partner Mike R. was treated, when he took off and went on vacation with his wife, after surviving our aviation adventure in New Mexico.

While Mike was gone, I was asked several times why he took trauma leave when nothing was "broken." When Mike returned from his so called "vacation," he was transferred to the Marine Group. Personally, I thought Mike was treated very poorly.

For the record, Senior Special Agent Mike R. went on to participate in a number of undercover marine operations, even though he was a veteran agent who could have enjoyed his last few years on the job doing as little as possible. Mike was the kind of guy, who would make up a plaque and present it to someone, who did a good job but was overlooked by the system. Besides being an exceptionally kind person, Mike was a true professional who was also incredibly brave. Clearly, he made a very important contribution throughout his career. In closing this chapter, it is my honor to publicly thank Mike R. for a job well done. Very few men are in your league.

A PREVIEW OF CONTROLLED DELIVERY BOOK II

Controlled Delivery Book II includes a number of high risk covert operations that involve larger quantities of drug contraband and the arrest of more significant violators. Even the undercover aircraft that we used in some of these operations, were more sophisticated and enabled us to meet the demands of more complex missions.

In the second half of this true story, The Blade Runner Squadron recruits some new talent to help us conduct some exceptionally dangerous missions. While working alongside the core group of undercover operatives, who were affiliated with this operation from the beginning, our newly hired personnel enabled us to expand our capabilities.

As described in Controlled Delivery Book I and II, our mission was to execute as many controlled delivery sting operations, aka transportation cases, as possible. Our objective was to infiltrate Colombian based smuggling organizations and seize large quantities of drug contraband, drug money and valuable drug assets.

In the process of conducting these operations, numerous major violators were arrested and record setting drug seizures were made. Even the smaller multi hundred kilogram cocaine cases that we worked, were major victories in our nation's Drug War.

Controlled Delivery Book II also reaffirms the fact, that The Drug War is a real conflict; one that includes the participation of U.S. law enforcement and U.S. Department of Defense personnel and assets. This becomes even more evident in CD Book II, when a much larger array of U.S. military aircraft and vessels are drafted into service, to provide critical assistance during some of our more elaborate covert air operations. These U.S. military assets come in especially handy, when our undercover aircraft begin operating at an international airport in Colombia and must be kept under surveillance on long range flights to destinations in the CONUS.

When Hurricane Andrew devastates parts of South Florida, undercover operations are temporarily shut down, as every available U.S. Customs Agent becomes a first responder. During this major natural disaster, my colleagues and I spent our days and nights providing assistance as required in the hardest hit areas of Dade County. While serving as first responders, two other agents and I come under sniper fire, while protecting a mobile surgical unit in a high crime area of South Florida. After surviving disaster duty, we return to the safety of directing and participating in high risk undercover air operations.

It's also in Book II, that we take on a different type of undercover mission and I go undercover as a cargo smuggler. During this undercover operation, I met a Korean violator who was involved in the smuggling and sale of counterfeit Chanel products from Korea.

By the time I completed my involvement in this cargo smuggling case, my line of duty physical injuries have gotten progressively worse. Even though I knew that my days of serving as a U.S. Customs Agent were numbered, I agreed to work undercover along the Mexican Border as a favor for a friend. In Controlled Delivery Book II, you will read what happened when I worked undercover for the last time on a machine gun trafficking case.

TO BE CONTINUED...

Made in the USA
San Bernardino, CA
17 March 2018